New Poets

of England and America

NEW POETS

OF ENGLAND AND AMERICA

Edited by Donald Hall

Robert Pack

Louis Simpson

Introduction by Robert Frost

A MERIDIAN BOOK

WORLD PUBLISHING

TIMES MIRROR

NEW YORK

AN ORIGINAL MERIDIAN BOOK

Published by The World Publishing Company
110 East 59th Street, New York, New York 10022
Published simultaneously in Canada by
Nelson, Foster and Scott, Ltd.
First printing August 1957
Fourteenth printing October 1971
Copyright © 1957 by The World Publishing Company
Library of Congress catalog card number: 57-10836
Printed in the United States of America

WORLD PUBLISHING
TIMES MIRROR

CONTENTS

New Poets

of England and America

Editors' Introduction

We have attempted to present selections from the poetry of a generation, and for convenience have included poets who are under forty or who would have been under forty at the time of the appearance of this publication. The poets represented in this anthology were born between 1917 and 1935. What characteristics are to be discovered in this poetry, we leave to the reader to determine. That poetry today is worthy of its inheritance, we hope we shall have shown in the following pages.

In the preparation of this volume we have read the work of more than three hundred poets. We regret the omission of certain work which individual editors wished included, and can only plead that this anthology represents a composite judgment. Our original aim was to print fewer poets and more poems by each, but to do so would have excluded many poets whose work we admire. It is hoped that in subsequent editions of this anthology poets who have been unavoidably omitted may be included.

Our selection of English poets may not be representative. Though we have read extensively in English books and manuscripts, we cannot claim to be familiar with all the work being done in England today. Nor can we be confident that our judgment of English poetry is as sure as it might be if we were living in England.

We dedicate this anthology, with gratitude, to Mr. Thomas Langbert, whose belief in the value of this undertaking made it possible.

March 20, 1957

Donald Hall
Robert Pack
Louis Simpson

Introduction by Robert Frost

MATURITY NO OBJECT

Maturity is no object except perhaps in education where you might think from all the talk the aim and end of everything was to get sophisticated before educated. Shakespeare says it is the right virtue of the medlar to be rotten before it is ripe. Overdevelop the social conscience and make us all social meddlers. But I digress before I begin. My theme is not education, but poetry and how young one has to be or stay to make it. And it is not schools in general I reflect on, only bad schools which something should be done about before they get much larger. My excuse is that school and poetry come so near being one thing. Poetry has been a great concern of school all down the ages. A large part of reading in school always has been and still is poetry; and it is but an extension from the metaphors of poetry out into all thinking, scientific and philosophic. In fact the poet and scholar have so much in common and live together so naturally that it is easy to make too much of a mystery about where they part company. Their material seems the same—perhaps differs a little in being differently come by and differently held in play. Thoroughness is the danger of the scholar, dredging to the dregs. He works on assignment and self-assignment with some sense of the value of what he is getting when he is getting it. He is perhaps too avid of knowledge. The poet's instinct is to shun or shed more knowledge than he can swing or sing. His most

10

available knowledge is acquired unconsciously. Something warns him dogged determination however profound can only result in doggerel. His danger is rhyming trivia. His depth is the lightsome blue depth of the air.

But I suppose the special distinction I was going to invest the poet with, that is making no object of maturity, was a mistake. It certainly belongs as much to the composer, the musician, the general, and I'm told the mathematician and the scientist. And it probably belongs to the scholar. Be that as it may, all poets I have ever heard of struck their note long before forty, the deadline for contributions to this book. The statistics are all in favor of their being as good and lyric as they will ever be. They may have ceased to be poets by the time appreciation catches up with them as Matthew Arnold complains somewhere. (I don't have to say exactly where because I'm not a scholar.) I have personal reasons to trust that they may go phasing on into being as good poets in their later mental ages. For my country's sake I might wish one or two of them an old age of epic writing. A good epic would grace our history. Landor has set an example in prolonging the lyric out of all bounds.

Maturity will come. We mature. But the point is that it is at best irrelevant. Young poetry is the breath of parted lips. For the spirit to survive, the mouth must find how to firm and not harden. I saw it in two faces in the same drawing room— one youth in Greek sculpture, the other manhood in modern painting. They were both noble. The man was no better than the boy nor worse because he was older. The poets of this group, many of them my friends and already known to many of us, need live to write no better, need only wait to be better known for what they have written.

The reader is more on trial here than they are. He is given his chance to see if he can tell all by himself without critical instruction the difference between the poets who wrote because they thought it would be a good idea to write and those who couldn't help writing out of a strong weakness for the muse, as for an elopement with her. There should be some way to tell that just as there is to tell the excitement of the morning from the autointoxication of midnight. Any distinction between maturity and immaturity is not worth making unless as a precaution. If school is going to proclaim a policy of maturing boys and girls ultimately it might become necessary for us to stay away from school or at least play hooky a good deal to season slowly out of doors rather than in an oven or in a tanning vat. And that seems too bad; for so many of us like school and want to go there.

As I often say a thousand, two thousand, colleges, town and gown together in the little town they make, give us the best audiences for poetry ever had in all this world. I am in on the ambition that this book will get to them—heart and mind.

KINGSLEY AMIS

Masters

That horse whose rider fears to jump will fall,
Riflemen miss if orders sound unsure;
They only are secure who seem secure;
  Who lose their voice, lose all.

Those whom heredity or guns have made
Masters, must show it by a common speech;
Expected words in the same tone from each
  Will always be obeyed.

Likewise with stance, with gestures, and with face;
No more than mouth need move when words are said,
No more than hand to strike, or point ahead;
  Like slaves, limbs learn their place.

In triumph as in mutiny unmoved,
These make their public act their private good,
Their words in lounge or courtroom understood,
  But themselves never loved.

The eyes that will not look, the twitching cheek,
The hands that sketch what mouth would fear to own,
These only make us known, and we are known
  Only as we are weak:

By yielding mastery the will is freed,
For it is by surrender that we live,
And we are taken if we wish to give,
  Are needed if we need.

Against Romanticism

A traveller who walks a temperate zone
   —Woods devoid of beasts, roads that please the foot—
Finds that its decent surface grows too thin:
   Something unperceived fumbles at his nerves.
To please an ingrown taste for anarchy
   Torrid images circle in the wood,
And sweat for recognition up the road,
   Cramming close the air with their bookish cries.
All senses then are glad to gasp: the eye
   Smeared with garish paints, tickled up with ghosts
That brandish warnings or an abstract noun;
   Melodies from shards, memories from coal,
Or saws from powdered tombstones thump the ear;
   Bodies rich with heat wriggle to the touch,
And verbal scents made real spellbind the nose:
   Incense, frankincense; legendary the taste
Of drinks or fruits or tongues laid on the tongue.
   Over all, a grand meaning fills the scene,
And sets the brain raging with prophecy,
   Raging to discard real time and place,
Raging to build a better time and place
   Than the ones which give prophecy its field
To work, the calm material for its rage,
   And the context which makes it prophecy.
Better, of course, if images were plain,
   Warnings clearly said, shapes put down quite still
Within the fingers' reach, or else nowhere;
   But complexities crowd the simplest thing,
And flaw the surface that they cannot break.
   Let us make at least visions that we need:
Let mine be pallid, so that it cannot
   Force a single glance, form a single word;
An afternoon long-drawn and silent, with
   Buildings free from all grime of history,
The people total strangers, the grass cut,
   Not long, voluble swooning wilderness,
And green, not parched or soured by frantic suns

Doubling the commands of a rout of gods,
Nor trampled by the havering unicorn;
    Let the sky be clean of officious birds
Punctiliously flying on the left;
    Let there be a path leading out of sight,
And at its other end a temperate zone:
    Woods devoid of beasts, roads that please the foot.

A Bookshop Idyll

Between the *gardening* and the *cookery*
    Comes the brief *Poetry* shelf;
By the Nonesuch Donne, a thin anthology
    Offers itself.

Critical, and with nothing else to do,
    I scan the Contents page,
Relieved to find the names are mostly new;
    No one my age.

Like all strangers, they divide by sex:
    Landscape near Parma
Interests a man, so does *The Double Vortex*,
    So does *Rilke and Buddha*.

'I travel, you see,' 'I think' and 'I can read'
    These titles seem to say;
But *I Remember You, Love is my Creed,*
    Poem for J.,

The ladies' choice, discountenance my patter
    For several seconds;
From somewhere in this (as in any) matter
    A moral beckons.

Should poets bicycle-pump the human heart
    Or squash it flat?
Man's love is of man's life a thing apart;
    Girls aren't like that.

We men have got love well weighed up; our stuff
    Can get by without it.
Women don't seem to think that's good enough;
    They write about it,

And the awful way their poems lay them open
    Just doesn't strike them.
Women are really much nicer than men:
    No wonder we like them.

Deciding this, we can forget those times
    We sat up half the night
Chock-full of love, crammed with bright thoughts, names,
    rhymes,
    And couldn't write.

Departure

For one month afterwards the eye stays true,
And sees the other's face held still and free
Of ornament; then tires of peering down
A narrow vista, and the month runs out.

Too lax, this eye will crave the merit of
A faithful sentry frozen at his post,
And not a movement seen; yet ranges over
Far other tracts, its object lost, corrupt.

Nor should I now swell to halloo the names
Of feelings that no one needs to remember,
Nor caper with my spray of wilted avowals
To clutter up your path I should wish clear.

Perhaps it is too late to crane the eye
And find you, distant and small, but as you are;
If not, I will retain you honestly blurred,
Not a bland refraction of sweet mirrors.

WILLIAM BELL

To a Lady on Her Marriage

My dear, when I was very young
and you not half as much again,
I found you single and unsung.
Oh then I only lived to pen
lamenting elegies. resigned
to die of love like better men
for both your body and your mind.

But even then I told you true,
(though you would pay no heed to me,)
'The days are drawing near when you
will ask no more for poetry
or flaming youth, content to find
a steady man, content if he
will love your body, not your mind.

'Joy is the rush of blood, the falling
or fallen pride of summer's lark
calling the leaves to hide him, calling ,
even the snows, even the dark.
Love is a mask, with death behind:
your beauty he will not remark,
nor love your body nor your mind.'

And though a torment as intense,
as tyrannous as then I had
awaits, I have learnt too much sense
to let her know when I am sad.
I'll say 'though love has made me blind
he has forgot to make me mad
to love your body and your mind.'

A Young Man's Song

(Pastourelle)

Maidens who this burning May
through the woods in quaint distress
wander till you find your way,
attend to what I have to say,
> but ask me nothing,
> ask me nothing,
ask me nothing you can guess.

Here I learned a year ago
this burden from a shepherdess:
'Love is wakefulness and woe,
'where it hurts you ought to know,
> 'so ask me nothing,
> 'ask me nothing,
'ask me nothing you can guess.'

Said I 'when such as you complain
'you cry to courtesy for redress:
'then may not I avenge your pain?'
but still she sang the same refrain,
> 'Ask me nothing,
> 'ask me nothing,
'ask me nothing you can guess.'

In the thicket where we hid
we found a primrose-bank to press,
and there I served her as she bid.
Let me shew you what we did!
> but ask me nothing,
> ask me nothing,
ask me nothing you can guess.

On a Dying Boy

Oh leave his body broken on the rocks
where fainting sense may drown beneath the sound
of the complaining surf. His spirit mocks
our ignorant attempts to hem it round:
as eagerly as body sought the ground
into its native ocean must it flow.
Oh let his body lie where it was found,
there's nothing we can do to help him now.

And hide his face under his tattered coat
until the women come to where he lies,
they come to bind the silence in his throat
and shut the eternal darkness in his eyes,
to wash the cold sweat of his agonies
and wash the blood that's clotted on his brow.
Cover his face from the unfriendly skies,
there's nothing we can do to help him now.

And watch even his enemies forget him,
the skies forget his sobs, the rocks his blood:
and think how neither rock nor sky dared let him
grow old enough for evil or for good;
and then forget him too. Even if we could
bring back the flower that's fallen from the bough,
bring back the flower that never left the bud,
there's nothing we can do to help him now.

Elegy IX

My dear, observe the rose! though she desire it
for every falling petal, must she miss
the marble's stiffness, when she might acquire it
by the transforming virtue of a kiss?
We were prepared for a remote defeat

before the winter's mustered powers, but this
    and all the anguish of it
were new to us, because no prophet
had warned us of the dryness and the heat.

It was the flaming summer, the deceiver
who settled on us like a falling flare
and lit our gazing faces with his fever,
so that our bodies seemed transfigured there,
and you especially became enchanted,
gazing across the empires of the air
      toward a world of flowers,
    and birds, a kinder world than ours
where winter finds that every grove is haunted.

For in your dream you wandered in a country
ringed by immaculate mountains, mountains where
a line of marble warriors kept sentry
gazing across the empires of the air,
watching the distant fronts of cloud, which seeming
as white and frozen as that carven stare
      acknowledged their defeat,
    for no extremity of cold nor heat
could interrupt the purpose of your dreaming.

Beside a fountain the philosophers
would sit and pour for you the flood of reason;
their tongues would make the fountain quiet here
in admiration—but the flowering season,
the falling flower, the fountain—all were fast,
unchangeable, against the changing treason
      of time and of old age.
    And there you even could assuage
the ever-changing fever of man's lust.

O set that intellectual perfection
upon a painter's canvas, for you can
no more presume to offer a prediction
of the degenerate temper of a man
desiring and rejecting your embraces.
Not even Breughel's hand or eye could scan
      and plot upon a chart

the fickle climates of the heart,
which crack and splinter those heroic faces.

There have been others, mightier far than you,
queens of the loyal earth and her profusion,
though not your perfect form, who would pursue
both happiness and the supreme illusion
that they could guard it somewhere far apart
from the heart's malice and the heart's confusion.
    But anarchy was making
  no truce with them until their breaking
armies fell about a broken heart.

And you, and you my dear, will guard no better
the part of happiness you try to hide,
weather and time and sorrow and time will batter
upon a heart grown brittle with your pride.
And only this forgotten verse will spare
your beauty when the soft seditious tide
    directs his charging breakers
  across your cities and your acres
where summer hovered like a falling flare.

Elegy X

(St. Peter)

Now Christendom bids her cathedrals call
no more to heaven: night and frost have taken
  the watchman from her wall.
O silent choirs, what bird will bid you waken
but he, the sun, the loudest bird of all?

Even while he was here I have denied
his agony, denied his resurrection.
  Now at his passiontide
his hands and feet are nailed for my inspection,
I plunge my fist into his wounded side.

The silence of these solitudes defies
the hollow throats of prophets: the apostle
    at length must close his eyes,
and silent now the blackbird and the throstle.
O silent choirs, what bird can bid you rise?

only a midnight weathercock, which crows
for dawn or spring to end the perjured trial.
    His raucous conscience knows
but one design to cancel by denial,
my last inverted cross among the snows,

a bed where all dishonesty of dress
and flesh is stripped for love's iconoclasm.
    And there I shall confess
when words have failed me, in my final spasm,
both love's precision and his nakedness.

While you, the accusing multitudes that throng
the empty terraces of my repentance,
    bear witness of the wrong,
and my exalted voice confirms the sentence,
o silent choirs, what can prevent your song?

Sonnet

You waken slowly. In your dream you're straying
into a garden at the forest's edge,
and there before you where a fountain's playing
a marble Syrinx crouches in the sedge,

the birds are singing there, but in the night,
in the deep woods your sleeping body lingers,
your naked mind surveys without delight
what would be paradise to eyes and fingers.

Only to hear the garden's quietness,
only to touch the carven girl's precision
with your accustomed body: this you desire,

but know that there you never can possess
never the saint's, never the lover's vision:
—you are the landscape that you would admire.

ROBERT BLY

The Puritan on His Honeymoon

Travelling south, leaves overflow the farms.
Day by day we watched the leaves increase
And the trees lie tangled in each other's arms.
Still generation, and calls that never cease
And rustlings in the brush; yesterday
She asked how long we had been on the way.
So in the afternoon we changed our route
And came down to the coast; everywhere
The same: fish, and the lobster's sensual eyes.
The natives sang for harvest, gave us fruit,
At night the monkeys sat beneath the trees.
All night the cries of dancers filled the air,
And last year's virgins pressed into the leaves.
Sometimes I think of your land, cold and fresh,
And try to think: what was the month we quit
Your northern land that seemed inhabited
By more than reproduction of the flesh?
I saw here, while the branches interknit
The monkeys gibbering by our bridal bed.

Barnfire During Church

And as we spoke the Nicene Creed we were called out
To fight the barn afire,
And here the summer's corn is born again
In reformation into air.

The children cry, back from the walls, among the men
And dart, and throw their snowballs in the fire.
The walls are folding; burning gold and rust,
The loft piles fire in air: the straw and chaff
Burn black the timid dampness of the night;
They churn the ancient wall-stones to a dust.

Where We Must Look for Help

The dove returns; it found no resting place;
It was in flight all night above the shaken seas;
Beneath ark eaves
The dove shall magnify the tiger's bed;
Give the dove peace.
The split-tail swallows leave the sill at dawn;
At dusk, blue swallows shall return.
On the third day the crow shall fly;
The crow, the crow, the spider-colored crow,
The crow shall find new mud to walk upon.

The Man Whom the Sea Kept Awake

I've heard the sea upon the troubled rocks
Waste this past night, with dreams more troubled still,
And where the images that you and I
Would smooth a sullen morning by? The fly,
Some mottled bird, the new brood of the fox?
O nothing will be born again, until
The monkish body and the eye can see
Down to the darkened sea's nobility
That now but seems a dancer on a bed
Glutting the clumsy, storm-delighted dead.

But now before another darkness and before
Another creaking of the hollow trees
That sang to mad and dead saints in the dark,

I'll hunt among the water-heavy bark
A worn, sun-warmed stone upon the shore
Where I can sit to still the arteries
Distracted by the night. Among birch and pine
Here stand the boulders in a forest line,
Once tall and tumbled by some bitter knee,
Or by the wind that blows in from the sea,

That blew the fig trees and the wild goats of Rome
And Greece to bits upon the Attic floor.
I find my stone and sit. Whatever I see
Increases the dream of the destructions of the sea.
Is it enough that we should have sad songs, on stones
To write away, by lines, the death of Thor?
When sparrows fall, they say its count is taken.
When one mouse shivers, the King upon his throne is shaken.
Let us turn our face to terror before we lose
The nine steps to the bottom of the sea.

A *Missouri Traveller Writes Home: 1830*

The spring rides down; from Judith and the Larb,
Straining and full, the choked Missouri, choked
With sticks and roots, and high with floating trees
Rides down, as my mind at this oakwood table.
For May unlocks the Crazy Hills
Pouring, as she has done before, the shattered snowfields
     down
Till the rumbling brown has burned the land away
A hundred feet below the plain
With spoils of snowfields from the Crazy Hills.
Day breaks, and the Pawnees on those cliffs
Above, shouting, keep pace with us;
The warrior trains like rocks against the sky:
At dawn we see the crumbling cliffs at first,
Then horse and rider, then the Western sky;
Those ash-grey horses black against the clouds!
Tall men, high, fierce, with shoulders as if brass

They lift long warbows made by the Dakotahs,
Above their Pawnee shields of black and white;
With cries and howls, all day they shriek on cliffs.
The buffalo, drinking at the shore, in herds
Hear, and shoulders humping, the buffalo stampede
Alarmed, up porch to porch, onto the plains of dust,
And I have heard the buffalo stampede
With muffled clatter of colliding horns.
On the whole, peril hangs above this land
Like smoke that floats at dawn above dead fires.

The Sioux believe all people, scalped or choked,
Are locked out of Paradise, yet I have seen
Small Sioux women hanging from scraggly trees;
On scaffolds stretch the acres of the dead,
Corroding in their sepulchres of air; at night
With cries, the Osage from their teepee doors,
Mourn the dead, cutting their arms, and screaming;
At dawn the buzzard flocks awake on trees, dew-damp,
And stretch their black wings toward the sun to dry.
Such are the few details that I have seen.

The River splits this country, and it seems
We see the Indians always walking Western banks,
Faced toward full sun, like nephews of the sun;
And there are signs of what will come: the whites,
With steel traps hanging, swung from saddle thongs,
Or flat Virginians, behind great round wheels:
All whites believe these Rees and Sioux and Kaws
And Mandans are not men, but damned as beasts:
Are damned; are held knit in damnation now
Like grasp of snakes, in Satan's grasp himself,
And like the serpent's hold, it is by death alone
To be released: The Sioux are still and silent
Generally, and I have watched them stand
By ones and twos upon the river's bank
As glum as Hudson's blankets winding them,
While shuttling steamboats smoke, labouring up
The breaking foam, beyond the cottonwoods,
Into the region of their dead and of their youth,
Pushed up, they say, by smoke; and they believe

The tribe of whites, like smoke, soon shall return
From whence it came: and therefore in both minds
The truth is absent; and the hands alone
Are like the willow trees, forever green
And undeceived: the hands continue killing.
The hands go on, the minds remain behind,
As if the concepts handled by the mind
Were lesser than the concepts of the hands,
As if a man achieves more than he knows;
Or if the pain of action were so great
And life so freezing and Medusa-faced,
That, like Medusa's head, it could be held
And not observed, lest eye's reward be stone.

The night grows old above this river boat.
Before I end, I shall include account
Of an incident tonight that moved my wonder.
At dusk we tied the boat to trees on shore;
No mortal boat in these night shoals can live.
At first I heard a cry: shuffling and cries
And muffled sounds on deckoak overhead
Drew me on deck, the air was chill, and there
I sensed, because these senses here are sharp
And must be, something living and unknown.
To night and North a crowd stared from the boatrail,
Upriver, nightward and North: a speck of white.
The thing was white: the resonance of night
Returned its grunts and whistlings on the air.
The frontier men swore in that river thicket
In ambush like the beasts they're modeled on,
Bristling for war, would be a thresh of Sioux;
The crew and gamblers nudged, to bait the settlers,
And arms nudged cry, "Along the river there's
Some settler's cow, Hereford or Poland China,
Some farmer could not nail tight enough in cribs,
And terrorizing frogs and catfish now."
But Mormons see some robe in that faint white,
In that dim white the angel of death, come
In cottonwoods to sign the Second Coming;
And on the river's border there they see
Some angel of Joseph upon the chill Missouri;

One man believed that there was nothing there,
As the moon too is false, and its white is false.
I sensed a fear, as if the wind protected it.
When the talk died, eight men, and I with them,
Set off, and moving overboard in dark,
With guns, protected by the thunder's noise,
Up the dark river, toward where the splashes rose,
So armed in case of Sioux, to our surprise
We found a white and wounded Northern Bear,
Shot in that day about the snout and head.
The pure-white bear, not native to these parts,
But to the Horns, or Ranges born, and shot
That morning, had turned downward South and East,
And had apparently through these dry plains
Passed South, to lay its burning paws and head
And lay its fever-proud and festered flesh
Within the cool Missouri's turbid bed.
Soon after, clouds of rain drove us indoors,
And lightning fell like sheets upon the sand,
Said to be sudden in these Western lands.
Minutes before it broke, a circling mass
Of split-tail swallows came and then were gone.
But now to bed. We disembark at dawn
And start to westward through the heavy grass.

PHILIP BOOTH

Heron

In the copper marsh
I saw a stilted heron
wade the tidal wash

and I, who caught no fish,
thought the grass barren
and that jade inlet harsh

until the quick-billed splash
of the long-necked heron
fulfilled my hunter's wish.

Then in the rising rush
of those great wings, far on
I saw the herring flash

and drop. And the dash
of lesser wings in the barren
marsh flew through my flesh.

The Wilding

While crabapple now is a windfall
of blossoms, why wait for a harvest
of worms? The wilding will shrivel
and sour this clearing, frost
will bite hard, and the crop
be lost.

But under woodpecker knock
in this rabbitrun wood, in May,
a sweet fern questionmark
whorls green as green is today,
and ferns ask no answer a swallow
can't fly.

When time is a troutlily yellow
as sun, what wildflowers weather
the high noon tomorrow?
Now jack-in-the-pulpits wither
for shade and there's maidenhair fern
to gather.

Now blossom is bloodroot is sap-run
is Spring, and true as arbutus

we're new. Words are a ruin
no animals heed, so kiss
me to silence: this wood
is for you.

Barred Islands

Between their sandspit ends
we rowed, two spruce islands
moored in a blue Maine bay.
And under the Sou'west sky
we rowed ashore to swim
for love, a summer whim
when our limbs were all July.

Riding in on the tide
with shipped oars, jade
shallows under us, we
both looked down at the play
of sun on seaweed gardens,
swaying whorls in the currents
we neither could see.

And then the kelp-grown slope
slid up to meet us, steep
as a hill below our hull:
sand, stone, and clamshell
dredged by waves, time-
shaped by tide and fathom;
and then the tide was full.

We floated on hope at flood,
and over, over, the tide-
sunk bar; there where the run
of current, the waving sun,
showed clear on the waterglass
sand, on the seawind grass,
how the islands were one.

Vermont: Indian Summer

Unseasonable
as bees in April,
rime in May,
or Orion high
in June,
     days lost
somewhere in August,
green days, dun,
return at noon
as numb-winged wasps
swim in the lapse
of weather:
        sun
and weathervane
are still; the cows
wait, hillside crows
caw down to barn
the first-frost burn
of sumac, maple,
and sideyard apple.
The sky is halo-
hazed, barn and silo
smell of baled hay,
corn-crib, and dry
harvest days;
       days,
goldenrod days:
and the dazzled wasps
climb numb in the lapse
of weather, lost
in what cannot last,
wings struck dumb,
in this other summer,
summer twice come.

Twelfth Night

At Twelfth Night twilight now
the greens burn bright: the dry-spined wreath
and bittersweet returned to frozen earth,
  Canada fir
  become the fire
that wreathes a ritual circle in the snow.

  The decorations are first
to flame: old mistletoe and holly
go up in a burst of charred berry, their holy
  roots tossed on,
  a burnt seed sown,
long after the symbol and song are lost.

  Uprooted meanings flare
like watchfires in this cold backyard.
A single star outshines the ice. Unheard,
  the Magi raise
  their prayer; a blaze
of balsam climbs the still and brittle air.

  At Twelfth Night twilight now
the tree must be the final torch,
a coronal to melt the dark; the branch
  that angels swung on,
  Christ hung on,
quick tinder lit to ebb the tidal snow.

  From slow bright smoke the tree
explodes in fire-veins, star-sparks rain
like fallen Pleiades. The green grain
  burns to warn
  the burner, turn
his back on ceremonial memory.

  No god's made manifest
from this raw bush. But who will light

a legend that he will not celebrate?
   In the quick match,
   the winter watch,
the burner is both burned and blessed.

North

North is weather, Winter, and change:
a wind-shift, snow, and how ice ages
shape the moraine of a mountain range.

At tree line the chiseled ledges
are ragged to climb; wind-twist trees
give way to the thrust of granite ridges,

peaks reach through abrasive centuries
of rain. The worn grain, the sleet-cut,
is magnified on blue Northwest days

where rock slides, like rip-tide, break out
through these geologic seas. Time
in a country of hills is seasonal light:

alpenglow, Northern lights, and tame
in October: Orion, cold hunter of stars.
Between what will be and was, rime

whites the foothill night and flowers
the rushes stilled in black millpond ice.
The dark, the nightfall temperatures

are North, and the honk of flyway geese
high over valley sleep. The woodland
is evergreen, ground pine, spruce,

and deadwood hills at the riverbend.
Black bear and mink fish beaver streams
where moose and caribou drink: beyond

the forests there are elk. Snowstorms
breed North like arctic birds that swirl
downhill, and in a blind wind small farms

are lost. At night the close cold is still,
the tilt world returns from sun to ice.
Glazed lichen is North, and snowfall

at five below. North is where rockface
and hoarfrost are formed with double grace:
love is twice warm in a cold place.

EDGAR BOWERS

From William Tyndale to John Frith *

The letters I, your lone friend, write in sorrow
Will not contain my sorrow: it is mine,
Not yours who stand for burning in my place.
Be certain of your fate. Though some, benign,
Will urge by their sweet threats malicious love
And counsel dangerous fear of violence,
Theirs is illusion's goodness proving fair—
Against your wisdom—worldly innocence
And just persuasions' old hypocrisy.
Making their choice, reflect what you become:
Horror and misery bringing ruin where
The saintly mind has treacherously gone numb;
Despair in the deceit of your remorse
As, doubly heretic, you waste your past
Recanting, by all pitied, honorless,
Until you choose more easy death at last.
Think too of me. Sometimes in morning dark
I let my candle gutter and sit here
Brooding, as shadows fill my cell and sky
Breaks pale outside my window; then the dear

Companionship we spent working for love
Compels me to achieve a double portion.
In spite of age, insanity, despair,
Grief, or declining powers, we have done
What passes to the living of all men
Beyond our weariness. The fire shall find
Me hidden here, although its pain be less
If you have gone to it with half my mind,
Leaving me still enough to fasten flesh
Against the stake, flesh absolute with will.
And should your human powers and my need
Tremble at last and grow faint, worn, and ill,
Pain be too much to think of, fear destroy,
And animal reluctance from the womb,
Endurance of your end's integrity,
Be strong in this: heaven shall be your tomb.

* John Frith, Tyndale's most loyal disciple, returned to Eng
land from the continent in 1533, when he was thirty years
old. He was arrested and burned at the stake. This letter
would have been written to Frith in prison from Tyndale in
Holland, where, not long after, he too was imprisoned and
burned at the stake for heresy.

Aix-La-Chappelle, 1945

How quietly in ruined state
The effigy of Charles the Great
Wastes in the rain! Baton and orb,
The rigid figure and the crown,
Tarnished by air and wet, absorb
His change, impassive in renown.

Northward along the Rhine, towns lie
Shattered by vague artillery:
Julich, Düren, whose Rathaus doors
The molten eagles seal, effaced,
Like Gladbach's partial walls and floors,
By snow impersonal as waste.

The South's white cities, terrible
With sensuous calm and beauty, fall
Through darkness to their fragrant streets.
France's smooth armor seeps her blood.
The European plain repeats
Its ageless night of ice and mud.

Despair shall rise. The dragon's gore
From off the torn cathedral floor
Forces his mind's dark cavity:
His sleep has been his innocence,
And his malignant growth shall be
Monstered by lucid violence.

The Wise Men

Far to the east I see them in my mind
Coming in every year to that one place.
They carry in their hands what they must find,
In their own faces bare what they shall face.

They move in silence, permanent and sure,
Like figurines of porcelain set with gold,
The colors of their garments bright and pure,
Their graceful features elegant and old.

They do not change: nor war nor peace define
Nor end the journey that each year the same
Renders them thus. They wait upon a sign
That promises no future but their name.

The Stoic: For Laura von Courten

All winter long you listened for the boom
Of distant cannon wheeled into their place.
Sometimes outside beneath a bombers' moon
You stood alone to watch the searchlights trace

Their careful webs against the boding sky,
While miles away on Munich's vacant square
The bombs lunged down with an unruly cry
Whose blast you saw yet could but faintly hear.

And might have turned your eyes upon the gleam
Of a thousand years of snow, where near the clouds
The Alps ride massive to their full extreme,
And season after season glacier crowds

The dark, persistent smudge of conifers.
Or seen beyond the hedge and through the trees
The shadowy forms of cattle on the furze,
Their dim coats white with mist against the freeze.

Or thought instead of other times than these,
Of other countries and of other sights:
Eternal Venice sinking by degrees
Into the very water that she lights;

Reflected in canals, the lucid dome
Of Maria dell'Salute at your feet,
Her triple spires disfigured by the foam.
Remembered in Berlin the parks, the neat

Footpaths and lawns, the clean spring foliage,
Where just short weeks before, a bomb unaimed
Had freed a raging lion from its cage,
Which in the mottled dark that trees enflamed

Killed one who hurried homeward from the raid.
And by yourself there standing in the chill
You must, with so much known, have been afraid
And chosen such a mind of constant will,

Which, though all time corrode with constant hurt,
Remains, until it occupies no space,
That which it is; and passionless, inert,
Becomes at last no meaning and no place.

Grove and Building

"Au soleil, dans l'immense forme du ciel pur . . ."
—Paul Valéry

When, having watched for a long time the trees
Scatter the sun among their shaded places,
You turn away, your face is many faces,
Each formed by the resistance of the leaves.

And through the dim contagion in your eyes
The agony of light which shade refuses
With bright decay a near façade infuses,
Drenched by the ebbing warmth of Paradise.

Its granite vaults the reach of passive trees,
And, shadowless, its final line of being
Extends a line beyond your shaded seeing
To train your sight on nothing that it sees.

There, at that moment of arrest, you feel
Against the blood veiling the eyes' repose
The prudent sun, the blood red solar Rose,
Unshadowed being turning like a wheel

At once clock-wise and also counter-wise;
Thus from its light whose motion is unending
All shadows turn and, on one axis bending,
Lose their umbrageous choice within your eyes.

The Mountain Cemetery

With their harsh leaves old rhododendrons fill
The crevices in grave plots' broken stones.
The bees renew the blossoms they destroy,

While in the burning air the pines rise still,
Commemorating long forgotten biers,
Whose roots replace the semblance of these bones.

The weight of cool, of imperceptible dust
That came from nothing and to nothing came
Is light within the earth and on the air.
The change that so renews itself is just.
The enormous, sundry platitude of death
Is for these bones, bees, trees, and leaves the same.

And splayed upon the ground and through the trees
The mountains' shadow fills and cools the air,
Smoothing the shape of headstones to the earth.
The rhododendrons suffer with the bees
Whose struggles loose ripe petals to the earth,
The heaviest burden it shall ever bear.

Our hard earned knowledge fits us for such sleep.
Although the spring must come, it passes too
To form the burden suffered for what comes.
Whatever we would give our souls to keep
Is only part of what we call the soul;
What we of time would threaten to undo

All time in its slow scrutiny has done.
For on the grass that starts about the feet
The body's shadow turns, to shape in time,
Soon grown preponderant with creeping shade,
The final shadow that is turn of earth;
And what seems won paid for as in defeat.

The Virgin Mary

The hovering and huge, dark, formless sway
That nature moves by laws we contemplate
We name for lack of name as order, fate,
God, principle, or primum mobile.

But in that graven image, word made wood
By skillful faith of him to whom she was
Eternal nature, first and final cause,
The form of knowledge knowledge understood
Bound human thought against the dark we find.
And body took the image of the mind
To shape in chaos a congruent form
Of will and matter, equal, side by side,
Upon the act of faith, within the norm
Of carnal being, blind and glorified.

CHARLES CAUSLEY

Recruiting Drive

Under the willow the willow
    I heard the butcher-bird sing,
Come out you fine young fellow
    From under your mother's wing.
I'll show you the magic garden
    That hangs in the beamy air,
The way of the lynx and the angry Sphinx
    And the fun of the freezing fair.

Lie down lie down with my daughter
    Beneath the Arabian tree,
Gaze on your face in the water
    Forget the scribbling sea.
Your pillow the nine bright shiners
    Your bed the spilling sand,
But the terrible toy of my lily-white boy
    Is the gun in his innocent hand.

You must take off your clothes for the doctor
    And stand as straight as a pin,

His hand of stone on your white breast-bone
　Where the bullets all go in.
They'll dress you in lawn and linen
　And fill you with Plymouth gin,
O the devil may wear a rose in his hair
　I'll wear my fine doe-skin.

My mother weeps as I leave her
　But I tell her it won't be long,
The murderers wail in Wandsworth Gaol
　But I shoot a more popular song.
Down in the enemy country
　Under the enemy tree
There lies a lad whose heart has gone bad
　Waiting for me, for me.

He says I have no culture
　And that when I've stormed the pass
I shall fall on the farm with a smoking arm
　And ravish his bonny lass.
Under the willow the willow
　Death spreads her dripping wings
And caught in the snare of the bleeding air
　The butcher-bird sings, sings, sings.

Ou Phrontis

To E. M. Forster

The bells assault the maiden air,
The coachman waits with a carriage and pair,
But the bridegroom says *I won't be there,*
　　I don't care!

Three times three times the banns declare
That the boys may blush and the girls may glare,
But the bridegroom is occupied elsewhere,
　　I don't care!

Lord, but the neighbours all will stare,
Their temperatures jump as high as a hare,
But the bridegroom says *I've paid my fare,*
   I don't care!

The bride she waits by the bed so bare,
Soft as a pillow is her hair,
But the bridegroom jigs with the leg of a chair,
   I don't care!

Say, but her father's a millionaire,
A girdle of gold all night will she wear,
You must your foolish ways forswear.
   I don't care!

Her mother will offer, if she dare,
A ring that is rich but not so rare
If you'll keep your friendship in repair.
   I don't care!

Her sisters will give you a plum and a pear
And a diamond saddle for your mare.
O bridegroom! For the night prepare!
   I don't care!

Her seven brothers all debonair
Will do your wishes and some to spare
If from your fancy you'll forbear.
   I don't care!

Say, but a maid you wouldn't scare
Now that you've got her in your snare?
And what about your son and heir?
   I don't care!

She'll leap she'll leap from the highest stair,
She'll drown herself in the river there,
With a silver knife her flesh she'll tear.
   I don't care!

Then another will lie in the silken lair
And cover with kisses her springing hair.

Another the bridal bed will share.
> *I don't care!*

I shall stand on my head on the table bare,
I shall kick my lily-white legs in the air,
I shall wash my hands of the whole affair,
> *I don't care!*

Note: The words *Ou phrontis* were carved by T. E. Lawrence over the door of his cottage at Clouds Hill, Dorset. They come from the story in Herodotus, on which this poem is based.

Cowboy Song

I come from Salem County
   Where the silver melons grow,
Where the wheat is sweet as an angel's feet
   And the zithering zephyrs blow.
I walk the blue bone-orchard
   In the apple-blossom snow,
Where the teasy bees take their honeyed ease
   And the marmalade moon hangs low.

My maw sleeps prone on the prairie
   In a boulder eiderdown,
Where the pickled stars in their little jam-jars
   Hang in a hoop to town.
I haven't see paw since a Sunday
   In eighteen seventy-three
When he packed his snap in a bitty mess-trap
   And said he'd be home by tea.

Fled is my fancy sister
   All weeping like the willow,
And dead is the brother I loved like no other
   Who once did share my pillow.
I fly the florid water
   Where run the seven geese round,

O the townsfolk talk to see me walk
    Six inches off the ground.

Across the map of midnight
    I trawl the turning sky,
In my green glass the salt fleets pass
    The moon her fire-float by.
The girls go gay in the valley
    When the boys come down from the farm,
Don't run, my joy, from a poor cowboy,
    I won't do you no harm.

The bread of my twentieth birthday
    I buttered with the sun,
Though I sharpen my eyes with lovers' lies
    I'll never see twenty-one.
Light is my shirt with lilies,
    And lined with lead my hood,
On my face as I pass is a plate of brass,
    And my suit is made of wood.

A Ballad for Katharine of Aragon

Queen of England, 1509-1533. Buried in Peterborough Ca-thedral

As I walked down by the river
Down by the frozen fen
I saw the grey cathedral
With the eyes of a child of ten.
O the railway arch is smoky
As the Flying Scot goes by
And but for the Education Act
Go Jumper Cross and I.

But war is a bitter bugle
That all must learn to blow
And it didn't take long to stop the song

In the dirty Italian snow.
O war is a casual mistress
And the world is her double bed
She has a few charms in her mechanised arms
But you wake up and find yourself dead.

The olive tree in winter
Casts her banner down
And the priest in white and scarlet
Comes up from the muddy town.
O never more will Jumper
Watch the Flying Scot go by
His funeral knell was a six-inch shell
Singing across the sky.

The Queen of Castile has a daughter
Who won't come home again
She lies in the grey cathedral
Under the arms of Spain.
O the Queen of Castile has a daughter
Torn out by the roots
Her lovely breast in a cold stone chest
Under the farmers' boots.

Now I like a Spanish party
And many O many the day
I have watched them swim as the night came dim
In Algeciras Bay.
O the high sierra was thunder
And the seven-branched river of Spain
Came down to the sea to plunder
The heart of the sailor again.

O shall I leap in the river
And knock upon paradise door
For a gunner of twenty-seven and a half
And a queen of twenty-four?
From the almond tree by the river
I watch the sky with a groan
For Jumper and Kate are always out late
And I lie here alone.

HENRI COULETTE

Intaglio

I have a picture in my room in which
Four gawky children strike a pose and stare
Out at the world without a worldly care.
Three girls and a boy in a paper hat:
The one too much a mouse to be a bitch,
The bitch, the actress, and the acrobat.

The roles I give them, half suggested by
The poses that they took, are meaningless,
For they are playing games. It is recess
Or summer—we have interrupted them.
They pose for us, with Agile romping by
And dark-eyed Pensive plucking at her hem.

This is my family. I dust them now
And then, and they return the courtesy
By never growing up. Thus, irony
Becomes a kind of family likeness, treasured
Not for the casual sameness of a brow
But for the attitudes one's mind has measured.

I knew an Agile once. To prove himself
The nimbler one, he pushed his books aside,
And crossed to Europe and the war, and died,
And his agility, which I believed a power
Then, then was gone, and his books on my shelf
Harvest the sunlit dust, hour after hour.

And there was Pensive, too, and everything
She touched was touched with fear. She married well,
Her people said, but marriage proves a hell
For those who marry but the flesh alone.
Who would have a known a turn of mind could bring
Such knowledge to a girl? Who would have known?

I think of her, the child with heavy heart,
Heavy with child, and, Child, I think of you
And all the follies you will journey through;
I know them as an author knows his book.
Action and thought are nothing if apart.
Love in a gesture, wisdom in a look—

These are the real births for which we die.
Outside, the neighbor children startle me,
Calling, "Allee, alleoutsinfree."
They cut for home. I hear a whirring skate
Fading through the darkness like a sigh.
I dust the frame and set the picture straight.

Antony and Cleopatra

[a sonnet sequence after Heredia]

I

Under the azure where the noon sun totters,
Its golden poop, its silk pavilions
As radiant as a galaxy of suns,
The ship flies in a heaven of blue waters

And from the hawk-like prow receives its name.
Gripping the rail with jewelled hands, she leans
Into the wind: the last of Egypt's queens,
The queen of sparrow-hawks, is out for game.

Here's Tarsus where the Roman Eagle rules
The empty market place; where, Prince of Fools,
Blond Bacchus draws a final, sober breath;

Where maid and eunuch whisper 'love and death,'
While Hawk and Eagle grouse and peck and lurch,
Two parakeets upon a single perch.

II

Glare! Shock! and it is done. An officer
Rallies the bronze platoons. The broken air

Echoes their cries and still their nostrils bear
Myrrh from the battlefield, the acrid myrrh.

Eyes of their comrades count the quiet dead.
Now, in the distance, like dead leaves, they see
The archers of Phraortes whirl and flee,
Glistening with sweat, their heads unhelmeted.

Under the floating purple, amid the blare
Of trumpeting monitors and level drums,
The eagles bow and point the way he comes,

Magnificent, reining his frightened mare—
This famous, bleeding Antony for whom
The incandescent sun becomes a plume.

III

The lovers pace the terrace nervously,
See Egypt dream beneath a sultry sky,
And hear the Nile, ambitious serpent, sigh
Through Sais and Bubastis for the sea.

The Roman feels beneath his stout cuirass—
Captive soldier cradled like a child—
Bending on his triumphant heart, the wild,
Barbaric body golden as his brass.

Winding his white face in her long black hair,
Her body drunk with lust, as light as air,
She offers up her lips and liquid eyes.

The Imperator bends to take his prize,
Sees in those gold-flecked eyes a troubled sea,
Immense and dark, where broken galleys flee.

DONALD DAVIE

At Knaresborough

'Broad acres, sir.' You hear them in my talk,
As tell-tale as a pigment in the skin.
Vowels as broad as all the plain of York
Proclaim me of this country and your kin.

And, gratified to have your guess endorsed,
You warm to me. I thaw, and am approved.
But, to be frank, the sentiment is forced,
When I pretend, for your sake, to be moved.

To feel so little, when his sympathies
Would be so much engaged (he would have said),
Surprised the poet too. But there it is,
The heart is not to be solicited.

Believe me, sir, I only ply my trade,
Which is to know when I am played upon.
You might have moved, you never shall persuade.
You grow too warm. I must be moving on.

The Evangelist

'My brethren . . .' And a bland, elastic smile
Basks on the mobile features of Dissent.
No hypocrite, you understand. The style
Befits a church that's based on sentiment.

Solicitations of a swirling gown,
The sudden vox humana, and the pause,
The expert orchestration of a frown
Deserve, no doubt, a murmur of applause.

The tides of feeling round me rise and sink;
Bunyan, however, found a place for wit.
Yes, I am more persuaded than I think;
Which is, perhaps, why I disparage it.

You round upon me, generously keen:
The man, you say, is patently sincere.
Because he is so eloquent, you mean?
That test was never patented, my dear.

If, when he plays upon your sympathies,
I'm pleased to be fastidious, and you
To be inspired, the vice in it is this:
Each does us credit, and we know it too.

The Garden Party

Above a stretch of still unravaged weald
In our Black Country, in a cedar-shade,
I found, shared out in tennis courts, a field
Where children of the local magnates played.

And I grew envious of their moneyed ease
In Scott Fitzgerald's unembarrassed vein.
Let prigs, I thought, fool others as they please,
I only wish I had my time again.

To crown a situation as contrived
As any in 'The Beautiful and Damned',
The phantom of my earliest love arrived;
I shook absurdly as I shook her hand.

As dusk drew in on cultivated cries,
Faces hung pearls upon a cedar-bough;
And gin could blur the glitter of her eyes,
But it's too late to learn to tango now.

My father, of a more submissive school,
Remarks the rich themselves are always sad.

There is that sort of equalizing rule;
But theirs is all the youth we might have had.

Remembering the 'Thirties

I

Hearing one saga, we enact the next.
We please our elders when we sit enthralled;
But then they're puzzled; and at last they're vexed
To have their youth so avidly recalled.

It dawns upon the veterans after all
That what for them were agonies, for us
Are high-brow thrillers, though historical;
And all their feats quite strictly fabulous.

This novel written fifteen years ago,
Set in my boyhood and my boyhood home,
These poems about 'abandoned workings,' show
Worlds more remote than Ithaca or Rome.

The Anschluss, Guernica—all the names
At which those poets thrilled or were afraid
For me mean schools and schoolmasters and games;
And in the process some-one is betrayed.

Ourselves perhaps. The Devil for a joke
Might carve his own initials on our desk,
And yet we'd miss the point because he spoke
An idiom too dated, Audenesque.

Raleigh's Guiana also killed his son.
A pretty pickle if we came to see
The tallest story really packed a gun,
The Telemachiad an Odyssey.

II

Even to them the tales were not so true
As not to be ridiculous as well:

The ironmaster met his Waterloo,
But Rider Haggard rode along the fell.

'Leave for Cape Wrath tonight!' They lounged away
On Fleming's trek or Isherwood's ascent.
England expected every man that day
To show his motives were ambivalent.

They played the fool, not to appear as fools
In time's long glass. A deprecating air
Disarmed, they thought, the jeers of later schools;
Yet irony itself is debonaire,

And, curiously, nothing now betrays
Their type to time's derision like this coy
Insistence on the quizzical, their craze
For showing Hector was a mother's boy.

A neutral tone is nowadays preferred.
And yet it may be better, if we must,
To find the stance impressive and absurd
Than not to see the hero for the dust.

For courage is the vegetable king,
The sprig of all ontologies, the weed
That beards the slag-heap with his hectoring,
Whose green adventure is to run to seed.

Homage to William Cowper

Mrs. Throckmorton's bull-finch sang a song
(Domesticate that comfortable bird!)
But still the deer has wandered from the herd,
The bard was not articulate for long.

A pasticheur of late-Augustan styles,
I too have sung the sofa and the hare,
Made nightmare ride upon a private air,
And hearths, extinguished, send a chill for miles.

This costive plan, this dense upholstery,
These mice and kittens, this constrictive rhyme,
These small Infernos of another time—
What's all this modish Hecuba to me?

Most poets let the morbid fancy roam.
The squalid rat broke through the finch's fence,
Which was a cage and still was no defence:
For Horror starts, like Charity, at home.

CATHERINE DAVIS

Nausea

Nothing will give delight.
What once was salt or sweet
Sickens the appetite
Like a corrupted meat.

Promiscuous disgust!
How shall I know or choose?
This loathing, like pure lust,
Taints all that I might use.

Like lust, this sick revulsion
Exhausts the flesh and bone,
Turns riot to compulsion,
And feeds itself alone.

Insights:

1. Passerculi

If you would have dark themes and high-flown words,
Great albatrosses drenched in sacredness,
Go read some other work; for I confess

I cannot make my verses to your taste.
And though they are not trifles made in haste,
Mine are to those such light things, little birds,
Sparrows among their kind, whose one last shift
Is shelter from the universal drift.

2.

Your kindness is no kindness now:
It is unkindness to allow
My unkind heart so to reveal
The differences it would conceal.
If I were, as I used to be,
As kind to you as you to me,
Or if I could but teach you how
To be unkind, as I am now,
That would be kindness of a kind,
To be again of a like mind.

3.

My self will flee, my shadow still pursue,
Whose self is but the shadow my self threw;
And while my unrest shall its rest undo,
My self, forsaking, still avenges you!

4.

In solitude, my thoughts hell-bent will flow,
But speech, breakwater, checks them as they go:
Converse with me—they reach you tame and slow.

5.

You ask sincerity,
That I be blind or rude:
If heart with tongue collude,
I see not what I see;
If tongue with heart agree,
Then you must bear the pain
Of injuries I sustain.

6. *This busy crowd*

They are not bees, this busy crowd,
They sting as hard and buzz as loud

And fly about, but do not mean:
Bohemian or Philistine,
Neither will bring, though both may thrive,
One drop of honey to the hive.

7.

Idleness, wretch, idleness ruins you!
Idleness works by more than mere inaction:
Exalts, among the great, great idlers, too,
And plunges you in riot and distraction!

8.

Beware, old scrounger, or, with winter come,
Your little impecuniosity
Will find at last the necessary sum
To cover all the waste there still must be:
All is the naked ground. And nothing, then,
Need fail you, who need never fail again.

9.

Comforting hope, how you have kept me warm!
Not that I have not gone, in freezing storm,
Head down against the wind, flat broke and sore,
But that I did not see myself before
As this mere fool, huddled, a shivering form
In last year's ragged things, and nothing more.

After a Time

After a time, all losses are the same.
One more thing lost is one thing less to lose;
And we go stripped at last the way we came.

Though we shall probe, time and again, our shame,
Who lack the wit to keep or to refuse,
After a time, all losses are the same.

No wit, no luck can beat a losing game;
Good fortune is a reassuring ruse:
And we go stripped at last the way we came.

Rage as we will for what we think to claim,
Nothing so much as this bare thought subdues:
After a time, all losses are the same.

The sense of treachery—the want, the blame—
Goes in the end, whether or not we choose,
And we go stripped at last the way we came.

So we, who would go raging, will go tame
When what we have we can no longer use:
After a time, all losses are the same;
And we go stripped at last the way we came.

KEITH DOUGLAS

Oxford

At home, as in no other city, here
summer holds her breath in a dark street
the trees nocturnally scented, lovers like moths
go by silently on the footpaths
and spirits of the young wait,
cannot be expelled, multiply each year.

In the meadows, walks, over the walls
the sunlight, far-travelled, tired and content,
warms the recollections of old men, touching
the hand of the scholar on his book, marching
through quadrangles and arches, at last spent
it leans through the stained windows and falls.

This then is the city of young men, of beginning,
ideas, trials, pardonable follies,
the lightness, seriousness and sorrow of youth.

And the city of the old, looking for truth,
browsing for years, the mind's seven bellies
filled, become legendary figures, seeming

Stones of the city, her venerable towers;
dignified, clothed by erudition and time.
For them it is not a city but an existence
outside which everything is a pretence:
within, the leisurely immortals dream
venerated and spared by the ominous hours.

Cairo Jag

Shall I get drunk or cut myself a piece of cake,
a pasty Syrian with a few words of English
or the Turk who says she is a princess—she dances
apparently by levitation? Or Marcelle, Parisienne
always preoccupied with her dull dead lover:
she has all the photographs and his letters
tied in a bundle and stamped *Décédé* in mauve ink.
All this takes place in a stink of jasmin.

But there are the streets dedicated to sleep
stenches and sour smells, the sour cries
do not disturb their application to slumber
all day, scattered on the pavement like rags
afflicted with fatalism and hashish. The women
offering their children brown-paper breasts
dry and twisted, elongated like the skull,
Holbein's signature. But this stained white town
is something in accordance with mundane conventions—
Marcelle drops her Gallic airs and tragedy
suddenly shrieks in Arabic about the fare
with the cabman, links herself so
with the somnambulists and legless beggars:
it is all one, all as you have heard.

But by a day's travelling you reach a new world
the vegetation is of iron

dead tanks, gun barrels split like celery
the metal brambles have no flowers or berries
and there are all sorts of manure, you can imagine
the dead themselves, their boots, clothes and possessions
clinging to the ground, a man with no head
has a packet of chocolate and a souvenir of Tripoli.

Vergissmeinicht

Three weeks gone and the combatants gone,
returning over the nightmare ground
we found the place again, and found
the soldier sprawling in the sun.

The frowning barrel of his gun
overshadowing. As we came on
that day, he hit my tank with one
like the entry of a demon.

Look. Here in the gunpit spoil
the dishonoured picture of his girl
who has put: *Steffi. Vergissmeinicht*
in a copybook gothic script.

We see him almost with content
abased, and seeming to have paid
and mocked at by his own equipment
that's hard and good when he's decayed.

But she would weep to see to-day
how on his skin the swart flies move;
the dust upon the paper eye
And the burst stomach like a cave.

For here the lover and killer are mingled
who had one body and one heart.
And death who had the soldier singled
has done the lover mortal hurt.

Homs, Tripolitania, 1943

Aristocrats

"I think I am becoming a God"

The noble horse with courage in his eye
clean in the bone, looks up at a shellburst:
away fly the images of the shires
but he puts the pipe back in his mouth.

Peter was unfortunately killed by an 88:
it took his leg away, he died in the ambulance.
I saw him crawling on the sand; he said
It's most unfair, they've shot my foot off.

How can I live among this gentle
obsolescent breed of heroes, and not weep?
Unicorns, almost,
for they are falling into two legends
in which their stupidity and chivalry
are celebrated. Each, fool and hero, will be an immortal.

The plains were their cricket pitch
and in the mountains the tremendous drop fences
brought down some of the runners. Here then
under the stones and earth they dispose themselves,
I think with their famous unconcern.
It is not gunfire I hear but a hunting horn.
                                   Enfidaville, Tunisia, 1943

Landscape with Figures

I

Perched on a great fall of air
a pilot or angel looking down
on some eccentric chart, a plain

dotted with useless furniture,
discerns drying on the sand vehicles
squashed dead or still entire, stunned
like beetles: scattered wingcases and
legs, heads, appear when the dust settles.

But you who like Thomas come
to poke fingers in the wounds
find monuments and metal posies.
On each disordered tomb
the steel is torn into fronds
by the lunatic explosive.

II

On sand and scrub the dead men wriggle
in their dowdy clothes. They are mimes
who express silence and futile aims
enacting this prone and motionless struggle
at a queer angle to the scenery,
crawling on the boards of the stage like walls,
deaf to the one who opens his mouth and calls
silently. The décor is a horrible tracery
of iron. The eye and mouth of each figure
bear the cosmetic blood and the hectic
colours death has the only list of.
A yard more and my little finger
could trace the maquillage of these stony actors:
I am the figure writhing on the backcloth.

Wadi Zem Zem, January, 1943

On a Return from Egypt

To stand here in the wings of Europe
disheartened, I have come away
from the sick land where in the sun lay
the gentle sloe-eyed murderers
of themselves, exquisites under a curse;
here to exercise my depleted fury.

For the heart is a coal, growing colder
when jewelled cerulean seas change
into grey rocks, grey water-fringe,
sea and sky altering like a cloth
till colour and sheen are gone both:
cold is an opiate of the soldier.

And all my endeavours are unlucky explorers
come back, abandoning the expedition;
the specimens, the lilies of ambition
still spring in their climate, still unpicked:
but time, time is all I lacked
to find them, as the great collectors before me.

The next month, then, is a window
and with a crash I'll split the glass.
Behind it stands one I must kiss,
person of love or death
a person or a wraith,
I fear what I shall find.

Egypt-England, 1943-44

Simplify Me When I'm Dead

Remember me when I am dead
and simplify me when I'm dead.

As the processes of earth
strip off the colour and the skin:
take the brown hair and blue eye

and leave me simpler than at birth,
when hairless I came howling in
as the moon entered the cold sky.

Of my skeleton perhaps,
so stripped, a learned man will say
"He was of such a type and intelligence," no more.

Thus when in a year collapse
particular memories, you may
deduce, from the long pain I bore

the opinions I held, who was my foe
and what I left, even my appearance
but incidents will be no guide.

Time's wrong-way telescope will show
a minute man ten years hence
and by distance simplified.

Through that lens see if I seem
substance or nothing: of the world
deserving mention or charitable oblivion,

not by momentary spleen
or love into decision hurled,
leisurely arrive at an opinion.

Remember me when I am dead
and simplify me when I'm dead.

Song

Do I venture away too far
from the hot coast of your love
whose southern virtues charmed me?
How long how long can I be safe,
for the poisonous sea and a cruel star
the one by day and one at night have charmed me.

And are you troubled with a fear
that I must be a seastruck lad
or that the devil armed me
with a compass in my head?
for the poisonous sea and a cruel star
the one by day and one at night have charmed me.

At night I see the hissing fire
when star and sea communicate
and they have alarmed me
by their interest and hate
for the poisonous sea and a cruel star
the one by day and one at night have charmed me.

O listen to the ship and hear
she sings all night a sailors' rune;
since the green water's claimed me
harm is coming to her soon
for the poisonous sea and a cruel star
the one by day and one at night have charmed me.

Yes, for I am doomed my dear
and I have jilted myself and you;
soon when the sea's embalmed me
I'll fade into the deceitful blue,
for the poisonous sea and a cruel star
the one by day and one at night have charmed me.

1942

Snakeskin and Stone

I praise a snakeskin or a stone:
a bald head or a public speech
I hate: the serpent's lozenges
are a calligraphy, and it is
truth these cryptograms teach,
the pebble is truth alone.
Complication belonging to the snake
who is as subtle as his gold, black, green—
it is right the stone is old
and smooth, utterly cruel and old.
These two are two pillars. Between
stand all the buildings truth can make,
a whole city, inhabited by lovers,
murderers, workmen and artists

not much recognized: all
who have no memorial
but are mere men. Even the lowest
never made himself a mask of words or figures.
The bald head is a desert
between country of life and country of death;
between the desolate projecting ears
move the wicked explorers, the flies
who know the dead bone is beneath
and from the skin the life half out
and dead words tumbled in heaps
in the papers lie in rows
awaiting burial. The speakers mouth
like a cold sea that sucks and spews them out
with insult to their bodies. Tangled they cruise
like mariners' bodies in the grave of ships.
Borrow hair for the bald crown,
borrow applause for the dead words;
for you who think the desert hidden
or the words, like the dry bones, living
are fit to profit from the world.
And God help the lover of snakeskin and stone.

DONALD FINKEL

The Clothing's New Emperor

Such as it is. Such as two men
Talking because there is nothing
Easier than to talk. All things
Momentary as that, as the flame

Between two mouths meeting
In simple speech, flame
Clothed in the commonest phrases,
Bent merely, as light bending

In water, and shaking. Such
As it is. Lips mouthing vowels
In a vacuum, as in a silent film,
Not empty, rather unheard speech,

Caught at the distance between
Two minds, talking because it is
Easy to talk. Nothing is
Given but the forms. They have seen

The clothes without the emperor.
Deceived by fleas, they see flesh
Under the shirt, blood rushing
Inside the sleeves and out of the collar.

An Esthetic of Imitation

Preferring resemblance to beauty,'
There were some who found more
Truth in Philoktetes' rotten legs
Than in the smooth buttocks
Of a hundred Venuses. There
Is something in certain events that
Drives one to repetition. The act
Is all; one says, This thing,
'Craftsmen, beggars, topers with rags,'
This thing.
                    With cheeks of silver,
Silanion inlaid the pallor of Iokaste.
Not life, rather this thing, which bangs
Silver into the real. Not there, rather
Before, or beside: 'the morning
After the taking of Troy, Odysseus
After slaying the suitors.'
                         Brother,
Nothing is real that has happened
Only once; and nothing can happen
Again, and still be true. One sings,
Not what was, but that it was;

What was true in flesh, is
Merely beautiful in silver.

The Sirens

The news lapped at us out of all
Horizons: the ticking night full
Of gods; sensed, heard the tactile

Sea turn in his bed, prickling
Among derelicts. When the song
Was clear enough, we spread our hair,

Caught it. Under the comb the strands
Whipped into fresh harmonies, untangled
Again. The wind took it, and he heard.

The droll ship swung leeward;
Caught sight of him (rather, could
Have seen, busy with the fugue)

Yanking his bonds, the strings of his wide
Neck drawn like shrouds, his scream
Caught in the sails.
                Now in a sea

Of wheat he rows, reconstructing.
In his ridiculous, lovely mouth the strains
Tumble into place. Do you think
Wax could have stopped us, or chains?

Hunting Song

The fox came lolloping, lolloping,
Lolloping. His tongue hung out
And his ears were high.
He was like death at the end of a string

When he came to the hollow
Log. Ran in one side
And out of the other. O
He was sly.

The hounds came tumbling, tumbling,
Tumbling. Their heads were low
And their eyes were red.
The sound of their breath was louder than death
When they came to the hollow
Log. They held at one end
But a bitch found the scent. O
They were mad.

The hunter came galloping, galloping,
Galloping. All damp was his mare
From her hooves to her mane.
His coat and his mouth were redder than death
When he came to the hollow
Log. He took in the rein
And over he went. O
He was fine.

The log, he just lay there, alone in
The clearing. No fox nor hound
Nor mounted man
Saw his black round eyes in their perfect disguise
(As the ends of a hollow
Log). He watched death go through him,
Around him and over him. O
He was wise.

Juan Belmonte, Torero

The first thing, I think, is a keen sense
Of the ridiculous. Before each corrida
To finger anew one's duties, one's motivations,
A housewife among suspicious vegetables.

Outside the mob shifts on its terrible
Haunches. It is strange: without them,
The whole thing is meaningless. The bull
Has more sense of his part. Many times I sit
Out there: I think to myself, how the hell
Can he do it? I see the bull tear out
Of the toril, and I am convinced that I should
Never be able to fight him.
                                        How much easier
In the old days. In Tablada, naked and dripping
Under the moon, losing the bull in the darkness;
Then suddenly the white horns, like the arms
Of a bathing girl.
                                Each time they expected
More, and each time I had less to give.
Now I no longer remember what is was that
I *meant* to give. The mob shakes its terrible
Hair. The old faenas are smoothed into
The sand. Glittering young men tread on it,
In their soft slippers and their bravery.

W. S. GRAHAM

Letter II

Burned in this element
To the bare bone, I am
Trusted on the language.
I am to walk to you
Through the night and through
Each word you make between
Each word I burn bright in
On this wide reach. And you,
Within what arms you lie,
Hear my burning ways
Across these darknesses

That move and merge like foam.
Lie in the world's room,
My dear, and contribute
Here where all dialogues write.

Younger in the towered
Tenement of night he heard
The shipyards with nightshifts
Of lathes turning their shafts.
His voice was a humble ear
Hardly turned to her.
Then in a welding flash
He found his poetry arm
And turned the coat of his trade.
From where I am I hear
Clearly his heart beat over
Clydeside's far hammers
And the nightshipping firth.
What's he to me? Only
Myself I died from into
These present words that move.
In that high tenement
I got a great grave.

Tonight in sadly need
Of you I move inhuman
Across this space of dread
And silence in my mind.
I walk the dead water
Burning language towards
You where you lie in the dark
Ascension of all words.
Yet where? Where do you lie
Lost to my cry and hidden
Away from the word's downfall?
O offer some way tonight
To make your love take place
In every word. Reply.
Time's branches burn to hear.
Take heed. Reply. Here
I am driven burning on

This loneliest element. Break
Break me out of this night,
This silence where you are not,
Nor any within earshot.
Break break me from this high
Helmet of idiocy.

Water water wallflower
Growing up so high
We are all children
We all must die.
Except Willie Graham
The fairest of them all.
He can dance and he can sing
And he can turn his face to the wall.
Fie, fie, fie for shame
Turn your face to the wall again.

Yes, laugh then cloudily laugh
Though he sat there as deaf
And worn to a stop
As the word had given him up.
Stay still. That was the sounding
Sea he moved on burning
His still unending cry.
That night hammered and waved
Its starry shipyard arms,
And it came to inherit
His death where these words merge.
This is his night writ large.
In Greenock the bright breath
Of night's array shone forth
On the nightshifting town.
Thus younger burning in
The best of his puny gear
He early set out
To write him to this death
And to that great breath
Taking of the sea,
The graith of Poetry.
My musing love lie down

Within his arms. He dies
Word by each word into

Myself now at this last
Word I die in. This last.

Baldy Bane

Shrill the fife, kettle the drum,
   My Queens my Sluts my Beauties
Show me your rich attention
   Among the shower of empties.
And quiet be as it was once
   It fell on a night late
The muse has felled me in this bed
   That in the wall is set.
Lie over to me from the wall or else
   Get up and clean the grate.

On such a night as this behind
   McKellar's Tanworks' wall
It seems I put my hand in hers
   As we played at the ball.
So began a folly that
   I hope will linger late,
Though I am of the kitchen bed
   And of the flannel sheet.
Lie over to me from the wall or else
   Get up and clean the grate.

Now pay her no attention now,
   Nor that we keep our bed.
It is yon hoodie on the gate
   Would speak me to the dead.
And though I am embedded here
   The creature to forget
I ask you one and all to come
   Let us communicate.

Lie over to me from the wall or else
  Get up and clean the grate.

Make yourself at home here.
  My words you move within.
I made them all by hand for you
  To use as your own.
Yet I'll not have it said that they
  Leave my intention out,
Else I, an old man, I will up
  And at that yella-yite.
Lie over to me from the wall or else
  Get up and clean the grate.

You're free to jig your fiddle or let
  It dally on the bow.
Who's he that bums his chat there,
  Drunk as a wheelbarrow?
Hey, you who visit an old man
  That a young wife has got,
Mind your brain on the beam there
  And watch the lentil pot.
Lie over to me from the wall or else
  Get up and clean the grate.

Now pay her no attention.
  I am the big bowbender.
These words shall lie the way I want
  Or she'll blacklead the fender.
No shallop she, her length and depth
  Is Clyde and clinker built.
When I have that one shafted I
  Allow my best to out.
Lie over to me from the wall or else
  Get up and clean the grate.

Full as a whelk, full as a whelk
  And sad when all is done.
The children cry me Baldy Bane
  And the great catches are gone.

But do you know my mother's tune,
    For it is very sweet?
I split my thumb upon the barb
    The last time I heard it.
Lie over to me from the wall or else
    Get up and clean the grate.

Squeeze the box upon the tune
    They call Kate Dalrymple O.
Cock your ears upon it and
    To cock your legs is simple O.
Full as a whelk, full as a whelk
    And all my hooks to bait.
Is that the nightshift knocking off?
    I hear men in the street.
Lie over to me from the wall or else
    Get up and clean the grate.

Move to me as you birl, Meg.
    Your mother was a great whore.
I have not seen such pas de bas
    Since up in Kirreimuir.
I waded in your shallows once,
    Now drink up to that.
It makes the blood go up and down
    And lifts the sneck a bit.
Lie over to me from the wall or else
    Get up and clean the grate.

Through the word and through the word,
    And all is sad and done,
Who are you that these words
    Make this fall upon?
Fair's fair, upon my word,
    And that you shall admit,
Or I will blow your face in glass
    And then I'll shatter it.
Lie over to me from the wall or else
    Get up and clean the grate.

If there's a joke between us
   Let it lie where it fell.
The exact word escapes me
   And that's just as well.
I always have the tune by ear.
   You are an afterthought.
But when the joke and the grief strike
   Your heart beats on the note.
Lie over to me from the wall or else
   Get up and clean the grate.

Full as a whelk, full as a whelk
   My brain is blanketstitched.
It is the drink has floored us
   And Meg lies unlatched.
Lie over to me, my own muse.
   The bed is our estate.
Here's a drink to caulk your seams
   Against the birling spate.
Lie over to me from the wall or else
   Get up and clean the grate.

Now pay her no attention, you.
   Your gears do not engage.
By and large it's meet you should
   Keep to your gelded cage.
My ooze, my merry-making muse,
   You're nothing to look at.
But prow is proud and rudder rude
   Is the long and short of that.
Lie over to me from the wall or else
   Get up and clean the grate.

Think of a word and double it.
   Admit my metaphor.
But leave the muscle in the verse,
   It is the Skerry Vore.
Can you wash a sailor's shirt
   And can you wash it white?
O can you wash a sailor's shirt
   The whitest in the fleet?

Lie over to me from the wall or else
  Get up and clean the grate.

Full as a whelk and ending,
  Surprise me to my lot.
The glint of the great catches
  Shall not again be caught.
But the window is catching
  The slow mend of light.
Who crossed these words before me
  Crossed my meaning out.
Lie over to me from the wall or else
  Get up and clean the grate.

Cry me Baldy Bane but cry
  The hoodie off the gate,
And before you turn away
  Turn to her last estate.
She lies to fell me on the field
  Of silence I wrote.
By whose endeavour do we fare?
  By the word in her throat.
Lie over to me from the wall or else
  Get up and clean the grate.

She lies to fell me on the field
  That is between us here.
I have but to lift the sneck
  With a few words more.
Take kindly to Baldy Bane, then
  And go your ways about.
Tell it in the Causewayside
  And in Cartsburn Street,
Lie over to me from the wall or else
  Get up and clean the grate.

Love me near, love me far.
  Lie over from the wall.
You have had the best of me
  Since we played at the ball.

I cross the Fingal of my stride
  With you at beauty heat.
And I burn my words behind me.
  Silence is shouted out.
Lie over to me from the wall or else
  Get up and clean the grate.

The Hill of Intrusion

The ear the answer
Hears the wrecked cry
Of the one-time
Holiday boy who
Feathered his oars
On a calm firth
Held still by hills.
Now grey rock clenches
Round the rower over-
Taken by rough
White-haired sea-troughs
That ride the foam
Of Time's bare back.
Wrecked pile of past
Events cindered
Into a charcoal
Of kindling power
And constellations
Of united hearts,
These make reply
To the flare flying
Off from the endangered
Watchman wornout.
The winds from a hill
Halfway Ben Narnain
And halfway hill
Of intrusion into
The silence between
My heart and those
Elements of nature

That are my food,
Sound out alarm
Over the baling
Prisoners of water
This night unsheltered.
The ear says more
Than any tongue.
The ear sings better
Than any sound
It hears on earth
Or waters perfect.
The ear the answer
Hears the caged cry
Of those prisoners
Crowded in a gesture
Of homesickness.

CHARLES GULLANS

Narcissus

Water, with lidless stare,
Invites a cool surmise,
Holds there his curious eyes,
Blind with the mid-day glare
    And false surprise.

The depths are yet opaque,
Because the glassy shelf
Returns him to himself,
Pure surface like the lake;
    Self cries to self.

He moves, and sun floods through,
The liquid vaults run clear.
Color is shadow here,
Thin azure and deep blue,
    Like sudden fear.

The silent depths disclose
With radiant pretence
A purer ambience
Than anything he knows,
  Bright innocence.

Calmly, the surface burns.
Intense, preoccupied,
Not pausing to decide,
He cleaves the russet ferns
  And moist bank-side,

Childlike and golden-thighed,
Sensuous, yet all too pure,
Impatient to secure
What life could not provide
  Nor love endure.

Autumn: An Ode

The late, retarding, and unsettled season
Works in the air with a distracting aim,
Loosing the heart from a distempered reason
To burn, like autumn, with low, sullen flame.

The year but deepens and protracts the lesion,
The heart surrenders to the time and place,
Leaves, casual and dull, with dull adhesion
Litter the garden beds, the green efface

As augurs of some final desolation;
But time delays, the year withholds the tides
That feeling needs to bring a consummation.
It is despair that, unresolved, abides.

Autumn's despair is summer's pride unending—
O pride, that like the summer's wealth assailed
Seems fallen, but to new resplendence bending,
Your true perfection in despair is veiled.

Solicitude is vain! a vain allegiance
To all the dead and dying fills the heart,
Unsatisfied forever, with its grievance,
To wish and want and find no perfect part.

Desiring nothing is complete possession
Or perfect pride put on to outface life;
The final and irrevocable cession
Is death alone, in which we leave the strife

Between the lusts of having and foregoing.
I would possess all in unmeasured part
Or all surrender to despise time's flowing
With perfect resignation in my heart.

Simplicity were but a last evasion,
Swift to destroy me; hesitance were still,
In limited and incomplete persuasion,
The calm of ignorance that bides its ill.

To one choice only and all else decrying
No perfect motion of my will assents.
To what end does the year perfect its dying,
The heart its pride? Aimless the year descends.

O pride of life, O pride in resignation,
Your malice lingers in the season's breath,
Joy unfulfilled, despair in consummation—
This progress to completion moves like death.

First Love

She fled in anguish; he pursued desire,
A god grown fleshly in a mortal fire.
Even in flight, what was revealed of her
Seemed fair, but what was hid still lovelier,
More tangible than all that then lay bare
To his impassioned eyes and her despair.

He followed blindly on her stumbling feet,
Reached for her white arms, and in rising heat
Lost sight of all but her retreating back
In the dense brush along the forest track.
He knew himself emerging from the shade
Into the riven sunlight of a glade
That broke upon his eyes. Trembling afresh,
Knowing his hand already on her flesh,
He plunged, intent, by matted bush and tree,
And then was startled from himself to see
Her brows descending toward a harsher mien
And where his hand touched flesh a quickened green.

Poema Morale

How foolishly I loved
Since you could not be moved
From disaffection:
Pity has always proved
To be rejection.

To what had I been true
In loving so? Not you,
But to illusion,
Cherished until you knew
Its full intrusion.

And if I love you still,
Why then, the heart is ill,
And ill in action,
Corrupting all the will
By its distraction.

I'll not love you again
Nor relive an old pain
In a changed fashion,
My heart has so long been
Calmed by dispassion.

To a Friend

Scorn me as reason, who am always there,
Loud at the gate, louder than your despair,
Crowding the edges of your meditation,
But think what bade me come to take that station.

I have not come, like conscience, unpreferred,
To call insistently and be deferred,
And not with pride, in which I am offended,
But dignity, separate and undefended.

There is not room for pride between such friends
As we have been, who need not make amends
For casual and chance differences of mind,
But ferity in us were still unkind.

I came at first upon your own request,
Now to be driven out like a rude guest
And nothing said of what has moved you so.
I find in silence your command to go,

But wonder still between the gate and door.
Now I have told you all and speak no more,
Think what you say, while I shall still be there,
My own voice silent in the morning air.

THOM GUNN

A Mirror for Poets

It was a violent time. Wheels, racks, and fires
In every writer's mouth, and not mere rant.
Certain shrewd herdsmen, in the twisted wires

Of penalty folding the realm, were thanked
For organising spies and secret police
By richness in the flock, which they could fleece.

Hacks in the Fleet and nobles in the Tower:
Shakespeare must keep the peace, and Jonson's thumb
Be branded (for manslaughter), to the power
Of irons Southampton's patronage was come.
Above all swayed the diseased and doubtful queen:
Her state canopied by the glamor of pain.

In this society the boundaries met
Of life and life, at danger; with no space
Being left between, except where might be set
That mathematical point whose time and place
Could not exist. Yet at this point they found
Arcadia, a fruitful permanent land.

The faint and stumbling crowds were dim to sight
Who had no time for pity or for terror:
Here moved the Forms, with their own pace and light,
In which an act or thought perceived its error.
The hustling details, calmed and relevant.
Here mankind might behold its whole extent.

Here in a cave the Paphlagonian King
Crouched, waiting for his greater counterpart
Who one remove from likelihood may seem,
But several nearer to the human heart.
In exile from dimension, change by storm,
Here his huge magnanimity was born.

Yet the historians tell us, life meant less,
It was a violent time, and evil-smelling.
Jonson howled "Hell's a grammar-school to this,"
But found renunciation well worth telling.
Winnowing with his flail of comedy
He showed coherence in society.

In street, in tavern, happening would cry
"I am myself, but part of something greater,

Find poets what that is, do not pass by,
For feel my fingers in your pia mater.
I am a cruelly insistent friend:
You cannot smile at me and make an end."

The Wound

The huge wound in my head began to heal
About the beginning of the seventh week.
Its valleys darkened, its villages became still:
Waiting, I did not move and dared not speak;
So reason might again be joined to will.

But constantly my mind returned to Troy.
After I sailed the seas I fought in turn
On both sides, sharing even Helen's joy
Of place, and growing up—to see Troy burn—
As Neoptolemus, that stubborn boy.

I lay and rested as prescription said.
Manoeuvred with the Greeks, or sallied out
Each day with Hector. Finally my bed
Became Achilles' tent, to which the lout
Thersites came reporting numbers dead.

I was myself: subject to no man's breath:
My own commander was my enemy.
And while my belt hung up, sword in the sheath,
Thersites shambled in and breathlessly
Cackled about my friend Patroclus' death.

I called for armour, rose, and did not reel.
But, when I thought, rage at his noble pain
Flew to my head, and turning I could feel
My wound break open wide. Over again
I had to let those storm-lit valleys heal.

Incident on a Journey

One night I reached a cave: I slept, my head
Full of the air. There came about daybreak
A red-coat soldier to the mouth, who said
'I am not living, in hell's pains I ache,
    But I regret nothing.'

His forehead had a bloody wound whose streaming
The pallid staring face illuminated.
Whether his words were mine or his, in dreaming
I found they were my deepest thoughts translated.
    '*I regret nothing*'

'Turn your closed eyes to see upon these walls
A mural scratched there by an earlier man,
And coloured with the blood of animals:
Showing humanity beyond its span,
    Regretting nothing.

'No plausible nostalgia, no brown shame
I had when treating with my enemies.
And always when a living impulse came
I acted, and my action made me wise.
    And I regretted nothing.

'I as possessor of unnatural strength
Was hunted, one day netted in a brawl;
A minute far beyond a minute's length
Took from me passion, strength, and life, and all.
    But I regretted nothing.

'Their triumph left my body in the dust;
The dust and beer still clotting in my hair
When I rise lonely, will-less. Where I must
I go, and what I must I bear.
    And I regret nothing.

'My lust runs yet and is unsatisfied,
My hate throbs yet but I am feeble-limbed;

If as an animal I could have died
My death had scattered instinct to the wind,
   Regrets as nothing.'

Later I woke. I started to my feet.
The valley light, the mist already going.
I was alive and felt my body sweet,
Uncaked blood in all its channels flowing.
   I would regret nothing.

Tamer and Hawk

I thought I was so tough,
But gentled at your hands
Cannot be quick enough
To fly for you and show
That when I go I go
At your commands.

Even in flight above
I am no longer free:
You seeled me with your love,
I am blind to other birds—
The habit of your words
Has hooded me.

As formerly, I wheel
I hover and I twist,
But only want the feel,
In my possessive thought,
Of catcher and of caught
Upon your wrist.

You but half civilise,
Taming me in this way.
Through having only eyes
For you I fear to lose,
I lose to keep, and choose
Tamer as prey.

Merlin in the Cave:
He Speculates Without a Book

This was the end and yet, another start:
Held by the arms of lust from lust I pace
About the dim fulfilment of my art,
Impatient in the flesh I eye a space
Where, warlock, once I might have left this place,
A form of life my tool, creeping across
The shelving rock as rank convolvulus.

The Rock. The space, too narrow for a hand.
Pressing my head between two slopes of stone
I peer at what I do not understand,
The movement: clouds, and separate rooks blown
Back on their flight. Where do they fly, alone?
I lost their instinct. It was late. To me
The bird is only meat for augury.

And here the mauve convolvulus falls in,
Its narrow stalk as fat and rich in sap
As I was rich in lusting to begin
A life I could have had and finished up
Years, years before. With aphrodisiac
I brought back vigour; oiled and curled my hair;
Reduced my huge obesity, to wear

The green as tightly girdled at my waist
As any boy who leapt about the court;
And with an unguent I made my chest
Fit for the iron plate. I still held short
Of wrestling as the boys did: from their sport
They slid back panting on the tiles to look
At one distinguished now by scent, not book.

Love was a test: I was all-powerful,
So failed, because I let no fault intrude.
A philosophic appetite. By rule

I calculated each fond attitude
But those that self-distrust makes more than mood,
The quick illogical motions, negative
But evidence that lovers move and live.

I watch the flux I never guessed: the grass;
The watchful animal that gnaws a root,
Knowing possession means the risk of loss;
Ripeness that rests an hour in the fruit.
Yet locked here with the very absolute
I challenged, I must try to break the hold:
This cave is empty, and is very cold.

I must grow back through knowledge, passing it
Like casual landmarks in a well-known land,
Great mausoleums over ancient wit,
Doors that would swing at my complacent hand;
And come at last, being glad to understand
The touched, the seen, and only those, to where
I find the earth is suddenly black and near.

And having reached the point where there remain
No knacks or habits, and these empty cells
Are matched by a great emptiness in my brain:
Unhampered by remembered syllables,
The youth I wasted at precocious spells
Will grow upon me, and my wants agree
In the sweet promiscuity of the bee.

And yet, the danger. All within my mind
Hovers complete, and if it never grows
It never rots; for what I leave behind
Contains no fight within itself: the rose
Is full and drops no petal, emblems doze
Perfect and quiet as if engraved in books,
Not like the fighting boys and wind-torn rooks

The bee's world and the rook's world are the same:
Where clouds do, or do not, let through the light;
Too mixed, unsimple, for a simple blame;
Belligerent: but no one starts the fight,

And nothing ends it but a storm or night.
Alchemists, only, boil away the pain,
And pick out value as one small dry grain.

And turned upon the flooding relative,
What could I do but start the quest once more
Towards the terrible cave in which I live,
The absolute prison where chance thrust me before
I built it round me on my study floor;
What could I do but seek the synthesis
As each man does, of what his nature is?

Knowing the end to movement, I will shrink
From movement not for its own wilful sake.
—How can a man live, and not act or think
Without an end? But I must act, and make
The meaning in each movement that I take.
Rook, bee, you are the whole and not a part.
This is an end, and yet another start.

The Corridor

A separate place between the thought and felt
The empty hotel corridor was dark.
But here the keyhole shone, a meaning spark.
What fires were latent in it! So he knelt.

Now, at the corridor's much lighter end,
A pierglass hung upon the wall and showed,
As by an easily decyphered code,
Dark, door, and man, hooped by a single band.

He squinted through the keyhole, and within
Surveyed an act of love that frank as air
He was too ugly for, or could not dare,
Or at a crucial moment thought a sin.

Pleasure was simple thus: he mastered it.
If once he acted as participant

He would be mastered, the inhabitant
Of someone else's world, mere shred to fit.

He moved himself to get a better look
And then it was he noticed in the glass
Two strange eyes in a fascinated face
That watched him like a picture in a book.

The instant drove simplicity away—
The scene was altered, it depended on
His kneeling, when he rose they were clean gone
The couple in the keyhole; this would stay.

For if the watcher of the watcher shown
There in the distant glass, should be watched too,
Who can be master, free of others; who
Can look around and say he is alone?

Moreover, who can know that what he sees
Is not distorted, that he is not seen
Distorted by a pierglass, curved and lean?
Those curious eyes, through him, were linked to these—

These lovers altered in the cornea's bend.
What could he do but leave the keyhole, rise,
Holding those eyes as equal in his eyes,
And go, one hand held out, to meet a friend?

Before the Carnival

a painting by Carl Timner

Look, in the attic, the unentered room,
A naked boy leans on the outspread knees
Of his tall brother lolling in costume,
Tights, vest, and cap, of one who on trapeze
Finds comfort farthest from complacencies.

Behind the little boy and acrobat
Through circling half-light from their down-shed musing
Hurries the miser in his double hat;
The dry guitar he holds is still, abusing
All others who play music of their choosing.

And lit by a sudden artificial beam
A smocked pretender with his instrument,
Knowing that he is fragment of a dream,
Smirks none the less with borrowed merriment
And twangs for approbation from the front.

Why should they listen when he sings about
The joy of others that he cannot share?
A sexual gossip with a doll-like pout
He cannot touch the objects of his stare:
A prodigal's reflections swimming there.

The boy, his brother's hand upon his arm,
Sees neither where the lava flow of chance
Overtook habit, for he feels the palm
Of him whose turning muscle's nonchalance
Transforms to clockwork their prepared advance.

He too must pick an instrument at length
For this is painted during carnival:
Shall it be then a simple rung of strength
Or these with many strings where well-trained skill
May touch one while it keeps the others still?

And both must dress for the trooping, but the man
Is yet too active and the boy too young
For cloak or fur of heavy thought. They scan
The pace of silence, by the dancers shown
Robes of bright scarlet, horns that were never blown.

The Nature of an Action

I

Here is a room with heavy-footed chairs,
A glass bell loaded with wax grapes and pears,

A polished table, holding down the look
Of bracket, mantelpiece, and marbled book.

Staying within the cluttered square of fact,
I cannot slip the clumsy fond contact:

So step into the corridor and start,
Directed by the compass of my heart.

II

Although the narrow corridor appears
So short, the journey took me twenty years.

Each gesture that my habit taught me fell
Down to the boards and made an obstacle.

I paused to watch the fly marks on a shelf,
And found the great obstruction of myself.

I reached the end but, pacing back and forth,
I could not see what reaching it was worth.

In corridors the rooms are undefined:
I groped to feel a handle in the mind.

Testing my faculties I found a stealth
Of passive illness lurking in my health.

And though I saw the corridor stretch bare,
Dusty, and hard, I doubted it was there;

Doubted myself, what final evidence
Lay in perceptions or in common sense?

III

My cause lay in the will, that opens straight
Upon an act for the most desperate.

That simple handle found, I entered in
The other room, where I had never been.

I found within it heavy-footed chairs,
A glass bell loaded with wax grapes and pears,

A polished table, holding down the look
Of bracket, mantelpiece, and marbled book.

Much like the first, this room in which I went.
Only my being there is different.

DONALD HALL

The Sleeping Giant

[A Hill, so Named, in Hamden, Connecticut]

The whole day long, under the walking sun
That poised an eye on me from its high floor,
Holding my toy beside the clapboard house
I looked for him, the summer I was four.

I was afraid the waking arm would break
From the loose earth and rub against his eyes
A fist of trees, and the whole country tremble
In the exultant labor of his rise;

Then he with giant steps in the small streets
Would stagger, cutting off the sky, to seize
The roofs from house and home because we had
Covered his shape with dirt and planted trees;

And then kneel down and rip with fingernails
A trench to pour the enemy Atlantic
Into our basin, and the water rush,
With the streets full and all the voices frantic.

That was the summer I expected him.
Later the high and watchful sun instead
Walked low behind the house, and school began,
And winter pulled a sheet over his head.

Je Suis Une Table

It has happened suddenly,
by surprise, in an arbor,
or while drinking good coffee,
after speaking, or before,

that I dumbly inhabit
a density; in language
nothing is to prevent it,
nothing to retain an edge.

Arrant ignorance presents,
later, words for a function,
but it is the weak pretense
of speech, by mere convention,

and there is nothing at all
but the work of years, nothing
to relieve on principle
now this intense thickening.

Habit of conversation
(thickly turned thing) may make none.

My Son, My Executioner

My son, my executioner,
    I take you in my arms,
Quiet and small and just astir,
    And whom my body warms.

Sweet death, small son, our instrument
    Of immortality,
Your cries and hungers document
    Our bodily decay.

We twenty-five and twenty-two,
    Who seemed to live forever,
Observe enduring life in you
    And start to die together.

I take into my arms the death
    Maturity exacts,
And name with my imperfect breath
    The mortal paradox.

The Body Politic

I shot my friend to save my country's life,
And when the happy bullet struck him dead,
I was saluted by the drum and fife
Corps of a high school, while the traitor bled.

I never thought until I pulled the trigger
But that I did the difficult and good.
I thought republics stood for something bigger,
For the mind of man, as Plato said they stood.

So when I heard the duty they assigned,
Shooting my friend seemed only sanity;

To keep disorder from the state of mind
Was mental rectitude, it seemed to me.

The audience dispersed. I felt depressed.
I went to where my orders issued from,
But the right number on the street was just
A rickety old house, vacant and dumb.

I tried to find the true address, but where?
Nobody told me what I really wanted;
Just secretaries sent me here and there
To other secretaries. I was daunted.

Poor Fred. His presence will be greatly missed
By children and by cronies by the score.
The State (I learn too late) does not exist;
Man lives by love, and not by metaphor.

Marriage

When in the bedded dark of night
I touch your body huddled tight,

Though each is singular and free
In numerous humanity,

I have some special knowledge then
That crosses and will cross again.

Abroad Thoughts from Home

My history extends
Where moved my tourist hands,
Who traveled on their own
Without a helping brain.

My hands that domineered
My body lacking mind
Pulled me around the globe
Like any country rube.

No more automaton,
Smarter and settled down,
I choose to move my hands
Which way my will extends.

I marvel now to mark
The geographic work
Done by my brainless touch
On every foreign latch.

In active consciousness
I now rehearse those trips
Which I no longer take
And only partly took.

Sestina

Hang it all, Ezra Pound, there is only the one sestina!
Or so I thought before, always supposing
The subject of them invariably themselves.
That is not true. Perhaps they are nearly a circle,
And they tell their motifs like party conversation,
Formally repetitious, wilfully dull,

But who are we to call recurrence dull?
It is not exact recurrence that makes a sestina,
But a compromise between a conversation
And absolute repetition. It comes from supposing
That there is a meaning to the almost-circle,
And that laws of proportion speak of more than themselves.

I think of the types of men who have loved themselves,
Who studious of their faces made them dull

To find them subtle; for the nearly a circle,
This is the danger. The introvert sestina
May lose its voice by childishly supposing
It holds a hearer with self-conversation.

When we are bound to a tedious conversation,
We pay attention to the words themselves
Until they lose their sense, perhaps supposing
Such nonsense is at very least less dull.
Yet if the tongue is held by a sestina,
It affirms not words but the shape of the unclosed circle.

The analogy: not the precise circle,
Nor the loose patching of a conversation
Describes the repetition of a sestina;
Predictable, yet not repeating themselves
Exactly, they are like life, and hardly dull,
And not destroyed by critical supposing.

Since there is nothing precise (always supposing)
Consider the spiraling, circular, not full-circle
As the type of existence, the dull and never dull
Predictable, general movement of conversation,
Where things seem often more, slightly, than themselves,
And make us wait for the coming, like a sestina.

And so we name the sestina's subject, supposing
Our lives themselves dwindle, an incomplete circle;
About which, conversation is not dull.

Munch's Scream

1. Observe. Ridged, raised, tactile, the horror
   of the skinned head is there. It is skinned
   which had a covering-up before,
   and now is nude, and is determined

   by what it perceives. The blood not Christ's,
   blood of death without resurrection,

winds flatly in the air. Habit foists
conventional surrender to one

response in vision, but it fails here,
where the partaking viewer is freed
into the under-skin of his fear.
Existence is laid bare, and married

to a movement of caught perception
where the unknown will become the known
as one piece of the rolling mountain
becomes another beneath the stone

which shifts now toward the happy valley
which is not prepared, as it could not
be, for the achieved catastrophe
which produces no moral upshot,

no curtain, epilogue, nor applause,
no Dame to return purged to the Manse,
(the Manse is wrecked)—not even the pause,
the repose of art that has distance.

2. We, unlike Munch, observe his The Scream
making words, since perhaps we too know
the head's "experience of extreme
disorder." We have made our bravo,

but such, of course, will never equal
the painting. What is the relation?
A word, which is at once richly full
of attributes: thinginess, reason,

reference, time, noise among others;
bounces off the firm brightness of paint
as if it had no substance, and errs
toward verbalism, naturally. Mayn't

we say that time cannot represent
space in art? "The fascination of

what's impossible" may be present,
motivating the artist to move.

So the poet, the talker, aims his
words at the object, and his words go
faster and faster, and now he is
like a cyclotron, breaking into

the structure of things by repeated
speed and force in order to lay bare
in words, naturally, unworded
insides of things, the things that are there.

MICHAEL HAMBURGER

A Song About Great Men

Pity those men who from the start
were martyrs to some dream or art,
who marched through continents or tried
to till the desert of the heart,
who won or lost the game and died.

Not Immortality but Time
flourished the whip that made them climb
frail Everests or try to hide
the grief of Adam in a rhyme;
they found or lost themselves and died.

Whether an empire or a book
was the rich bait upon the hook
that landed them, do not deride
the rare explorers who forsook
their native shelters, bit and died.

Pity old Abelard who drove
angels and devils from his love,

and Casanova's foolish pride
in pushing what he could not move:
they won or lost the game and died.

Pity the men whose vast desire
was both the fuel and the fire,
who could not, though we can, divide
the plucking finger from the lyre,
but set their souls to words and died.

Between the poles of love and death
they too were torn and spent their breath
in vain endeavours to decide
between the garden and the wreath,
and still endeavoured when they died.

Pity those men who from the start
defied the desert of the heart,
the victims of some crazy pride
in love, in armies or in art,
who won or lost their game and died.

A Poet's Progress

Like snooker balls thrown on the table's faded green,
rare ivory and weighted with his best ambitions,
at first his words are launched: not certain what they mean,
he loves to see them roll, rebound, assume positions
which—since not he—some higher power has assigned.
But now the game begins: dead players, living critics
are watching him—and suddenly one eye goes blind,
the hand that holds the cue shakes like a paralytic's,
till every thudding, every clinking sound portends
new failure, new defeat. Amazed, he finds that still
it is not he who guides his missiles to their ends
but an unkind geometry that mocks his will.

If he persists, for years he'll practice patiently,
lock all the doors, learn all the tricks, keep noises out,

though he may pick a ghost or two for company
or pierce the room's inhuman silence with a shout.
More often silence wins; then soon the green felt seems
an evil playground, lawless, lot to time, forsaken,
and he a fool caught in the water weeds of dreams
whom only death or frantic effort can awaken.

At last, a master player, he can face applause,
looks for a fit opponent, former friends, emerges;
but no one knows him now. He questions his own cause
and has forgotten why he yielded to those urges,
took up a wooden cue to strike a coloured ball.
Wise now, he goes on playing; both his house and heart
unguarded solitudes, hospitable to all
who can endure the cold intensity of art.

From the Note-Book of a European Tramp

XI

The townsman on his yielding bed
Thinks that the world will end when he
On the bare floorboards lies instead.
He also who was forced to see
The mind's own mattresses ripped up
And many a recipient head
Smashed like a saucer or a cup
Feels that by rights he should be dead.

True, there are moments when he finds
That metaphysics was no more
Than luxury of idle minds,
Soft padding round a rotten core—
Particularly in the Spring
When Chaos, ever young, unbinds
Gods who are game for anything
And demi-gods of various kinds.

In winter, though he's far from sure,
He says his prayers just in case
A word in the right place might cure
His pangs, redeem all men's disgrace;
And still it seems a little weird
That the earth's axle is secure
When all the nightmares he most feared
Prosper in daylight and endure.

The Death of an Old Man

Muttering at the crowd, indifferent
faces which could not understand that he,
an island full of wilting flowers pent
in by the foolish, the forgetting sea,
was rare and beautiful, quite suddenly
he plunged into the traffic, his neck bent
low like a fighting bull's who seems intent
on the quick blade but, bleeding, cannot see.

Then he awoke, his body broken, knew
what had happened. In the dusk his mind
began its last descent, let pain review
the landscape he could neither leave behind
nor take away; for who will now unwind
his memory, relive past love, renew
the music and the silences that grew
within him for a life-time, intertwined?

In October . . .

In October the pregnant woman walked by the river
When autumn's failing green on the water's face
Conjures a world without depth, a landscape of glass.
She saw leaves and their images meet and saw them severed,

From the tall trees, glowing, a flicker of red fall down,
Leaves of the weeping willows drop and drown,
Cracking that mirror of green, the immaculate water.
'Tears of time,' she thought; 'O my son or daughter
Due to be born with the lambs and, like them, slaughtered
By the sudden thrust in war, slow waste in peace,
To wonder, to hope for a while, then glimmer passionless.
Man's grief I perpetuate, which else might cease.'

Faint, but golden, the sun broke through the haze;
She saw dead leaves assembled on the river's bed,
Water-weeds groping for food, their green unshed,
And above, new buds, minute, on the naked boughs.
'Nameless you are,' she thought, 'my son or daughter,
Nameless as unborn leaves, dead leaves and the water,
A particle, passing but blessed, between always and never.
Man's joy I perpetuate, the tree and the river,
Summer's unbroken mirror, the cracking glass
And the stillness that spreads where leaf and image have
     passed;
We are only the bed, not the source or the giver.'

ELIZABETH B. HARROD

Summer Afternoon

Manchester, Massachusetts

Withdrawn on this warm ledge I lie
And watch the green sea-bubbled rocks
Or tiring, turn to see how looks
The parched blue desert of the sky.

The inchoate clouds together drawn
Formed, drifted and re-formed till they
In shapes of the immortals lay,
Bathing in the bright afternoon.

From these strange sands I walked along,
The great bell-throated sea, the air
A mighty pulse, a humming sphere—
Admit, O ears, the Sirens' song!

Ulysses all, we are all restrained
Within this body, from it rapt
By the bright sea from whose waves crept
The form by which we are enchained.

Great Mother of our flesh and blood
Who rocked us dreaming in the womb,
"Come home come home come home come home,
She calls to her unfilial brood.

What nourishes the seed lays waste
The fertile earth; these tidal chants
Bemuse the mind and lure the sense,
And those green lips are death to taste.

Alien by virtue of our breath,
We must shut out with many tears
The surging voices in our ears
Or in sea-song be drowned to death.

August Night, 1953

We lie by towering hollyhocks
And watch the moon drip down the stalks
To spill on us from every leaf;
While higher still all whorled and bright
The Milky Way bathes us in light
Till sense alone compels belief.

Caught up by earth we seem to prove
The real existence of our love.
And from this fire of transience
We make of sex the sacrament

To fix in us our frail intent—
A paradox of permanence.

Sonnet Against the Too-Facile Mystic

[After reading *After Many a Summer Dies the Swan*]

Secret in bed the lustful with soft cries
And fervent hands the local pulse entreat
And lie abandoned to its dying beat
Rapt in the circling of each other's thighs;
While foamy-lipped the epileptic lies
Beside the curb, and wondering in the street,
The children gather curious at his feet,
Appalled, entranced, with fixed and eager eyes.

And lotus-postured and annihilate,
The patient mystic in his ecstasies,
Purged from himself, needs no more contemplate
Who is the Godhead now and one with these,
Indifferent the path to this estate,
Through fits of thought or raptures of disease.

Calvinist Autumnal

By these slow shadows and the frosted air
All the rich swollen grapes of summer laden
With honey, heavy with light, are trodden
Into the wine of autumn's atmosphere.

And in this winey time the year grows mellow;
All sensual beauty ripens and decays;
The trees as death stirs in them are ablaze
With crimson, scarlet, purple, bronze, and yellow

It is the sweet sap makes the maple flame;
Each burns at last according to its flesh.

Body and leaf fall in immortal ash,
The mind consents to death and bears the blame.

Yet with such grace the year comes to its death,
In such a glory of burning is consumed,
The bright air trembles into stillness, dimmed
With the spicy smoke of its expiring breath.

If Heaven's not one great motion of delight
Circling Thy Presence with a constant praise,
And yet as bright soul or as sensual blaze
All dying life dies in or into light;

So that, as Calvin had it, angels tell
Among their joys the burning of the damned
That mingles with the choirs of the redeemed
The reek and phosphorescent haze of Hell;

Still I would love Thee so that I may be
Even a stub-end flickering in Thy sight.
Oh, in the final shadow of Thy light,
Christ, let me shine—or burn autumnally!

JOHN HEATH-STUBBS

The Old King

I am so old a king that I remember
How three oak-forests have sprouted and grown and died
Around this hall, and the generations
Of strong young men drinking ale under the shade of them,
But now I am content to sleep.

My beard is grown long and fine like cobwebs;
The soft dust has fallen upon my shoulders;
The mice playing around me do not heed me at all;
It's little warmth I find in these embers.

There were proud queens with yellow hair, white breasts,
Walking the earth when I was young;
I had a long straight sword and their castles to storm;
It's little warmth I find in these embers.

Their faces are fallen in and their beauty gone,
And no-one remembers, no-one remembers;
I could be sorrowful thinking of what I have lost,
But now I am content to sleep.

It's little warmth I find in these embers
But now I am content to sleep.

Churchyard of St. Mary Magdalene, Old Milton

Here, where my father lies under the ornamental plum,
Geese step in the next farm-field, while to the Rectory elms
The rooks fly home. *Dominus exaltatio mea*—
The eagle rising with its sprig of acorns.

Feet deep in sticky clay, under the kempt grasses,
Under the anglo-saxon, and the celtic crosses,
The Indian judges lie, the admirals, the solicitors,
The eccentric ladies, and the shopkeepers,
The unenterprising who would not go to the town,
The charwoman with a cleft palate, the jobbing gardener,
And the four Germans who fell, some few years back,
Out of a sky of trouble, smashed
In an empty field—these have
Their regulation crosses too, of wood,
And scattered flowers, left by the prisoners:
The old woman whom I meet
Remarks that after all they were somebody's sons
And we would do as much for our people.

"The writer returns to the scene of his childhood"—
Where he loitered and looked at the rooks and the geese and
    the turkeys,

Or sought for wild barley by the churchyard gate—
The caterpillar-grass
Whose insect heads climb slowly up your sleeve;
The rootless writer, filling his town lungs
With a gust of country air. A grey afternoon,
And in the sky, the promise of evening's rain.

Where people come to take the air and die,
Ending their lives here on an adequate pension,
A sickly child, brought there by careful parents,
Might mend in the salt breeze. From six to twenty-four
Home was this scattered residential village of bungalows,
Of gabled villas, and neglected fallows,
Crazy paving, gravel, and tarmac. Now he comes back
And stands unrecognized among these graves.

The church here under John, that lackland king,
(The guide-book says), rebuilt under Elizabeth:
(The tower still stands, four-square, looks down upon
The village green, a row of shops, a garage
Crimson and yellow with petrol-pumps,
A line of cottages, a blacksmith's forge—
A child, I remember that darkness and smoke and music—
Two adjacent public-houses, the "George" and "Wheatsheaf,"
And the post-office store, where stands behind the jumble
Of picture-postcards, cigarettes, and buttons,
The dusty case with its stuffed gannet and guillemot).
Rebuilt under Elizabeth, restored under Victoria,
(The green distempered walls, peeling to white patches,
Which took, at sermon time, the shapes of islands—
White islands, in a green smooth-glistening sea).

Lie here the serfs, the yeomen, and the gentry,
Under their mounds, and single stones, and vaults yellow
    with lichen;
Of all those faces, one only gazes still—
Queen Anne's colonel, in effigy, pompous his armour,
His helmet beside him, a rigleted wig of stone
Framing his vacant brow. His sword, that steel blade,
Which he drew against the French, is hung above him
Over the blurred inscription, on the left of the porch.

A torch borne in the wind, a drift of sparks and smoke
As the racer rounds the track in the bright sunlight,
Dust-puff, and dream, and shadow. . . .
A drop of rain, a large, warm drop,
A rustle in the tresses of the elm,
A breath of perfume, twitched by the light breeze,
From the fading flowers laid on the Italian marble—
But these evoke the sudden splendour of bright hair
Unloosed from the darkness of a penitent snood,
Sweetness, and the splintering of the alabaster-sealed heart;
Somewhere among these tombs a woman's voice is sobbing;
Among these fragments grope the white and delicate hands
Of the Anointer of the Dead, who comes in the dark hour
Bringing her spices for the early dawn.

A fountain of lamentation above the firmament, a human
River of tears, that knows all streets, alleys, and dark courts,
And bears upon its little waves
Sticks and straws and draggled cigarette-ends,
The gutter's refuse and corruption, on
Past Roman causeways, through black hearts of cities.
A girl, mad as grief, trudging the hard roads;
A woman, with a few ripe ears, in a country of famine;
The august queen of the shrunken banks of Nile,
Who seeks the body of her murdered Lord;
A girl, sorry as sin, and broken as contrition.

Lady of Magdala's tower, and the dower of Bethany,
You who are called patron here, forgive
The little lives, partial and fugitive existences,
The gestures of love frozen in a pose of propriety,
And starved desire, with malice that lies on a turning bed;
Forgive the tyrannies of the hearthstone, and the small poli-
    tics
Of the local interest, the lonely and the dull.
Ask pardon for the community without a heart, and the be-
    trayal
Of the backward years and the uncomplaining dead.
Carry these lives, these parts of lives, these yellow leaves
Drifted in autumn from the tree of the world,
On tides of intercession, down

To a sea thirsty with love, where the breakers lift
White triumphing hands—insatiable;
And the free gull tacks to the courteous southern stars,
With arched and frost-pale pinion:
Oh, in Death's garden be
Prime witness of the only Resurrection.

A Charm Against the Toothache

Venerable Mother Toothache
Climb down from the white battlements,
Stop twisting in your yellow fingers
The fourfold rope of nerves;
And to-morrow I will give you a tot of whisky
To hold in your cupped hands,
A garland of anise-flowers,
And three cloves like nails.

And tell the attendant gnomes
It is time to knock off now,
To shoulder their little pick-axes,
Their cold-chisels and drills.
And you may mount by a silver ladder
Into the sky, to grind
In the cracked polished mortar
Of the hollow moon.

By the lapse of warm waters,
And the poppies nodding like red coals,
The paths on the granite mountains,
And the plantation of my dreams.

The Death of Digenes Akritas

I'm that distinguished twice-born hero
And imperial partisan,

Destroyer of the Turk and Tartar,
Bulgar and Paulician.

Take your bread and meat and brandy
While they still keep out the cold;
A black wind whistles down the mountain,
Charon has me in his hold.

I, on marches of the Empire,
Prop of all the crumbling themes,
Have turned back the Emperor's enemies
By the fast and bloody streams.

The Pope of Rome in a purple surplice,
The Sultan by Euphrates' brink,
Should they hear my name referred to,
Take more water with their drink.

I have seen the golden Emperor
Sitting under a golden tree,
Commanding Sappho and Anacreon
To praise me with their balladry.

Once I met the Queen of the Vampyres
In a green and gracious place,
For three nights fought with her, and left her,
A knife-wound in her hooded face.

I have encountered the pterodactyl,
Manticor, and rhinoceros;
Hunting where it was not permitted
Brought me to this unhappy pass.

Oh swift and swift comes through the forest
That white deer with the silver horns;
Who follows that unlikely quarry,
Drained of manhood he returns.

For three months of a silent winter
I chased him through the glassy wood;

And when he turned and knelt for pity,
Took out my knife and drew his blood.

The Lady of the Mountains feeds him
Among her inaccessible rocks;
His eyes are cleaner than cold water,
Between his eyes the crucifix.

When my horoscope was casting
Ares ruled the troubled sky;
I was born upon a Tuesday
And on Tuesday I must die.

You can take and break my rifle,
Take my pipe and tinder-box;
Lay me decent, light a candle,
Keep the ritual orthodox.

Epitaph

Mr. Heath-Stubbs as you must understand
Came of a gentleman's family out of Staffordshire
Of as good blood as any in England
But he was wall-eyed and his legs too spare.

His elbows and finger-joints could bend more ways than one
And in frosty weather would creak audibly
As to delight his friends he would give demonstration
Which he might have done in public for a small fee.

Amongst the more learned persons of his time
Having had his schooling in the University of Oxford
In Anglo-Saxon Latin ornithology and crime
Yet after four years he was finally not preferred.

Orthodox in beliefs as following the English Church
Barring some heresies he would have for recreation

Yet too often left these sound principles (as I am told)
    in the lurch
Being troubled with idleness, lechery, pride and dissipation.

In his youth he would compose poems in prose and verse
In a classical romantic manner which was pastoral
To which the best judges of the Age were not averse
And the public also but his profit was not financial.

Now having outlived his friends and most of his reputation
He is content to take his rest under these stones and grass
Not expecting but hoping that the Resurrection
Will not catch him unawares whenever it takes place.

ANTHONY HECHT

The Vow

In the third month, a sudden flow of blood.
The mirth of tabrets ceaseth, and the joy
Also of the harp. The frail image of God
Lay spilled and formless. Neither girl nor boy,
But yet blood of my blood, nearly my child.
    All that long day
Her pale face turned to the window's mild
    Featureless grey.

And for some nights she whimpered as she dreamed
The dead thing spoke, saying: "Do not recall
Pleasure at my conception. I am redeemed
From pain and sorrow. Mourn rather for all
Who breathlessly issue from the bone gates,
    The gates of horn,
For truly it is best of all the fates
    Not to be born.

"Mother, a child lay gasping for bare breath
On Christmas Eve when Santa Claus had set
Death in the stocking, and the lights of death
Flamed in the tree. O, if you can, forget
You were the child, turn to my father's lips
    Against the time
When his cold hand puts forth its fingertips
    Of jointed lime."

Doctors of Science, what is man that he
Should hope to come to a good end? *The best
Is not to have been born.* And could it be
That Jewish diligence and Irish jest
The consent of flesh and a midwinter storm
    Had reconciled,
Was yet too bold a mixture to inform
    A simple child?

Even as gold is tried, Gentile and Jew.
If that ghost was a girl's, I swear to it:
Your mother shall be far more blessed than you.
And if a boy's, I swear: The flames are lit
That shall refine us; they shall not destroy
    A living hair.
Your younger brothers shall confirm in joy
    This that I swear.

La Condition Botanique

    Romans, rheumatic, gouty, came
  To bathe in Ischian springs where water steamed,
Puffed and enlarged their bold imperial thoughts, and which
Later Madame Curie declared to be so rich
    In radioactive content as she deemed
    Should win them everlasting fame.

    Scattered throughout their ice and snow
  The Finns have built airtight cabins of log
Where they may lie, limp and entranced by the sedative purr

Of steam pipes, or torment themselves with flails of fir
  To stimulate the blood, and swill down grog,
    Setting the particles aglow.

    Similarly the Turks, but know
  Nothing of the more delicate thin sweat
Of plants, breathing their scented oxygen upon
Brooklyn's botanical gardens, roofed with glass and run
  So to the pleasure of each leafy pet,
    Manured, addressed in Latin, so

    To its thermostatic happiness—
  Spreading its green and innocence to the ground
Where pipes, like Satan masquerading as the snake,
Coil and uncoil their frightful liquid length, and make
  Gurglings of love mixed with a rumbling sound
    Of sharp intestinal distress—

    So to its pleasure, as I said,
  That each particular vegetable may thrive,
Early and late, as in the lot first given Man,
Sans interruption, as when Universal Pan
  Led on the Eternal Spring. The spears of chive,
    The sensitive plant, showing its dread,

    The Mexican flytrap, that can knit
  Its quilled jaws pitilessly, and would hurt
A fly with pleasure, leading Riley's life in bed
Of peat moss and of chemicals, and is thoughtfully fed
  Flies for the entrée, flies for the dessert,
    Fruit flies for fruit, and all of it

    Administered as by a wife—
  Lilith our lady, patroness of plants,
Who sings, *Lullay myn lykyng, myn owyn dere derlyng,*
Madrigals nightly to the spiny talk in sterling
  Whole notes of admiration and romance—
    This, then, is what is called The Life.

    And we, like disinherited heirs,
  Old Adams, can inspect the void estate

At visiting hours: the unconditional garden spot,
The effortless innocence preserved, for God knows what,
   And think, as we depart by the toll gate:
     No one has lived here these five thousand years.

     Our world is turned on points, is whirled
     On wheels, Tibetan prayer wheels, French verb wheels,
The toothy wheels of progress, the terrible torque
Insisting, and in the sky, even above New York
   Rotate the marvelous four-fangled seals
     Ezekiel saw. The mother-of-pearled

     Home of the bachelor oyster lies
     Fondled in fluent shifts of bile and lime
As sunlight strikes the water, and it is of our world,
And will appear to us sometime where the finger is curled
   Between the frets upon a mandolin,
     Fancy cigar boxes, and eyes

     Of ceremonial masks; and all
     The places where Kilroy inscribed his name,
For instance, the ladies' rest room in the Gare du Nord,
The iron rump of Buddha, whose hallowed, hollowed core
   Admitted tourists once but all the same
     Housed a machine gun, and let fall

     A killing fire from its eyes
     During the war; and Polyphemus hurled
Tremendous rocks that stand today off Sicily's coast
Signed with the famous scrawl of our most traveled ghost;
   And all these various things are of our world.
     But what's become of Paradise?

     Ah, it is lodged in glass, survives
     In Brooklyn, like a throwback, out of style,
Like an incomprehensible veteran of the Grand
Army of the Republic in the reviewing stand
   Who sees young men in a mud-colored file
     March to the summit of their lives,

     For glory, for their country, with the flag
     Joining divergent stars of North and South

In one blue field of heaven, till they fall in blood
And are returned at last unto their native mud—
   The eyes weighed down with stones, the sometimes mouth
     Helpless to masticate or gag

   Its old inheritance of earth.
In the sweat of thy face shalt thou manage, said the Lord.
And we, old Adams, stare through the glass panes and wince,
Fearing to see the ancestral apple, pear, or quince,
   The delicacy of knowledge, the fleshed Word,
     The globe of wisdom that was worth

   Our lives, or so our parents thought,
  And turn away to strengthen our poor breath
And body, keep the flesh rosy with hopeful dreams,
Peach-colored, practical, to decorate the bones, with schemes
   Of life insurance, Ice-Cream-After-Death,
     Hormone injections, against the *mort'*

   Saison, largely to babble praise
  Of Simeon Pyrites, patron saint
Of our Fools' Paradise, whose glittering effigy
Shines in God's normal sunlight till the blind men see
   Visions as permanent as artists paint:
     The body's firm, nothing decays

   Upon the heirloom set of bones
  In their gavotte. Yet we look through the glass
Where green lies ageless under snow-stacked roofs in steam-
Fitted apartments, and reflect how bud and stem
   Are wholly flesh, and the immaculate grass
     Does without buttressing of bones.

   In open field or public bed
  With ultraviolet help, man hopes to learn
The leafy secret, pay his most outstanding debt
To God in the salt and honesty of his sweat,
   And in his streaming face manly to earn
     His daily and all-nourishing bread.

Samuel Sewall

Samuel Sewall, in a world of wigs,
Flouted opinion in his personal hair;
For foppery he gave not any figs,
But in his right and honor took the air.

Thus in his naked style, though well attired,
He went forth in the city, or paid court
To Madam Winthrop, whom he much admired,
Most godly, but yet liberal with the port.

And all the town admired for two full years
His excellent address, his gifts of fruit,
Her gracious ways and delicate white ears,
And held the course of nature absolute.

But yet she bade him suffer a peruke,
"That One be not distinguished from the All";
Delivered of herself this stern rebuke
Framed in the resonant language of St. Paul.

"Madam," he answered her, "I have a Friend
Furnishes me with hair out of His strength,
And He requires only I attend
Unto His charity and to its length."

And all the town was witness to his trust:
On Monday he walked out with the Widow Gibbs,
A pious lady of charm and notable bust,
Whose heart beat tolerably beneath her ribs.

On Saturday he wrote proposing marriage,
And closed, imploring that she be not cruel,
"Your favorable answer will oblige,
Madam, your humble servant, Samuel Sewall."

The Origin of Centaurs

"But to the girdle do the gods inherit,
 Beneath is all the fiend's."
                                    —King Lear

This mild September mist recalls the soul
      To its own lust;
   On the enchanted lawn
It sees the iron top of the flagpole
   Sublimed away and gone
Into Parnassian regions beyond rust;
And would undo the body to less than dust.

Sundial and juniper have been dispelled
      Into thin air.
   The pale ghost of a leaf
Haunts those uncanny softnesses that filled
   And whitely brought to grief
The trees that only yesterday were there.
The soul recoils into its old despair,

Knowing that though the horizon is at hand,
      Twelve paltry feet
   Refuse to be traversed,
And form themselves before wherever you stand
   As if you were accursed;
While stones drift from the field, and the arbor-seat
Floats toward some *millefleurs* world of summer heat.

Yet from the void where the azalea bush
      Departed hence,
   Sadly the soul must hear
Twitter and cricket where should be all hush,
   And from the belvedere
A muffled grunt survives in evidence
That love must sweat under the weight of sense.

Or so once thought a man in a Greek mist—
      Who set aside

The wine-cup and the wine,
And that deep fissure he alone had kissed,
    All circumscribing line,
Moved to the very edge in one swift stride
And took those shawls of nothing for his bride.

Was it the Goddess herself? Some dense embrace
    Closed like a bath
Of love about his head;
Perfectly silent and without a face.
    Blindfolded on her bed,
He could see nothing but the aftermath:
Those powerful, clear hoofprints on the path.

GEOFFREY HILL

Asmodai

I

They, after the slow building of the house,
Furnished it; brought warmth under the skin.
Tiles, that a year's rough wind could rattle loose,
Being close pressed still kept storms out and storms in.
(Of all primed and vain citadels, to choose
This, to choose this of all times to begin!)
Acknowledging, they said, one who pursues
Hobbies of serious lust and indoor sin,
Clearly they both stood, lovers without fear,
Might toy with fire brought dangerously to hand
To tame, not exorcise, spirits; though the air
Whistled abstracted menace, could confound
Strength by device, by music reaching the ear,
Lightning conducted forcibly to the ground.

II

The night, then; bravely stiffen; you are one
Whom stars could burn more deeply than the sun,

Guide-book martyr. You, doubtless, hear wings,
Too sheer for cover, swift; the scattered noise
Of darkness looming with propitious things;
And nests of rumour clustered in the world.
So drummed, so shadowed, your mere trudging voice
Might rave at large while easy truths were told,
Bad perjurable stuff, to be forgiven
Because of this lame journey out of mind.
A tax on men to seventy-times-seven,
A busy vigilance of goose and hound,
Keeps up all guards. Since you are outside, go,
Closing the doors of the house and the head also!

The Turtle Dove

Love, that drained her, drained him she'd loved, though each,
For the other's sake, forged passion upon speech,
Bore their close days through sufferance towards night
Where she at length grasped sleep and he lay quiet

As though needing no questions, now, to guess
What her secreting heart could not well hide.
Her caught face flinched in half-sleep at his side.
Yet she, by day, modelled her real distress,

Poised, turned her cheek to the attending world
Of children and intriguers and the old,
Conversed freely, exercised, was admired,
Being strong to dazzle. All this she endured

To affront him. He watched her rough grief work
Under the formed surface of habit. She spoke
Like one long undeceived but she was hurt.
She denied more love, yet her starved eyes caught

His, devouring, at times. Then, as one self-dared,
She went to him, plied there; like a furious dove

Bore down with visitations of such love
As his lithe, fathoming heart absorbed and buried.

The Re-Birth of Venus

And now the sea-scoured temptress, having failed
To scoop out of horizons what birds herald—
Tufts of fresh soil—shakes off an entire sea,
Though not as the dove, harried. Rather, she,

A shark hurricaned to estuary-water
(The lesser hunter almost by a greater
Devoured) but unflurried, lies, approaches all
Stayers, and searchers of the fanged pool.

In Memory of Jane Frazer

When snow like sheep lay in the fold
And winds went begging at each door,
And the far hills were blue with cold,
And a cold shroud lay on the moor,

She kept the siege. And every day
We watched her brooding over death
Like a strong bird above its prey.
The room filled with the kettle's breath.

Damp curtains glued against the pane
Sealed time away. Her body froze
As if to freeze us all, and chain
Creation to a stunned repose.

She died before the world could stir.
In March the ice unloosed the brook
And water ruffled the sun's hair,
And a few sprinkled leaves unshook.

Gideon at the Well

[For Janice]

Nudging and thrusting to the light
Crocuses snuff the air. The Sun
Melts with his breath the frost of night
Scrawled like a snail-track on the stone.

Primroses thread the hills, the starved
Flanks of the soil; drenched valleys lie
Heavy as fleece—the sign I craved—
And still my tongued heart, rough and dry,

Can find no respite from its thirst.
The stones, the bruised lips of this well,
Yield me a honeycomb of dust.
No brimming of the springs can quell

My crackling wounds, no oil of love
Assuage them. Being sealed and chosen,
I raise my staff: the armies move,
As out of rock, as floods unfrozen.

God's Little Mountain

Below, the river scrambled like a goat,
Dislodging stones. The mountain stamped its foot,
Shaking, as from a trance. And I was shut
With wads of sound into a sudden quiet.

I thought the thunder had unsettled heaven,
All was so still. And yet the sky was cloven
By flame that left the air cold and engraven.
I waited for the word that was not given,

Pent up into a region of pure force,
Made subject to the pressure of the stars;
I saw the angels lifted like pale straws;
I could not stand before those winnowing eyes

And fell, until I found the world again.
Now I lack grace to tell what I have seen;
For though the head frames words the tongue has none,
And who will prove the surgeon to this stone?

Genesis

I

Against the burly air I strode,
Where the tight ocean heaves its load,
Crying the miracles of God.

And first I brought the sea to bear
Upon the dead weight of the land;
And the waves flourished at my prayer,
The rivers spawned their sand.

And where the streams were salt and full
The tough pig-headed salmon strove,
Curbing the ebb and the tide's pull,
To reach the steady hills above.

II

The second day I stood and saw
The osprey plunge with triggered claw,
Feathering blood along the shore,
To lay the living sinew bare.

And the third day I cried: "Beware
The soft-voiced owl, the ferret's smile,
The hawk's deliberate stoop in air,

Cold eyes, and bodies hooped in steel,
Forever bent upon the kill."

III

And I renounced, on the fourth day,
This fierce and unregenerate clay,

Building as a huge myth for man
The watery Leviathan,

And made the glove-winged albatross
Scour the ashes of the sea
Where Capricorn and Zero cross,
A brooding immortality—
Such as the charmed phoenix has
In the unwithering tree.

IV

The phoenix burns as cold as frost;
And, like a legendary ghost,
The phantom-bird goes wild and lost,
Upon a pointless ocean tossed.

So, the fifth day, I turned again
To flesh and blood and the blood's pain.

V

On the sixth day, as I rode
In haste about the works of God,
With spurs I plucked the horse's blood.

By blood we live, the hot, the cold,
To ravage and redeem the world:
There is no bloodless myth will hold.

And by Christ's blood are men made free
Though in close shrouds their bodies lie
Under the rough pelt of the sea;

Though Earth has rolled beneath her weight
The bones that cannot bear the light.

JOHN HOLLANDER

The Lady's-Maid Song

When Adam found his rib was gone
He cursed and sighed and cried and swore,
And looked with cold resentment on
The creature God had used it for.
All love's delights were quickly spent
And soon his sorrows multiplied;
He learned to blame his discontent
On something stolen from his side.

And so in every age we find
Each Jack, destroying every Joan,
Divides and conquers womankind
In vengeance for the missing bone;
By day he spins out quaint conceits
With gossip, flattery and song
And then at night, between the sheets
He wrongs the girl to right the wrong.

Though shoulder, bosom, lip and knee
Are praised in every kind of art,
Here is Love's true anatomy:
His rib is gone; he'll have her heart.
So women bear the debt alone
And live eternally distressed,
For though we throw the dog his bone
He wants it back with interest.

The Fear of Trembling

[for George Kateb]

If it is true that we no longer seek
To avoid the three peculiar trees that grow

At the edge of the wood, it is because we know
That even the wood itself can hold no terrors.
If, without fear of falling, we can speak
Three times of the devil, ignore the fatal errors
Of leaving nail-parings and bits of hair about,
Or even our impress in wrinkles on a sheet,
It is because of too many occasions
On which the devil never appears. And suasions
That spiky crones have urged on images
Crudely depicting us too often meet
With scorn, or any of the various stages
Of nonchalance, and are put down, without

Any benefit of dramaturgy
By which to frighten the old bitches back
(To make white magic is to believe in black).
And we have lost the less accessible fear
Of pushing past seers, and the sober clergy
Of the God in his normal forms, crossing the blear
Ravines and craggy slopes to come upon
The cave of the Wolf-Zeus, where the blinding sun
Beats on the rocky wall, but where we cast
No shadow. For, likewise, when our last
Guests have departed, and the night's debris
Grows pale at dawn, the Uninvited one
Whose name we could not remember turns out to be
Someone with an identity of his own

And no real *Doppelgänger* after all.
Thus, as we lose our terror of the night,
The Sun-God's sadduccees are put to flight,
Dispersing underground, and carrying
The relics of Certainty with them, as a pall
Of unreal darkness blurs their exiting.
Their sun sets and our sky grows colder: we
Are left in the hardrock desert, bare of tree
And stripped of mirage, that Locke looked out and saw
Under the setting sunlight, faint and raw;
All the sure horrors have vanished from a world
Bathed in the twilight of Probability

That sent the heebie-jeebies down, and hurled
Them, screaming, into the fringes of mystery,

The margins of truth. Well then, we have got
Our landscape plain enough now, and the rope
Of Illusion, hung in front of us like Hope
Has been withdrawn. But, peering across the sand,
We are unaccustomed to so much nothing. What,
Then, if we tremble a little? To understand
Exactly what it means to shiver, when
We have grown used to the chilly air, is, then,
Perhaps to know that our knowledge of what is true
Of the world casts doubt on what we thought we knew
About ourselves, or at least by how it was
We came to know it. And when other men
With other minds stare at our hands, it is
Because theirs tremble too, and only in

Such signs and portents do we know our fear
To lie. For only in the fear of trembling,
When all the physical spectres disappear,
Are the unknowable present dangers clear:
Watch how we shake! We cannot be dissembling,
We cannot be deceived; something resembling
Something frightening, even now, is here.

Horas Tempestatis Quoque Enumero
The Sundial

When in the festival of August heat
The air stops throbbing over the balustrades
Bordering the terrazzo, and for a moment
The white pilasters on the Older Wing,
No longer mixed with the rough pink of the wall,
Regain the intransigency of their marble,
A second of stillness halts the processional
Of hours on the heels of hotter hours,

Winding their turn and then their counterturn
And stand. The concrete lions of the steps
Seem always at the moment of fidgeting
And the house cats are no less motionless,
Their tails on the verge of twitching, never now, but
    Always the following second.

Then servants clamor for the city. Rifts
And cracks in the masonry appear much wider
Than we had ever thought them. Tufts of grass
Thrust out through the cracked base of the sundial
While wilting morning glory menaces
Its bronze ingenuous face with blurring shadows:
Only then can we feel the sudden storm
To be overdue for the fraction of the instant,
For the darkening wind is upon us then, the heat
Fractures like concrete, mirrored in the sky
By the thinnest of cracks across the clouds, and followed
By the expectedly delayed report
That is always graver than we care to think,
    Rumbling out of the darkness.

Then sundial and birdbath (which is which now?) run
Over into the lawn, and bubbling puddles
Drip down the steps. Neglected, by a wall,
Two marble *putti* weep as they are bathed,
Still leering through the rusty stains about
Their mouths. The ruin and the summerhouse
Are empty, but through the trumpeting downpour, some-
    where,
Inside the long windows, Leopoldine is playing
Her *Gradus ad Parnassum,* while nearby
A Chinese philosopher on a silk screen shrinks
From the thunder he has always held to be
The ultimate disorder, as the wind
Wrinkles a painted heron on the bank
    Barely suggested behind him.

The hour of storm goes by unmarked, and when
The lowering sun hangs over the afternoon,

Making gold veins in all the marble again,
Revealing crystals in the carpeted lawns;
When the air is clear and cool with a new stillness,
The girls emerge from the house with laughter and teacups
(The youngest stands on a swing in the oldest elm
Facing her visitor from the city, who
Is tall and thin in black clothes, swinging back
And forth like the slowest of water-clocks) only then
Does the cool shadow on the sundial show
The elapsed time of a distant age, the drip
Of water from its bronzed ostensive finger
Still falling at ever slower intervals,
    Dropping (the swing slowing) dropping . . .

I cannot but wonder what you meant last month
When, recounting for us an old hour of storm
You invoked implausible landscapes, as you said:
"We had a quarrel once, and after the quarrel
He left, and I went home and wept, and then
Still weeping, I played pingpong with my sisters . . ."
And your weeping echoed in another Europe
Of houses to which we would never be invited,
The girls in long white dresses, and the game
Disconsolate enough to last an hour
While the storm raged on outside the draperies,
Spattering the terrace; while the sundial
Said nothing, remembering everything, as the rain
    Slowly eroded its features.

When such heat sends us fleeing from the city,
Pursues, and then gives up its chase, the thunder
Blows its retreating blasts. But to be left
Stranded in another time, outside
Some city—Dublin or St. Petersburg,
Salzburg or Prague—with no trains and the roads
Impassably muddy is to be confronted
With one's own dream entire, with the side
Of the image one never sees, the sundial in darkness,
Or cracked from its base and lying in one of the cellars,
Numbering storm-tossed hours, but telling nothing,
Until, before the vision dissolves, we can see

The marble house, the park, the filmy girls
   Standing and swinging in silence;
The unambiguous shadow on the sundial
Cast by the last glance of departing sunlight,
   Measuring always this moment.

Paysage Moralisé

Astonished poplars hide
Their faces in leafy hands
Pale-green with feigned horror

As, by a fountain's side,
Daphnis misunderstands
Chloe, and makes an error.

Too soon, too soon, he plunges
His hand under the mound
Of taffeta around her!

And so alas she flinches,
Leaps up from the ground
And makes for the grove behind her,

Flinging the old reproach
At lingering Daphnis, who
Had snatched at her only

Because he felt too much
A flatterer, who knew
Of how to praise the lonely.

Under a soupy tree
Mopes Daphnis, joined by all
The brown surrounding landscape:

Even in Arcady
Ego needs must spoil
Such a beautiful friendship.

JOHN HOLLOWAY

Journey Through the Night

At the first hour from dawn
The traveller in the window seat
Rubbed his eyes, woke from a daze,
Brushed his rough hair back with great
Podgy fingers, gave a yawn,
Cleared the pane's white dewy haze,
Then stared so eagerly, it might
Have been his home place come in sight.

But at the second hour from dawn
The traveller in the window seat
Suddenly turned away from the world
As though he saw some thing too sweet
Or too bitter to be borne;
And when he met my glance, he curled
His body to the wall, and wept
I thought; but it may be he slept.

At the third hour from dawn
The ticket man rolled back the door:
The traveller blurted out that he
Wanted another ticket for
Some other place, somewhere further on;
He spoke shortly, confusedly;
But I saw he did not know,
Now, where in the world to go.

The Light

Water the ground with his tears,
For those who die in pain

Nourish most opulently
The incomprehensible grain
That we hoard warm and high
Against murrained years.

Let the loud priest rehearse
With book, candle and bell,
To exorcise the evil,
And leave no place but Hell
For the kind fertility devil:
God bless the curse.

Let the trained observer
Find the perennial root
Of the malady,
Stamp on it with his foot.
But the sick man must die
Before he can recover.

The white dress of folly
Is the dress of the bride,
Because of the hair-fine
Barriers that divide
And therefore also join,
Crazy things and holy.

Elegy for an Estrangement

One had grown almost affluent: one had
Almost deliberately chosen to be poor.
Each of them knew the other's choice was bad,
And, at the same time, each became unsure.
    They grew less intimate than before.
    Yet both had once known pain
And much bewilderment, that no overt act
Could quite convey the intimacy they felt.
And then, had been bewildered over again
To find this as true with women, as with men.

For one, that find was a vague flaw; whereby
The act he coveted might just be dulled
A trifle. But if he ignored it confidently
The two-backed beast could still turn hollow gold
   And he grasp all its vault might hold.
      But for the other one
It was a plain enigma; that he thought
About until it had perplexed him quite:
He being forced to spend much time alone,
And evaluate many more things than he had done.

It was before this time that they had walked
Together home from school: seen scaffolds grow
Like bamboos down long modern streets, and talked
Of how they both would make the future go
   Into a pattern fine to show;
      Or strolled on holidays
Over the dip-slope and chill showery rim
Down to the villages planting out the plain,
Where the quiet chalk, at last, a hundred ways,
Gives tongue, and globes the streams with mimulus.

Later, around a college quad', they spoke
Of subtler things: and understood them well.
One preferred Aristotle or blunt Locke,
And one, Spinoza's calm unlikely tale:
   But none of these could half reveal
      To either one of them
How by some gentle yet insistent art
To amalgam things that now trended apart;
Or how unlikely it was, any golden stream
Would gush from the wilder uplands not of place, but time.

Time by its formal definition moves
To a sidereal or a solar rhythm
Too big to watch: perplexed among its grooves
Each tried to fashion and perfect his system,
   And both drew slowly to them
      Whatever they could find
(Like pieces for a puzzle) to complete
The equilibrium of the closed circuit.

The few inter-connexions that remained
Troubling them less . . . as they grew more purblind.

Theirs was the typical case: not in one night,
But over years, as their great scheme, each tried,
Like a bold landscape-gardener, to create
A whole new Nature, calm and rectified.
   And each one watched his dream subside.
      Yet never saw the change,
For by enharmony, dream and act were blent:
Or seemed to be so, as their sense grew blunt.
The fragments, though, grew harder to arrange.
They could not be so intimate. It was strange.

And then they sealed the rock: heretical
When least they glimpsed it. Each of them contrived
To ignore the little tinkling passing bell.
The god expired too slow to be revived.
   Yet even so he was short-lived,
      And thus they knew much pain:
Weeds choked the garden, the diagrams all turned
Into grey scribbles. Hollow gold all spent.
A flowerless river skulking through a plain.
Streets of an endless town. Night falls in rain.

Warning to a Guest

Against the flare and descant of the gas
I heard an old woman in a shop maintain
This fog comes when the moon is on the wane:
   And ten full days must pass
Before the crescent mows it in like grass.
   Shun the black puddles, the scrub hedge
Down to the sea. Keep to the wet streets where
Mercury and sodium flood their sullen fire.
Tonight, do not disturb the water's edge.

There'll be no storm, I know: having often gone,
In storm or calm, where the strong tide has flowed

Right to the tunnel underneath the road
   Along the formless dune.
But this is the third quarter of the moon
  In fog. There'll be no drench and roar
Of breakers: the quiet tide will drift
Idly among the pebbles, and then sift
Back to the sea. Yet shun that dark foreshore.

There'll be no sound: except the echoing
Horn of a baffled ship, shut out from home,
And the small birds that skirt the stranded foam.
    Dunlin and sanderling
Feed through the night, or lightly they take wing
  Down the soft fog. So sharp their pulse
Trills, and their dram of blood burns up so clear,
Each minute, in their bright sight, makes a year.
But you may catch the note of something else.

I have watched you, as you have visited at this house,
And know, from knowing myself, that you will be
Quick to people the shore, the fog, the sea,
    With all the fabulous
Things of the moon's dark side. No, stay with us.
  Do not demand a walk tonight
Down to the sea. It makes no place for those
Like you and me who, to sustain our pose,
Need wine and conversation, colour and light.

ELIZABETH JENNINGS

Delay

The radiance of that star that leans on me
Was shining years ago. The light that now
Glitters up there my eye may never see,
And so the time lag teases me with how

Love that loves now may not reach me until
Its first desire is spent. The star's impulse
Must wait for eyes to claim it beautiful
And love arrived may find us somewhere else.

Winter Love

Let us have winter loving that the heart
May be in peace and ready to partake
Of the slow pleasure spring would wish to hurry
Or that in summer harshly would awake,
And let us fall apart, O gladly weary,
The white skin shaken like a white snowflake.

Weathercock

A hard tin bird was my lover
Fluttering with every breeze
To north and west would hover
In fierce extremities
But I would never find
Him quietly in the south
Or in the warmest east
And never near my mouth
And never on my breast.

A hard bird swinging high
Glinting with gold and sun
Aloft swung in the sky
Ready to run
O would I were that sun
He swings to with desire
Could see my love's gold eye
And feel his fire.

Identity

When I decide I shall assemble you
Or, more precisely, when I decide which thoughts
Of mine about you fit most easily together,
Then I can learn what I have loved, what lets
Light through the mind. The residue
Of what you may be goes. I gather

Only as lovers or friends gather at all
For making friends means this—
Image and passion combined into a whole
Pattern within the loving mind, not her or his
Concurring there. You can project the full
Picture of lover or friend that is not either.

So then assemble me,
Your exact picture firm and credible,
Though as I think myself I may be free
And accurate enough.
That you love what is truthful to your will
Is all that ever can be answered for
And, what is more,
Is all we make each other when we love.

The Climbers

To the cold peak without their careful women
(Who watching children climbing into dreams
Go dispossessed at home). The mountain moves
Away at every climb and steps are hard
Frozen along the glacier. Every man
Tied to the rope constructs himself alone.

And not the summit reached nor any pole
Touched is the wished embrace, but still to move

And as the mountain climbs to see it whole
And each mind's landscape growing more complete
As sinews strain and all the muscles knot.

One at the peak is small. His disappointment
The coloured flag flown at the lonely top,
And all the valley's motive grown obscure.
He envies the large toilers halfway there
Who still possess the mountain by desire
And, not arriving, dream in no resentment.

The Idler

An idler holds that rose as always rose,
Will not, before the bud discloses it
Within a later season, in his thought
Unwrap the flower and force the petals open
And wish in mind a different rose to happen.

So will not colour it with his own shadow
As we contrive, living beyond the present,
To move all things away from their own moment
And state another time for us. O who
Watches may yet make time refuse to grow.

So has his subtle power wiser than ours
And need elaborate no peace at all.
Watch how a landscape kindest is to idlers
Helping their shiftlessness grow to new powers,
Composing stillness round their careless will.

A Way of Looking

It is the association after all
We seek, we would retrace our thoughts to find

The thought of which this landscape is the image,
Then pay the thought and not the landscape homage.
It is as if the tree and waterfall
Had their first roots and source within the mind.

But something plays a trick upon the scene:
A different kind of light, a stranger colour
Flows down on the appropriated view.
Nothing within the mind fits. This is new.
Thought and reflection must begin again
To fit the image and to make it true.

Not in the Guide-Books

Nobody stays here long;
  Deliberate visitors know
There is nothing here the guide-books show,
  No ruin or statue to sustain
Some great emotion in their stone.
  So visitors soon go.

Some travellers stay a little
  To collect wine or corn
And here breathe in the over-subtle
  Smell of places worn
Not by a marvellous death or battle
  But by their insignificance brought down.

Yet good, a place like this,
  For one grown tired of histories
To shape a human myth,
  A story but for his
Delight, where he might make the place
  His own success
Building what no one else had bothered with—
  A simple life or death.

Beyond Possession

Our images withdraw, the rose returns
To what it was before we looked at it.
We lift our look from where the water runs
And it's pure river once again, we write
No emblems on the trees. A way begins
Of living where we have no need to beat
The petals down to get the scent of rose
Or sign our features where the water goes.

All is itself. Each man himself entire,
Not even plucking out his thought, not even
Bringing a tutored wilfulness to bear
Upon the rose, the water. Each has given
Essence of water back to itself, essence of flower,
Till he is yoked to his own heart and driven
Inward to find a private kind of peace
And not a mind reflecting his own face.

Yet must go deeper still, must move to love
Where thought is free to let the water ride,
Is liberal to the rose giving it life
And setting even its own shadow aside;
Till flower and water blend with freedom of
Passion that does not close them in and hide
Their deepest natures; but the heart is strong
To beat with rose and river in one song.

Communication

No use to speak, no good to tell you that
A love is worn away not by the one
Who leaves but by the one who stays and hopes,
Since you would rather have the hoping still

Than be yourself again. What can I say
Who know, better than you, the one who has
Moved on, away, not loving him at all?

And certainly to you I would relinquish
This knowledge held in other ways of feeling
Though dressed up in the properties of passion
Looked at by you. Something is deeply held
By me who never deeply searched at all
And we are not yet wise enough or subtle
To offer anyone a state of mind.

This the particular problem, and I search
A power over our general condition,
Where love is like a landscape we can change
And where desire may be transformed to friendship
If friendship gives the really wanted knowledge,
Where we can see the end and have the power
To take the journey there a different way,
And we can move our minds as we move houses:
Where love is more than lucky in the land.

Mirrors

Was it a mirror then across a room,
A crowded room of parties where the smoke
Rose to the ceiling with the talk? The glass
Stared back at me a half-familiar face
Yet something hoped for. When at last you came
It was as if the distant mirror spoke.

That loving ended as all self-love ends
And teaches us that only fair-grounds have
The right to show us halls of mirrors where
In every place we look we see our stare
Taunting our own identities. But love
Perceives without a mirror in the hands.

Escape and Return

Now from the darkness of myself
I turn to let the lightness in.
Is it the raging of the sun
Or my own thoughts made free again?
I between hills of light and light
Stand and, composed of my own doubt,
Wonder where they, where I begin.

For I would travel from the mind
And move beyond the intellect
And search and search until I find
Identity clear in total act;
Then learn how landscape is combined
With images we mint and make
From the mind's fret and the bones' ache.

And I would feel the invading vision
Without a self to stand and watch,
Without these hands to trap and touch;
Bodiless I would prove my passion
By learning the character of each
Landscape or person that I love,
Clothing them only with contemplation.

Out of this will to be beyond
Myself I come, return again
Into the struggling thoughts within
The boundaries of my own mind.
Yet something of those loves, that land
Batters and batters on my thought,
And, once more separate in the heart,
I feel the images that strained
Within me join the landscape drained
Of everything but its own light.

Answers

I kept my answers small and kept them near;
Big questions bruised my mind but still I let
Small answers be a bulwark to my fear.

The huge abstractions I kept from the light;
Small things I handled and caressed and loved.
I let the stars assume the whole of night.

But the big answers clamoured to be moved
Into my life. Their great audacity
Shouted to be acknowledged and believed.

Even when all small answers build up to
Protection of my spirit, still I hear
Big answers striving for their overthrow

And all the great conclusions coming near.

In the Night

Out of my window late at night I gape
And see the stars but do not watch them really,
And hear the trains but do not listen clearly;
Inside my mind I turn about to keep
Myself awake, yet am not there entirely.
Something of me is out in the dark landscape.

How much am I then what I think, how much what I feel?
How much the eye that seems to keep stars straight?
Do I control what I can contemplate
Or is it my vision that's amenable?
I turn in my mind, my mind is a room whose wall
I can see the top of but never completely scale.

All that I love is, like the night, outside,
Good to be gazed at, looking as if it could
With a simple gesture be brought inside my head
Or in my heart. But my thoughts about it divide
Me from my object. Now deep in my bed
I turn and the world turns on the other side.

DONALD JUSTICE

In Bertram's Garden

Jane looks down at her organdy skirt
As if *it* somehow were the thing disgraced,
For being there, on the floor, in the dirt,
And she catches it up about her waist,
Smooths it out along one hip,
And pulls it over the crumpled slip.

On the porch, green-shuttered, cool,
Asleep is Bertram, that bronze boy,
Who, having wound her around a spool,
Sends her spinning like a toy
Out to the garden, all alone,
To sit and weep on a bench of stone.

Soon the purple dark must bruise
Lily and bleeding-heart and rose,
And the little Cupid lose
Eyes and ears and chin and nose,
And Jane lie down with others soon,
Naked to the naked moon.

Beyond the Hunting Woods

I speak of that great house
Beyond the hunting woods,

Turreted and towered
In nineteenth-century style,
Where fireflies by the hundreds
Leap in the long grass,
Odor of jessamine
And roses, canker-bit,
Recalling famous times
When dame and maiden sipped
Sassafras or wild
Elderberry wine,
While far in the hunting woods
Men after their red hounds
Pursued the mythic beast.

I ask it of a stranger,
In all that great house finding
Not any living thing,
Or of the wind and the weather,
What charm was in that vine
That they should vanish so,
Ladies in their stiff
Bone and clean of limb,
And over the hunting woods
What mist had maddened them
That gentlemen should lose
Not only the beast in view
But Belle and Ginger too,
Nor home from the hunting woods
Ever, ever come?

Counting the Mad

This one was put in a jacket,
This one was sent home,
This one was given bread and meat
But would eat none,
And this one cried No No No No
All day long.

This one looked at the window
As though it were a wall,
This one saw things that were not there,
This one things that were,
And this one cried No No No No
All day long.

This one thought himself a bird,
This one a dog,
And this one thought himself a man,
An ordinary man,
And cried and cried No No No No
All day long.

Sestina

I woke by first light in a wood
Right in the shadow of a hill
And saw about me in a circle
Many I knew, the dear faces
Of some I recognized as friends.
I knew that I had lost my way.

I asked if any knew the way.
They stared at me like blocks of wood.
They turned their backs on me, those friends,
And struggled up the stubborn hill
Along that road which makes a circle.
No longer could I see their faces.

But there were trees with human faces.
Afraid, I ran a little way
But must have wandered in a circle.
I had not left that human wood;
I was no farther up the hill.
And all the while I heard my friends

Discussing me, but not like friends.
Through gaps in trees I glimpsed their faces.

(The trees grow crooked on that hill.)
Now all at once I saw the way:
Above a clearing in the wood
A lone bird wheeling in a circle

And in that shadowed space the circle
Of those I thought of still as friends.
I drew near, calling, and the wood
Rang and they turned their deaf faces
This way and that, but not my way.
They rose and danced upon the hill.

And it grew dark. Behind the hill
The sun slid down, a fiery circle;
Screeching, the bird flew on her way.
It was too dark to see my friends.
But then I saw them, and their faces
Were leaning above me like a wood.

They round me circle on the hill.
But what is wrong with my friends' faces?
Why have they changed that way to wood?

ELLEN DE YOUNG KAY

Tiresias' Lament

I touch and recollect
Less than the shape and shade
Of formal colonnade.
Unwilling architect

Of the uncloistered mind,
I compass touch and time,
Trace lines on the sublime.
Ridiculous and blind,

I stumble in the crowd;
Fools—still they envy me
For this thin prophecy—
Time's cheat, and living's shroud.

Men, I have known your might,
Women, your subtler grace;
Seen in love's double face
Love's singular delight;

And now what am I made?
Less than each one I was,
The present gives small pause
To my time-ruined shade.

I curse the blackened sun;
Sight was too dear a cost
For this, which shall be lost
Before what is, is done.

Cante Hondo

"Cuando por la calle voy
La gente me miran mucho,
A mi alma, a mi cara, a mi sombra
A ver quien soy . . ."

The hands of beggars peddle cigarets;
White hands that never work, with long, black nails.
Made idle in obscure, plague-haunted jails,
They beg to live, and die in living debts.

Cowed, insolent, the preying hands proceed
In desperation toward the carrion—
A tourist, sweating in the shame and sun,
His lowered stare on print he cannot read.

Refused, the beggars do not go away;
Their sullen eyes accuse the fortunate

More with incomprehension than with hate.
And what is there to do, and what to say?

Impatient to excuse my soul's retreat,
I try to blame a culture not my own.
But finally man faces man alone;
How shall I meet these faces that I meet?

The shadows cross and leave mine in the sand,
Black as the women's stark, habitual dress;
And passing them I feel the loneliness
Inherent in the people of this land.

For each one lives the memory of death,
And each from birth accepts the death to come.
Under the brazen bells the poor are dumb,
And count their days with incense in their breath.

Life is a ritual, a master plan;
Death they accept, and poverty and pain.
And as all men must bear the loss and gain,
They seek to comprehend not God, but man.

The people watch me closely as I go,
They watch my prosperous shadow and my face—
The testimony of a carefree race—
They seek my soul which I shall never know.

Who is the strange one? Is it you or I?
My face, my soul, my shadow, hold a mask
Before the question all mankind may ask.
How can I tell them I have no reply?

To a Blue Hippopotamus

Egyptian, c. 1950 B.C.

Millions who pass you see
But incongruity;

Fail now to reconcile
The river horse, the Nile
Your pasture, rapid, blue,
With that bare dungeoned zoo
Where your descendants dwell,
Mocked in their three-walled hell.

None have observed your pace,
Swift underwater grace,
Or rest like river gods
Feeding on sacred pods
In shallows by the bank.
They picture but the rank
Straw, the abrupt cement,
Nutshells and excrement.

Who know but cramp and noise,
Smile at your easy poise;
Who have not seen you swim
Can only damn as whim
That you, instead of mud,
Wear lotus, bloom and bud;
Who rush past will not span
Four thousand years of man.

Yet some Egyptian youth
Saw, not in whim but truth,
The river horse submerge
Under cerulean surge,
Prisoned in lotus. We
Who condescendingly
Smile at the primitive,
The simplified, who live

Magnified incidents;
Which of us has the sense,
Perspective, or the power
To cast beast, river, flower—
One moment's entity—
In such simplicity

Of whole, perfect with part;
In such immobile art?

The Magnanimous

The Ethics put it well:
It is a sin to sell
Great spirit for the fee
Of inadvertency,
To counterfeit his pose
Who boasts he little knows.

The all unequal mind,
As it is bound, must bind;
Those who are set apart
In work, in self, in art,
Are suppliant to the mass
Bound so that none surpass.

Thus are the real elect
Forced to an unreal sect,
Seeking the world among
Their species, their own tongue,
A word, a nod, a wife
To realize their life.

And between word and word,
Acclimate to the absurd,
They court their own chagrin,
Self-deprecate, they sin—
Being less than they would be,
Is not humility.

Humility is vain
In the deluded brain;
Socrates was no fool
Yet fools repeat his rule,

See not what he would show
Who knew he did not know.

He gave his world the lie,
Arrogant went to die;
Misunderstood as proud,
Pride was his worldly shroud;
None but his gods and he
Knew his humility.

MELVIN WALKER LA FOLLETTE

Hunt

All day it had been raining; now, the leaves
Were crisp and wet with light. It was not late
Yet; bright, the clouds were bright; but it was cold,
And in your small shivering you let me hold
Your head against my chest, and in that great
Alone it was only the light of the leaves
That was watching us. Our breath was clouds, a stump
Steamed quietly, a goldfinch landed on a clump
Of thistle, and started to sing; and it was good
To be warm with you in that untrammeled wood.
But time broke around us like glass, our friendly park
Grew bristling, we stood apart. From the dark
Trees came a red fox, running. Then
The dogs closed in, and finally, the men.

Didactic Sonnet

Love the unholy, that frost which quickens summer
And crispens the thighs like a thorn or a rose
As you lie sleeping; clasp to your belly

The lizard of the great sun, and love him, too.
Admit that you are breathless, like a harried runner,
But do not trade your scepter for fanciful clothes;
Instead of Pegasus, ride on the back of a saddle-green filly
To the moon's other window, and using this platform, screw
Yourself up to the summit of stars. The setting hen
Who hatches shooting stars will love you then,
Even though you steal her eggs for your mother's ocean.
But you must take care, for the sparkling motion
Of star-eggs falling into water causes fog. Fear fog,
For he shall eat your sweetbreads, like a dog.

Summerhouse

There have been three storms in my heart
Since the apricot blossomed; the gourd
Where the purple martens nested is empty;
Oh, goodbye. There is one room that I
Must not touch. It is furnished with a hoard
Of treasures. I recall, with a start,
There was something in June I forgot,
When the storm clouds fumed, lazy and hot,
Over the orchard. In July, I could fling
Dry clods at the noisy birds. Something
Spoke. That was the second storm. In August
A whirlwind filled my mouth with dust,
And I cried. It is September; the lost
Room is locked, my heart is attuned to frost.

The Blue Horse

That summer we saw the Blue Horse.
We tamed him. His sky-splashed mane
Hummed with the current of surcharged hoofs
That flowed into our stony lane.

His love for us was infinite:
The head held high; the tender mouth
That never knew a bit; the eyes
Compassionate as rain that follows drouth.

We loved him; loved, but not because
He was blue and blue horses are rare—
He taught us love; he tamed *us*, too—
Our wild minds learned new meanings for care.

Winter: the Blue Horse was with us still;
The mane now ragged; the eyes still bright
But brightness now admixed with pain;
We taught him hate; we showed him fright.

For Christmas found us listening in the church
To cruel stories; worshiping the star of war;
Our fear forgot his love—forgot
His grief at the sickly fear we bore.

We fought among ourselves: we killed;
The more we fought, the more we feared;
The Blue Horse cried often; you struck me
One day and the Blue Horse disappeared.

We found him when the snow had melted—
Rotted eyes; the mouth become a leer—
He tamed us with his eager love—
We killed him with our feeble fear.

The Ballad of Red Fox

Yellow sun yellow
Sun yellow sun,
When, oh, when
Will red fox run?

When the hollow horn shall sound,
When the hunter lifts his gun
And liberates the wicked hound,
Then, oh, then shall red fox run.

Yellow sun yellow
Sun yellow sun,
Where, oh, where
Will red fox run?

Through meadows hot as sulphur,
Through forests cool as clay,
Through hedges crisp as morning
And grasses limp as day.

Yellow sky yellow
Sky yellow sky,
How, oh, how
Will red fox die?

With a bullet in his belly,
A dagger in his eye,
And blood upon his red red brush
Shall red fox die.

JOSEPH LANGLAND

Aria for Flute and Oboe

Contending with her streams, renascent stars
In the damp halo of dusk, he fondled night
Falling upward under the valley cliffs
And floating deeply out of raspberry vines
Through fragrant thickets sprung in burroak trees
Into its rare and racy luminescence.

Venus inflamed and all her stippled gods
Impaled him through their plunging distances.

Asleep in the down of summer, at that light
Crickets uplept, blinking their feet, and frogs
Trilled in their valleyponds of scummy water;
An owl hollowed his roundly solemn note
While aftersilence shivered and night mist came
Stealing through undershades with wispy hands
To stroke him out of substance. Into the vague
Mounds of neighboring hills a moonsad fox
Yipped for his fellows; when wood echoes lost
That brightness in blunt rocks, a mourning dove
Shaped in the subtle whorls of his ear's shell
Its brief and windy sorrows, hesitant flutes
Saying the wind was down and fireflies still
Raging in sultry grasses . . .
                              Then, then
When choking dust and rock beat back his heart,
A stunning fish gone dull in rainbow leaping,
Then what is a boy to do, himself on fire
With phosphorescent darkness, his milkwhite
Limbs limp in starlight, the downy face
A whole moon in the leaves, his body flung
Like a green twig in moss on limestone rocks,
With doves mourning and owls taunting and frogs
Burbling in watery bottoms, crickets harping
Arpeggios over the bone, the furred fox
Crying in haunts that the summer wind is down
In all the hills, then what is a boy to do
When, pale as stars, his hands shimmer in leaves,
Smothered in music, and flames sleep in the earth
And stars wash over his limbs in the mothering night?

Winter Juniper

Above these bleak Wyoming plains,
These high plateaus

Where water seldom rises through the rock,
This twisting cedar grows.
Splitting through sharp and sandy grains
Of buried cliffs, its fragrant seedlings mock
Deep humus soils and rains.

Under a bright December sun
This cedar pricks
With waxed and polished stems the arid air,
Pivots angular sticks,
Quivers in western winds; they run
Through and away. Here with such final care
Its tortured life is done,

And done, and done again, until
The grained wood
Spirals into a balance, a defense,
A grace. One night I stood
Under the moon in a midnight chill,
Caught in that alien axis, grown immense
In that green will.

War

When my young brother was killed
By a mute and dusty shell in the thorny brush
Crowning the boulders of the Villa Verde Trail
On the island of Luzon,

I laid my whole dry body down,
Dropping my face like a stone in a green park
On the east banks of the Rhine;

On an airstrip skirting the Seine
His sergeant brother sat like a stick in his barracks
While cracks of fading sunlight
Caged the dusty air;

In the rocky rolling hills west of the Mississippi
His father and mother sat in a simple Norwegian parlor
With a photograph smiling between them on the table
And their hands fallen into their laps
Like sticks and dust;

And still other brothers and sisters,
Linking their arms together,
Walked down the dusty road where once he ran
And into the deep green valley
To sit on the stony banks of the stream he loved
And let the murmuring waters
Wash over their blood-hot feet with a springing crown of
   tears.

Hunters in the Snow: Brueghel

Quail and rabbit hunters with tawny hounds,
Shadowless, out of late afternoon
Trudge toward the neutral evening of indeterminate form.
Done with their blood-annunciated day
Public dogs and all the passionless mongrels
Through deep snow
Trail their deliberate masters
Descending from the upper village home in lovering light.
Sooty lamps
Glow in the stone-carved kitchens.

This is the fabulous hour of shape and form
When Flemish children are gray-black-olive
And green-dark-brown
Scattered and skating informal figures
On the mill ice pond.
Moving in stillness
A hunched dame struggles with her bundled sticks,
Letting her evening's comfort cudgel her
While she, like jug or wheel, like a wagon cart
Walked by lazy oxen along the old snowlanes,

Creeps and crunches down the dusky street.
High in the fire-red dooryard
Half unhitched the sign of the Inn
Hangs in wind
Tipped to the pitch of the roof.
Near it anonymous parents and peasant girl,
Living like proverbs carved in the alehouse walls,
Gather the country evening into their arms
And lean to the glowing flames.

Now in the dimming distance fades
The other village; across the valley
Imperturbable Flemish cliffs and crags
Vaguely advance, close in, loom
Lost in nearness. Now
The night-black raven perched in branching boughs
Opens its early wing and slipping out
Above the gray-green valley
Weaves a net of slumber over the snow-capped homes.
And now the church, and then the walls and roofs
Of all the little houses are become
Close kin to shadow with small lantern eyes.
And now the bird of evening
With shadows streaming down from its gliding wings
Circles the neighboring hills
Of Hertogenbosch, Brabant.

Darkness stalks the hunters,
Slowly sliding down,
Falling in beating rings and soft diagonals.
Lodged in the vague vast valley the village sleeps.

Willows

Willows are trees of life. They ride
Their limp boughs to their feeding ground
And sound
Their roots in their immediate countryside.

Like them, I, too, survive
By circular and seasonal disguise;
One golden childhood willow kept my eyes
In a huge green honey hive;

Those twigs and saplings of indifferent dreams
Blooming upon their mountain meadowlands
Sprang in my hands
Like shadows on the upper willow streams.

Now down they run like water to broad plumes
Of delta beds
And toss their palaces of tangled heads
In green felicities of trailing rooms

While rivers in the silted sands dispute,
With sea-borne gravity,
The overflowing tree,
The plunging siphon root.

That thirst would drink the creek beds dry:
Or so I thought. But minnow schools
Sparkle in willow pools,
Shifting their golden flecks in that bright eye.

So have I lain in depths while vision pearled
Over the clouded surfaces of things
In dense imaginings
With one eye squinting upward into the world

Out of my willowy sleep. That memory calls
Where the old willow tells
Of disembodied cities of floating bells
Tumbling simultaneously through waterfalls.

The spring floods flash. Believe me, one cannot
Casually remember now
All jewels hidden under the willow bough,
In all begetting time what one begot.

When I am an old man and dying, almost lost
On the northern slopes of death, a stiff reed
Trembling from husk to seed,
My flutes all cracked with frost,

I will translate myself into a brown
Paradise of willow roots, a whole
Country of mountain meadows for the soul
Dreaming toward natural grace in a green town.

Ecclesiastes

Out of the icy storms the white hare came
Shivering into a haven of human arms;
It was not love but fear that made him tame.

He lay in the arms of love, having no name
But comfort to address. Shaking alarms
Out of the icy storms, the white hare came

Across the haunted meadows crackling with game.
What evil eye pinpointed his soft charms?
It was not love but fear. That made him tame

Among the chilling hail and scattering aim.
Helpless against the sport of ancient farms,
Out of the icy storms the white hare came

Thinking, perhaps, it leaped through icy flame,
Thinking, with instinct, hate or trust disarms.
It was not love. But fear that made him tame

Leaped again in his heart; his flesh became
Translated into havens. From sudden harms
Out of the icy storms the white hare came;
It was not love but fear that made him tame.

Pruners: Conca di Marini

Pruners have come again among the vineyards;
They ride the terraced mountain on their ladders
To clip the grapevines hanging in these arbors.
               I heard their winter shears
               Go cleanly by these stairs.

Among the wild disorder of our twigs
Over the outer edges, frugal snips
Devour half the vines, and willow slips
               Bind up the bloodless stems
               In greys and gold reds.

Someone must train the vines (no spring has come)
Trying a few pale tendrils in the air;
Now they are clean, stripped to a winter stare.
               In less becoming more,
               Consider what is lost.

This shock will keep the vines asleep till March.
They would not dare affront their keeper's eyes
Though he is full of wine, in nothing wise
               Except these ritual chores.
               Economy of words.

For who would let a senseless love of sun
Updraw him, or a warm unseasonal rain,
Only to gaze at winter once again?
               The mild unsparing grooms
               Keep the essential roots

And pile the clippings on their women's backs
To ride the hearths and ovens of these hills
Where food and wine and fire have their wills
               And the rank autumn grapes
               Rise in their winter flames.

PHILIP LARKIN

Deceptions

'Of course I was drugged, and so heavily I did not regain my consciousness till the next morning. I was horrified to discover that I had been ruined, and for some days I was inconsolable, and cried like a child to be killed or sent back to my aunt.'—Mayhew, *London Labour and the London Poor.*

Even so distant, I can taste the grief,
Bitter and sharp with stalks, he made you gulp.
The sun's occasional print, the brisk brief
Worry of wheels along the street outside
Where bridal London bows the other way,
And light, unanswerable and tall and wide,
Forbids the scar to heal, and drives
Shame out of hiding. All the unhurried day
Your mind lay open like a drawer of knives.

Slums, years, have buried you. I would not dare
Console you if I could. What can be said,
Except that suffering is exact, but where
Desire takes charge, readings will grow erratic?
For you would hardly care
That you were less deceived, out on that bed,
Than he was, stumbling up the breathless stair
To burst into fulfilment's desolate attic.

Church Going

Once I am sure there's nothing going on
I step inside, letting the door thud shut.
Another church: matting, seats, and stone,

And little books; sprawlings of flowers, cut
For Sunday, brownish now; some brass and stuff
Up at the holy end; the small neat organ;
And a tense, musty, unignorable silence,
Brewed God knows how long. Hatless, I take off
My cycle-clips in awkward reverence,

Move forward, run my hand around the font.
From where I stand, the roof looks almost new—
Cleaned or restored? Someone would know: I don't.
Mounting the lectern, I peruse a few
Hectoring large-scale verses, and pronounce
'Here endeth' much more loudly than I'd meant.
The echoes snigger briefly. Back at the door
I sign the book, donate an Irish sixpence,
Reflect the place was not worth stopping for.

Yet stop I did: in fact I often do,
And always end much at a loss like this,
Wondering what to look for; wondering, too,
When churches fall completely out of use
What we shall turn them into, if we shall keep
A few cathedrals chronically on show,
Their parchment, plate and pyx in locked cases,
And let the rest rent-free to rain and sheep.
Shall we avoid them as unlucky places?

Or, after dark, will dubious women come
To make their children touch a particular stone;
Pick simples for a cancer; or in some
Advised night see walking a dead one?
Power of some sort or other will go on
In games, in riddles, seemingly at random;
But superstition, like belief, must die,
And what remains when disbelief has gone?
Grass, weedy pavement, brambles, buttress, sky,

A shape less recognisable each week,
A purpose more obscure. I wonder who
Will be the last, the very last, to seek
This place for what it was; one of the crew

That tap and jot and know what rood-lofts were?
Some ruin-bibber, randy for antique,
Or Christmas-addict, counting on a whiff
Of gown-and-bands and organ-pipes and myrrh?
Or will he be my representative,

Bored, uninformed, knowing the ghostly silt
Dispersed, yet tending to this cross of ground
Through suburb scrub because it held unspilt
So long and equably what since is found
Only in separation—marriage, and birth,
And deaths, and thoughts of these—for whom was built
This special shell? For, though I've no idea
What this accoutred frowsty barn is worth,
It pleases me to stand in silence here;

A serious house on serious earth it is,
In whose blent air all our compulsions meet,
Are recognized, and robed as destinies.
And that much never can be obsolete,
Since someone will forever be surprising
A hunger in himself to be more serious,
And gravitating with it to this ground,
Which, he once heard, was proper to grow wise in,
If only that so many dead lie round.

Toads

Why should I let the toad *work*
    Squat on my life?
Can't I use my wit as a pitchfork
    And drive the brute off?

Six days of the week it soils
    With its sickening poison—
Just for paying a few bills!
    That's out of proportion.

Lots of folk live on their wits:
    Lecturers, lispers,
Losels, loblolly-men, louts—
    They don't end as paupers;

Lots of folk live up lanes
    With fires in a bucket,
Eat windfalls and tinned sardines—
    They seem to like it.

Their nippers have got bare feet,
    Their unspeakable wives
Are skinny as whippets—and yet
    No one actually *starves*.

Ah, were I courageous enough
    To shout *Stuff your pension!*
But I know, all too well, that's the stuff
    That dreams are made on:

For something sufficiently toad-like
    Squats in me, too;
Its hunkers are heavy as hard luck,
    And cold as snow,

And will never allow me to blarney
    My way to getting
The fame and the girl and the money
    All at one sitting.

I don't say, one bodies the other
    One's spiritual truth;
But I do say it's hard to lose either,
    When you have both.

Poetry of Departures

Sometimes you hear, fifth-hand,
As epitaph:

He chucked up everything
And just cleared off,
And always the voice will sound
Certain you approve
This audacious, purifying,
Elemental move.

And they are right, I think.
We all hate home
And having to be there:
I detest my room,
Its specially-chosen junk,
The good books, the good bed,
And my life, in perfect order:
So to hear it said

He walked out on the whole crowd
Leaves me flushed and stirred,
Like *Then she undid her dress*
Or *Take that you bastard;*
Surely I can, if he did?
And that helps me stay
Sober and industrious.
But I'd go today,

Yes, swagger the nut-strewn roads,
Crouch in the fo'c'sle
Stubbly with goodness, if
It weren't so artificial,
Such a deliberate step backwards
To create an object:
Books; china; a life
Reprehensibly perfect.

At Grass

The eye can hardly pick them out
From the cold shade they shelter in,

Till wind distresses tail and mane;
Then one crops grass, and moves about
—The other seeming to look on—
And stands anonymous again.

Yet fifteen years ago, perhaps
Two dozen distances sufficed
To fable them: faint afternoons
Of Cups and Stakes and Handicaps,
Whereby their names were artificed
To inlay faded, classic Junes—

Silks at the start: against the sky
Numbers and parasols: outside,
Squadrons of empty cars, and heat,
And littered grass: then the long cry
Hanging unhushed till it subside
To stop-press columns on the street.

Do memories plague their ears like flies?
They shake their heads. Dusk brims the shadows.
Summer by summer all stole away,
The starting-gates, the crowds and cries—
All but the unmolesting meadows.
Almanacked, their names live; they

Have slipped their names, and stand at ease,
Or gallop for what must be joy,
And not a fieldglass sees them home,
Or curious stop-watch prophesies:
Only the groom, and the groom's boy,
With bridles in the evening come.

Next, Please

Always too eager for the future, we
Pick up bad habits of expectancy.

Something is always approaching; every day
Till then we say,

Watching from a bluff the tiny, clear
Sparkling armada of promises draw near.
How slow they are! And how much time they waste,
Refusing to make haste!

Yet still they leave us holding wretched stalks
Of disappointment, for, though nothing balks
Each big approach, leaning with brasswork prinked,
Each rope distinct,

Flagged, and the figurehead with golden tits
Arching our way, it never anchors; it's
No sooner present than it turns to past.
Right to the last

We think each one will heave to and unload
All good into our lives, all we are owed
For waiting so devoutly and so long.
But we are wrong:

Only one ship is seeking us, a black-
Sailed unfamiliar, towing at her back
A huge and birdless silence. In her wake
No waters breed or break.

Places, Loved Ones

No, I have never found
The place where I could say
This is my proper ground,
Here I shall stay;
Nor met that special one
Who has an instant claim
On everything I own
Down to my name;

To find such seems to prove
You want no choice in where
To build, or whom to love;
You ask them to bear
You off irrevocably,
So that it's not your fault
Should the town turn dreary,
The girl a dolt.

Yet, having missed them, you're
Bound, none the less to act
As if what you settled for
Mashed you, in fact;
And wiser to keep away
From thinking you still might trace
Uncalled-for to this day
Your person, your place.

ROBERT LAYZER

Saint's Parade

After the squealing brass
The thick-legged saint appears,
Dressed in a dead smile
And carved by Roman spears.

Needles of light impale
The shadowed innocence
Where boys with carbon hair
Match blades for fifty cents.

Saint Rocco of the Banknotes
With a treasury of wounds
Displays his painted mercies
To the bleeding afternoon.

The shops along the street
Give oil and vinegar
To soothe the massive hurt,
Garlic to please the martyr.

The butcher's wife is selling
The buttons of the saint,
Wearing a yellow shirt.
The sun begins to faint . . .

But the girls come and sprinkle
The lavender of their hearts
On the gasping red piazza
Where the young men play darts.

The Sleeping Beauty

I

No, nothing is asleep in this demesne
  Of scrub pine, washed-out oak; the wet
    Intrudes on every cache,
    And feathered throats complain
That the rude wind is tramping through the brush
    In streams of sweat.

There are deep holes beneath the sodden thatch
  And under rocks and rotten logs,
    Where you may press your eyes
    Like fingers on a latch
Opening caverns pungent with surprise:
    Three watchful dogs

With eyes as big as candles or chime-clocks
  Sit on a heaped-up treasury
    And will not wink or doze.
    But where's the tinder box

To fetch the sleeping princess in her nightclothes
    For privacy,

Or kindle the vault where Juliet lies asleep
    Dreaming of sunlight on a sheet?
      Under the spongy turf
      Not closeted or deep
A girl lies dead: and the dying needles beat
    On her face like surf.

II

Turn over again. The reins of day are reversed,
    And sleep the overrider spurs
      His foaming mount to death.
      Intolerable thirst
Evokes the dripping forest whose moist breath
    Dunned in your ears.

The wind said: "It is because the thrushes sing
    How beauty innocent of pain
      Transfigures all this brake,
      That I am ravaging.
Woe to the antic sparrow when I shake
    My jagged mane."

Pain is certain. "There may be heaven, there must
    Be hell." The sleeping virgin dreams
      Enchanted harmonies
      Within her house of dust;
But now the grinding tempest racks the trees,
    Big vacant seams

Divulge the treasures of the fissured earth:
    A grave springs open and at last,
      Brushing the dirt aside
      With hideous pangs of birth,
The sleeping beauty wakes, immortal bride,
    And holds you fast.

The Lawn Roller

Too many summers out of the way of a trowel
Has given the clover and dandelion a feast,
And now it's as easy to temper the whim of the soil
As argue the sun into crouching from west to east.

Down at the end of the street a sun-glazed man
Has three hundred pounds of water inside a drum
Rolling and pressing a naked torso of lawn
Into flat perfection, ripe for the gardener's thumb.

The bare and close is where I began, but somehow
Only wild things grew out of my ministries,
Or extravagant tame. Astonished, I watched them swallow
The plot like Africans eating their enemies

Not out of malice but a respect for kinship.
What could succeed? The peony changed a bed
Of oil and ease for a ·fierce alien worship,
The rose lay down beside the ragweed's head

And everything the lascivious earth raised up
From a cold slumber, threw off sheets of clay
To fold the sunlight in an amorous grip.
It was too late to prune the jungle away,

Or too injurious for the eye stained green
To crop an inch of greenness. The twentieth spring
Found me in this delirium eyeing the scene
With a lawn roller's contempt for rioting

Abundance, and a sunstruck tenderness.
I watched and waited. Later it seemed the moon,
Cold as the face of Helen in her distress,
Was looking through the branches, hard and alone.

The Insult

On the hottest day of the year I rode the mail
To Waterloo Strand and Seaside Macedon
Where, tanned like Egyptians in their Louis-Quatorze
Bath chairs, the sumptuous pleasure-loving dead
Felt no reproach, not even the tart harangue
Of the sea slapping their feet. I counted on this.

Those basking moguls thought they scented blood
When out of my deep pouch like an angler I pulled
The mail. They pressed me in a sweating circle,
Filling the air with adolescent mewings
For local news (which I had early disguised)
Of that untarnished county beyond the wave.

They soon divined the insult of my game.
I took my exit as they began to grate
Their grim vexation; but a decrepit Greek
Collared me with the force of twenty youths
(Though blind) and at my insolence sternly chewed:
This is a dream. Where is your lost beloved?

Elegy

I

Whenever we touched, I thought of the Lying-in Hospital.
Those women were big as the houses they hoped to fill,
Not slender like you: too bulky to be desired
But swollen and snug as after a Thanksgiving dinner.
They were digesting some really important secret
And I remembered, when you moved out of my arms,
That we had our own secrets to fill the room.

II

We slept. I dreamed or simply remembered a room
Where the laughter of nursing mothers lay like the hum
Of telephones on the air. A woman sat
On the edge of her bed and combed her hair and laughed,
Bare to the waist, the gentle curve of her back
Partly in shadows of the late afternoon
And partly illumined by my clear desire.

III

Your hand had slipped from mine and I was afraid
To wake you, if I took you in my arms,
From that ambiguous dream that smoothed your face
Into the semblance of complete content.
The moonlight picked out objects in the room.
What did I lack? The bed and books were there,
Your breathing, and the secrets of the room.

ROBERT LOWELL

Her Dead Brother

I

The Lion of St. Mark's upon the glass
Shield in my window reddens, as the night
Enchants the swinging dories to its terrors,
And dulls your distant wind-stung eyes; alas,
Your portrait, coiled in German-silver hawsers, mirrors
The sunset as a dragon. Enough light
Remains to see you through your varnish. Giving
Your life has brought you closer to your friends;
Yes, it has brought you home. All's well that ends:
Achilles dead is greater than the living;

My mind holds you as I would have you live,
A wintering dragon. Summer was too short
When we went picnicking with telescopes
And crocking leather handbooks to that fort
Above the lank and heroned Sheepscot, where its slopes
Are clutched by hemlocks—spotting birds. I give
You back that idyll, Brother. Was it more?
Remember riding, scotching with your spur
That four-foot milk-snake in a juniper?
Father shellacked it to the ice-house door.

Then you were grown; I left you on your own.
We will forget that August twenty-third,
When Mother motored with the maids to Stowe,
And the pale summer shades were drawn—so low
No one could see us; no, nor catch your hissing word,
As false as Cressid! Let our deaths atone:
The fingers on your sword-knot are alive,
And Hope, that fouls my brightness with its grace,
Will anchor in the narrows of your face.
My husband's Packard crunches up the drive.

II

(Three months later)

The ice is out: the tidal current swims
Its blocks against the launches as they pitch
Under the cruisers of my Brother's fleet.
The gas, uncoiling from my oven burners, dims
The fact above this bottled *Water Witch*,
The knockabout my Brother fouled and left to eat
Its heart out by the Boston Light. My Brother,
I've saved you in the ice-house of my mind—
The ice is out. . . . Our fingers lock behind
The tiller. We are heeling in the smother,

Our sails, balloon and leg-o'-mutton, tell
The colors of the rainbow; but they flap,
As the wind fails, and cannot fetch the bell. . . .
His stick is tapping on the millwheel-step,
He lights a match, another and another—

The Lord is dark, and holy is His name;
By my own hands, into His hands! My burners
Sing like a kettle, and its nickel mirrors
Your squadron by the Stygian Landing. Brother,
The harbor! The torpedoed cruisers flame,

The motor-launches with their searchlights bristle
About the targets. You are black. You shout,
And cup your broken sword-hand. Yes, your whistle
Across the crackling water: *Quick, the ice is out.* . . .
The wind dies in our canvas; we were running dead
Before the wind, but now our sail is part
Of death. O Brother, a New England town is death
And incest—and I saw it whole. I said,
Life is a thing I own. Brother, my heart
Races for sea-room—we are out of breath.

New Year's Day

Again and then again . . . the year is born
To ice and death, and it will never do
To skulk behind storm-windows by the stove
To hear the postgirl sounding her French horn
When the thin tidal ice is wearing through.
Here is the understanding not to love
Our neighbor, or tomorrow that will sieve
Our resolutions. While we live, we live

To snuff the smoke of victims. In the snow
The kitten heaved its hindlegs, as if fouled,
And died. We bent it in a Christmas box
And scattered blazing weeds to scare the crow
Until the snake-tailed sea-winds coughed and howled
For alms outside the church whose double locks
Wait for St. Peter, the distorted key.
Under St. Peter's bell the parish sea

Swells with its smelt into the burlap shack
Where Joseph plucks his hand-lines like a harp,
And hears the fearful *Puer natus est*
Of Circumcision, and relives the wrack
And howls of Jesus whom he holds. How sharp
The burden of the Law before the beast:
Time and the grindstone and the knife of God.
The Child is born in blood, O child of blood.

The Holy Innocents

Listen, the hay-bells tinkle as the cart
Wavers on rubber tires along the tar
And cindered ice below the burlap mill
And ale-wife run. The oxen drool and start
In wonder at the fenders of a car,
And blunder hugely up St. Peter's hill.
These are the undefiled by woman—their
Sorrow is not the sorrow of this world:
King Herod shrieking vengeance at the curled
Up knees of Jesus choking in the air,

A king of speechless clods and infants. Still
The world out-Herods Herod; and the year,
The nineteen-hundred forty-fifth of grace,
Lumbers with losses up the clinkered hill
Of our purgation; and the oxen near
The worn foundations of our resting-place,
The holy manger where their bed is corn
And holly torn for Christmas. If they die,
As Jesus, in the harness, who will mourn?
Lamb of the shepherds, Child, how still you lie.

Between the Porch and the Altar

I
Mother and Son

Meeting his mother makes him lose ten years,
Or is it twenty? Time, no doubt, has ears
That listen to the swallowed serpent, wound
Into its bowels, but he thinks no sound
Is possible before her, he thinks the past
Is settled. It is honest to hold fast
Merely to what one sees with one's own eyes
When the red velvet curves and haunches rise
To blot him from the pretty driftwood fire's
Façade of welcome. Then the son retires
Into the sack and selfhood of the boy
Who clawed through fallen houses of his Troy,
Homely and human only when the flames
Crackle in recollection. Nothing shames
Him more than this uncoiling, counterfeit
Body presented as an idol. It
Is something in a circus, big as life,
The painted dragon, a mother and a wife
With flat glass eyes pushed at him on a stick;
The human mover crawls to make them click.
The forehead of her father's portrait peels
With rosy dryness, and the schoolboy kneels
To ask the benediction of the hand,
Lifted as though to motion him to stand,
Dangling its watch-chain on the Holy Book—
A little golden snake that mouths a hook.

II
Adam and Eve

The farmer sizzles on his shaft all day. .
He is content and centuries away
From white-hot Concord, and he stands on guard.

Or is he melting down like sculptured lard?
His hand is crisp and steady on the plough.
I quarreled with you, but am happy now
To while away my life for your unrest
Of terror. Never to have lived is best;
Man tasted Eve with death. I taste my wife
And children while I hold your hands. I knife
Their names into this elm. What is exempt?
I eye the statue with an awed contempt
And see the puritanical façade
Of the white church that Irish exiles made
For Patrick—that Colonial from Rome
Had magicked the charmed serpents from their home,
As though he were the Piper. Will his breath
Scorch the red dragon of my nerves to death?
By sundown we are on a shore. You walk
A little way before me and I talk,
Half to myself and half aloud. They lied,
My cold-eyed seedy fathers when they died,
Or rather threw their lives away, to fix
Sterile, forbidding nameplates on the bricks
Above a kettle. Jesus rest their souls!
You cry for help. Your market-basket rolls
With all its baking apples in the lake.
You watch the whorish slither of a snake
That chokes a duckling. When we try to kiss,
Our eyes are slits and cringing, and we hiss;
Scales glitter on our bodies as we fall.
The Farmer melts upon his pedestal.

III

Katherine's Dream

It must have been a Friday. I could hear
The top-floor typist's thunder and the beer
That you had brought in cases hurt my head;
I'd sent the pillows flying from my bed,
I hugged my knees together and I gasped.
The dangling telephone receiver rasped
Like someone in a dream who cannot stop
For breath or logic till his victim drop

To darkness and the sheets. I must have slept,
But still could hear my father who had kept
Your guilty presents but cut off my hair.
He whispers that he really doesn't care
If I am your kept woman all my life,
Or ruin your two children and your wife;
But my dishonor makes him drink. Of course
I'll tell the court the truth for his divorce.
I walk through snow into St. Patrick's yard.
Black nuns with glasses smile and stand on guard
Before a bulkhead in a bank of snow,
Whose charred doors open, as good people go
Inside by twos to the confessor. One
Must have a friend to enter there, but none
Is friendless in this crowd, and the nuns smile.
I stand aside and marvel; for a while
The winter sun is pleasant and it warms
My heart with love for others, but the swarms
Of penitents have dwindled. I begin
To cry and ask God's pardon for our sin.
Where are you? You were with me and are gone.
All the forgiven couples hurry on
To dinner and their nights, and none will stop.
I run about in circles till I drop
Against a padlocked bulkhead in a yard
Where faces redden and the snow is hard.

IV

At the Altar

I sit at a gold table with my girl
Whose eyelids burn with brandy. What a whirl
Of Easter eggs is colored by the lights,
As the Norwegian dancer's crystalled tights
Flash with her naked leg's high-booted skate,
Like Northern Lights upon my watching plate.
The twinkling steel above me is a star;
I am a fallen Christmas tree. Our car
Races through seven red-lights—then the road
Is unpatrolled and empty, and a load
Of ply-wood with a tail-light makes us slow.

I turn and whisper in her ear. You know
I want to leave my mother and my wife,
You wouldn't have me tied to them for life . . .
Time runs, the windshield runs with stars. The past
Is cities from a train, until at last
Its escalating and black-windowed blocks
Recoil against a Gothic church. The clocks
Are tolling. I am dying. The shocked stones
Are falling like a ton of bricks and bones
That snap and splinter and descend in glass
Before a priest who mumbles through his Mass
And sprinkles holy water; and the Day
Breaks with its lightning on the man of clay,
Dies amara valde. Here the Lord
Is Lucifer in harness: hand on sword,
He watches me for Mother, and will turn
The bier and baby-carriage where I burn.

After the Surprising Conversions

September twenty-second, Sir: today
I answer. In the latter part of May,
Hard on our Lord's Ascension, it began
To be more sensible. A gentleman
Of more than common understanding, strict
In morals, pious in behavior, kicked
Against our goad. A man of some renown,
An useful, honored person in the town,
He came of melancholy parents; prone
To secret spells, for years they kept alone—
His uncle, I believe, was killed of it:
Good people, but of too much or little wit.
I preached one Sabbath on a text from Kings;
He showed concernment for his soul. Some things
In his experience were hopeful. He
Would sit and watch the wind knocking a tree
And praise this countryside our Lord has made.
Once when a poor man's heifer died, he laid

A shilling on the doorsill; though a thirst
For loving shook him like a snake, he durst
Not entertain much hope of his estate
In heaven. Once we saw him sitting late
Behind his attic window by a light
That guttered on his Bible; through that night
He meditated terror, and he seemed
Beyond advice or reason, for he dreamed
That he was called to trumpet Judgment Day
To Concord. In the latter part of May
He cut his throat. And though the coroner
Judged him delirious, soon a noisome stir
Palsied our village. At Jehovah's nod
Satan seemed more let loose amongst us: God
Abandoned us to Satan, and he pressed
Us hard, until we thought we could not rest
Till we had done with life. Content was gone.
All the good work was quashed. We were undone.
The breath of God had carried out a planned
And sensible withdrawal from this land;
The multitude, once unconcerned with doubt,
Once neither callous, curious nor devout,
Jumped at broad noon, as though some peddler groaned
At it in its familiar twang: "My friend,
Cut your own throat. Cut your own throat. Now! Now!"
September twenty-second, Sir, the bough
Cracks with the unpicked apples, and at dawn
The small-mouth bass breaks water, gorged with spawn.

Salem

In Salem seasick spindrift drifts or skips
To the canvas flapping on the seaward panes
Until the knitting sailor stabs at ships
Nosing like sheep of Morpheus through his brain's
Asylum. Seaman, seaman, how the draft
Lashes the oily slick about your head,
Beating up whitecaps! Seaman, Charon's raft

Dumps its damned goods into the harbor-bed,—
There sewage sickens the rebellious seas.
Remember, seaman, Salem fishermen
Once hung their nimble fleets on the Great Banks.
Where was it that New England bred the men
Who quartered the Leviathan's fat flanks
And fought the British Lion to his knees?

The North Sea Undertaker's Complaint

Now south and south and south the mallard heads,
His green-blue bony hood echoes the green
Flats of the Weser, and the mussel beds
Are sluggish where the webbed feet spanked the lean
Eel grass to tinder in the take-off. South
Is what I think of. It seems yesterday
I slid my hearse across the river mouth
And pitched the first iced mouse into the hay.
Thirty below it is. I hear our dumb
Club-footed orphan ring the Angelus
And clank the bell-chain for St. Gertrude's choir
To wail with the dead bell the martyrdom
Of one more blue-lipped priest; the phosphorous
Melted the hammer of his heart to fire.

As a Plane Tree by the Water

Darkness has called to darkness, and disgrace
Elbows about our windows in this planned
Babel of Boston where our money talks
And multiplies the darkness of a land
Of preparation where the Virgin walks
And roses spiral her enamelled face
Or fall to splinters on unwatered streets.

Our Lady of Babylon, go by, go by,
I was once the apple of your eye;
Flies, flies are on the plane tree, on the streets.

The flies, the flies, the flies of Babylon
Buzz in my ear-drums while the devil's long
Dirge of the people detonates the hour
For floating cities where his golden tongue
Enchants the masons of the Babel Tower
To raise tomorrow's city to the sun
That never sets upon these hell-fire streets
Of Boston, where the sunlight is a sword
Striking at the withholder of the Lord:
Flies, flies are on the plane tree, on the streets.

Flies strike the miraculous waters of the iced
Atlantic and the eyes of Bernadette
Who saw Our Lady standing in the cave
At Massabielle, saw her so squarely that
Her vision put out reason's eyes. The grave
Is open-mouthed and swallowed up in Christ.
O walls of Jericho! And all the streets
To our Atlantic wall are singing: "Sing,
Sing for the resurrection of the King."
Flies, flies are on the plane tree, on the streets.

Mr. Edwards and the Spider

I saw the spiders marching through the air,
Swimming from tree to tree that mildewed day
    In latter August when the hay
    Came creaking to the barn. But where
        The wind is westerly,
Where gnarled November makes the spiders fly
Into the apparitions of the sky,
    They purpose nothing but their ease and die
Urgently beating east to sunrise and the sea;

What are we in the hands of the great God?
It was in vain you set up thorn and briar
   In battle array against the fire
    And treason crackling in your blood;
     For the wild thorns grow tame
And will do nothing to oppose the flame;
Your lacerations tell the losing game
You play against a sickness past your cure.
How will the hands be strong? How will the heart endure?

A very little thing, a little worm,
Or hourglass-blazoned spider, it is said,
   Can kill a tiger. Will the dead
   Hold up his mirror and affirm
    To the four winds the smell
And flash of his authority? It's well
If God who holds you to the pit of hell,
Much as one holds a spider, will destroy,
Baffle and dissipate your soul. As a small boy

On Windsor Marsh, I saw the spider die
When thrown into the bowels of fierce fire:
   There's no long struggle, no desire
   To get up on its feet and fly—
    It stretches out its feet
And dies. This is the sinner's last retreat;
Yes, and no strength exerted on the heat
Then sinews the abolished will, when sick
And full of burning, it will whistle on a brick.

But who can plumb the sinking of that soul?
Josiah Hawley, picture yourself cast
   Into a brick-kiln where the blast
   Fans your quick vitals to a coal—
    If measured by a glass,
How long would it seem burning! Let there pass
A minute, ten, ten trillion; but the blaze
Is infinite, eternal: this is death.
To die and know it. This is the Black Widow, death.

The Dead in Europe

After the planes unloaded, we fell down
Buried together, unmarried men and women;
Not crown of thorns, not iron, not Lombard crown,
Not grilled and spindle spires pointing to heaven
Could save us. Raise us, Mother, we fell down
Here hugger-mugger in the jellied fire:
Our sacred earth in our day was our curse.

Our Mother, shall we rise on Mary's day
In Maryland, wherever corpses married
Under the rubble, bundled together? Pray
For us whom the blockbusters marred and buried;
When Satan scatters us on Rising-day,
O Mother, snatch our bodies from the fire:
Our sacred earth in our day was our curse.

Mother, my bones are trembling and I hear
The earth's reverberations and the trumpet
Bleating into my shambles. Shall I bear,
(O Mary!) unmarried man and powder-puppet,
Witness to the Devil? Mary, hear,
O Mary, marry earth, sea, air and fire;
Our sacred earth in our day is our curse.

Where the Rainbow Ends

I saw the sky descending, black and white,
Not blue, on Boston where the winters wore
The skulls to jack-o'-lanterns on the slates,
And Hunger's skin-and-bone retrievers tore
The chickadee and shrike. The thorn tree waits
Its victim and tonight
The worms will eat the deadwood to the foot
Of Ararat: the scythers, Time and Death,

Helmed locusts, move upon the tree of breath;
The wild ingrafted olive and the root

Are withered, and a winter drifts to where
The Pepperpot, ironic rainbow, spans
Charles River and its scales of scorched-earth miles
I saw my city in the Scales, the pans
Of judgment rising and descending. Piles
Of dead leaves char the air—
And I am a red arrow on this graph
Of Revelations. Every dove is sold
The Chapel's sharp-shinned eagle shifts its hold
On serpent-Time, the rainbow's epitaph.

In Boston serpents whistle at the cold.
The victim climbs the altar steps and sings:
"Hosannah to the lion, lamb, and beast
Who fans the furnace-face of IS with wings:
I breathe the ether of my marriage feast."
At the high altar, gold
And a fair cloth. I kneel and the wings beat
My cheek. What can the dove of Jesus give
You now but wisdom, exile? Stand and live,
The dove has brought an olive branch to eat.

WILLIAM H. MATCHETT

Packing a Photograph from Firenze

1.

This house that has been our home has been condemned
To be demolished as part of a master plan
That calls for enlarging the institution next door.
Overnight, on the torn, raw ground, they will graft a new,
Of course modern, stainless, leakproof research
Laboratory, with interphone system and guards.

Here, where the staircase creaks and the furnace complains,
Where brown fingers have clutched the plaster through
        countless rains,
Steel and concrete will shield the tempered air.
Here, where the ashtrays have spilled the warm ends of
        thought
While the coffee grew cold, none being afraid to speak,
Where we have lain locked through long nights and were
        loath to arise
On grey winter mornings when chickadees came to the
        window,
In sound-proof cells on registered pads
The approved will doodle death with indelible ink.

2.

The artery sings in the wrist, *time passes, time passes;*
Youth, though it swings with the cadence, is deaf to the song,
Which is its horror, poignancy and salvation.
Michelangelo's David, firm, with the poised repose
Of a hidden lion, drawn by the will of the blood,
Sling in hand, muses of greater Goliaths.
If this were the boy portrayed, not the image given
To life in the lifeless stone, if this were the flesh
That now is the dust of ageless mutations of dust,
The flesh, defiant, perplexed, ashamedly lonely,
Then in the depth of the chest, in the ribs' cave,
Would lurk, unperceived, the treacherous final plague,
The twisted limb, the sagging physique, the intense
And fussy attention to each misbeat of the pulse.
But the stone that stands transcends the David that died,
Though he died a king. Is it better to make an end
Than to face the interminable pains and the diminutions?
Perhaps it is progress, this pure research into killing;
The suddenly dead avoid their slow decay.

3.

I hear the mouse in the laundry and know that fall
Has arrived to drive him in again; on the lawn
The last of the leaves are collecting in drifts at the base
Of the purple beech. One straggling chrysanthemum
Dips and drips bronze-gold on the crusted earth.

This clear, suspended moment before the frost
Is the time for turning the compost and mulching the rose,
Spreading the wholesome corruption that feeds
Through the probable winter to the impossible spring.
But let it pass. Why enrich the soil
That will never produce? A jungle of structural steel,
Though rooted firmly in humus as black as war,
Is no less barren. A buried seed that is warmed
By a basement floor will unwrap the tallow coil
From its pallid core and, seeking the sun, will rot.
So it comes to an end, breaking the usual cycle;
The frame is ravaged behind the evicted soul.

4.

The affections, ever conservative, cling to the forms
Worn smoothest by custom, resisting even improvement,
Content, when pressed, with the shreds of a wretched past.
Eppur si muove. I would not wish to be
The hierophant proscribing Galileo.
Yet truth is not false because the affections agree.
This is not science, this furious drive for extinction,
The spurious promise of power perverts cognition
While the single-minded pursuit of enslavable facts
Neglects the very ravines where the victims lie strangled.
I must affirm this ill-proportioned house
And the earth around it, even the mouse and the staircase.
All change is not progress, nor is all age decline.
There is more to be drawn from the line of the silvered limbs
Of the purple beech, more from the silvered line
Of David's limbs, more from the intercourse
Of hearts, fertile minds, dirty fingers and growing things
Than from all the sterilized data of destruction.

But the time has arrived for removing all we can save
In an echoing search through painfully naked rooms
Where stark, dark wallpaper celebrates each missing picture,
Revealing the silent advance of ceaseless change.
We have been warned. We clasp our belongings. We flee.
Yet slowly, inexorably, the future pursues
With the final knowledge of all that we shall lose:
In the fall of this house all houses stand condemned.

Water Ouzel

for Dora Willson

Follow back from the gull's bright arc and the osprey's
     plunge,
Past the silent heron, erect in the tidal marsh,
Up the mighty river, rolling in mud. Branch off
At the sign of the kingfisher poised on a twisted snag.
Not deceived when the surface grows calm, keep on,
Past the placidity of ducks, the delusive pastoral dreams
Drawn down by the effortless swallows that drink on the
     wing.
With the wheat fields behind you, do not neglect to choose
At every juncture the clearest and coldest path.
Push through the reeds where the redwing sways,
Climb through the warnings of hidden jays,
Climb, climb the jostling, narrowing stream
Through aspen sunlight into the evergreen darkness
Where chattering crossbills scatter the shreds of cones.
Here at last at the brink of the furthest fall,
With the water dissolving to mist as it shatters the pool be-
     low,
Pause beneath timber-line springs and the melting snow.
Here, where the shadows are deep in the crystal air,
So near a myriad beginnings, after so long a journey,
Expecting at least a golden cockatoo
Or a screaming eagle with wings of flame,
Stifle your disappointment, observe
The burgher of all this beauty, the drab
Citizen of the headwaters; struggle to love
The ridiculous ouzel, perched on his slippery stone
Like an awkward, overblown catbird deprived of its tail.
Not for him the limitless soaring above the storm,
Or the surface-skimming, or swimming, or plunging in.
He walks. In the midst of the turbulence, bathed in spray,
From a rock without foothold into the lunging current
He descends a deliberate step at a time till, submerged,

He has walked from sight and hope. The stream
Drives on, dashes, splashes, drops over the edge,
Too swift for ice in midwinter, too cold
For life in midsummer, depositing any debris,
Leaf, twig or carcass, along the way,
Wedging them in behind rocks to rot,
Such as these not reaching the ocean.

Yet, lo, the lost one emerges unharmed,
Hardly wet as he walks from the water.
Undisturbed by beauty or terror, pursuing
His own few needs with a nerveless will,
Nonchalant in the torrent, he bobs and nods
As though to acknowledge implicit applause.
This ceaseless tic, a trick of the muscles shared
With the solitary sandpiper, burlesqued
By the teeter-bob and the phoebe's tail,
Is not related to approbation. The dipper,
Denied the adventure of uncharted flight
Over vast waters to an unknown homeland, denied
Bodily beauty, slightly absurd and eccentric,
Will never attain acclaim as a popular hero.
No prize committee selects the clown
Whose only dangers are daily and domestic.

Yet he persists, and does not consider it persisting.
On a starless, sub-zero, northern night,
When all else has taken flight into sleep or the south,
He, on the edge of the stream, has been heard to repeat
The rippling notes of his song, which are clear and sweet.

Old Inn on the Eastern Shore

On stifling summer days
While a listless peacock strays
Through the overgrown boxwood maze,
Scratching for insects and seeds

Among prehensile weeds,
The giant magnolia bleeds.
Each ravished ivory bud
Drops tarnished petals of blood
Whose heavy fragrance collects
In stagnant pools and infects
The pulsing air. No skill
Can protect the tainted will
From paralysis or death.
Merely to draw your breath
Is effort enough for the day,
As wilting lungs obey
The example of decay.
Brickdust drifts from the wall
In response to the crystal call
Of the oriole whose nest
Hangs from the loveliest
Branch of the oak like a shy
Tear on the cheek of the sky.
The afternoon creeps by
As slowly as the tide
Creeps into the cove to hide
The fetid mud where the sedge
Lines the channel's edge,
Bringing salt from the ocean
With imperceptible motion,
And bringing, at last, a breeze
That rummages through the trees,
Trails its fingers over the lawn
Stifles a heavy yawn
And curls at your feet and dies.
The silence magnifies
Each distant, diminutive sound—
The sturdy, steady pound
Of a pump across the river,
The spluttering of a flivver
On the county road, the drone
Of a sleepless locust, the groan
Of the sleeping spaniel—each noise
Accumulates and destroys
Any chance of comfort or rest.

A fitful nap is the best
You can wish for.

                    Here is the end
Of all dreams. Here you suspend
Hope, pride, ambition,
In unclouded recognition.
Who would have thought that grace
Would seek out such a place?
Who would have suspected that light
Sufficient for second sight
Might linger here as a ghost,
Haunting the innermost
Heart of the boxwood maze,
Like the darkly shimmering rays
From a mythical pirate's cache,
Seeping out, not in a flash
Of insight, but slowly pervading
The afternoon, slowly persuading
Your eyes to turn inward and stare
At the emptiness honored there?
Caught, too weak to resist
The knowledge, too weak to insist
On turning your back, you must face
The evaded commonplace.
Your senses coalesce
In a multiple consciousness,
For your cognizance does not prevent
Awareness of sound and scent,
And this insight does not float
In an atmosphere vaguely remote
But anchors to here and now,
This place, the white oak bough,
The oriole's nest, the sweet
Sickly smell of magnolia, the heat
Reflected from red brick walls,
These, and the figure that sprawls
Uncomfortably in the shade,
You, and your wish to evade
The knowledge, that too is clear,
As is the mounting fear

Of your helplessness, hot and tired,
Lacking the will-power required.

   It will pass. The insight will fade
With the sunset, and you will persuade
Yourself, as the evening grows cool,
That you have been playing the fool,
Allowing yourself to suppose
You had seen some truth in the throes
Of prostration, some horrible truth
Of deception and wasted youth,
The fantasies of a brain
Suffering under the strain
Of a long, hot, humid day,
Too exhausted to read or to play
The radio. You will rise
With the first of the fireflies
And, knowing yourself no sinner,
Will go in to bathe before dinner.

THOMAS McGRATH

Against the False Magicians

for Don Gordon

The poem must not charm us like a play:
See, in the war-torn city, that reckless, gallant
Handsome lieutenant turn to the wet-lipped blonde
(Our childhood fixation) for one sweet desperate kiss
In the broken room, in blue cinematic moonlight—
Bombers across that moon, and the bombs falling,
The last train leaving, the regiment departing—
And their lips lock, saluting themselves and death:
And then the screen goes dead and all go home . . .
Ritual of the false imagination.

The poem must not charm us like the fact:
A warship can sink a circus at forty miles,
And art, love's lonely counterfeit, has small dominion
Over those nightmares that move in the actual sunlight.
The blonde will not be faithful, nor her lover ever return,
Nor the note be found in the hollow tree of childhood—
This dazzle of the facts would have us weeping
The orphaned fantasies of easier days.

It is the charm which the potential has
That is the proper aura for the poem.
Though ceremony fail, though each of your grey hairs
Help string a harp in the landlord's heaven,
And every battle, every augury,
Argue defeat, and if defeat itself
Bring all the darkness level with our eyes—
It is the poem provides the proper charm,
Spelling resistance and the living will,
To bring to dance a stony field of fact
And set against terror exile or despair
The rituals of our humanity.

Remembering That Island

Remembering that island lying in the rain
(Lost in the North Pacific, lost in time and the war)
With a terrible fatigue as of repeated dreams
Of running, climbing, fighting in the dark,
I feel the wind rising and the pitiless cold surf
Shaking the headlands of the black north.

And the ships come in again out of the fog—
As real as nightmare I hear the rattle of blocks
When the first boat comes down, the ghostly whisper of feet
At the barge pier—and wild with strain I wait
For the flags of my first war, the remembered faces,
And mine not among them to make the nightmare safe.

Then without words, with a heavy shuffling of gear,
The figures plod in the rain, in the shoreside mud,
Speechless and tired; their faces, lined and hard,
I search for my comrades, and suddenly—there—there—
Harry, Charlie, and Bob, but their faces are worn, old,
And mine is among them. In a dream as real as war

I see the vast stinking Pacific suddenly awash
Once more with bodies, landing on all beaches,
The bodies of dead and living go back to appointed places,
A ten year old resurrection,
And myself once more in the scourging wind, waiting, wait-
    ing
While the rich oratory and the lying famous corrupt
Senators mine our lives for another war.

Ode for the American Dead in Korea

1.

God love you now, if no one else will ever,
Corpse in the paddy, or dead on a high hill
In the fine and ruinous summer of a war
You never wanted. All your false flags were
Of bravery and ignorance, like grade school maps:
Colors of countries you would never see—
Until that weekend in eternity
When, laughing, well armed, perfectly ready to kill
The world and your brother, the safe commanders sent
You into your future. Oh, dead on a hill,
Dead in a paddy, leeched and tumbled to
A tomb of footnotes. We mourn a changeling: you:
Handselled to poverty and drummed to war
By distinguished masters whom you never knew.

2.

The bee that spins his metal from the sun,
The shy mole drifting like a miner ghost

Through midnight earth—all happy creatures run
As strict as trains on rails the circuits of
Blind instinct. Happy in your summer follies,
You mined a culture that was mined for war:
The state to mold you, church to bless, and always
The elders to confirm you in your ignorance.
No scholar put your thinking cap on nor
Warned that in dead seas fishes died in schools
Before inventing legs to walk the land.
The rulers stuck a tennis racket in your hand,
An Ark against the flood. In time of change
Courage is not enough: the blind mole dies,
And you on your hill, who did not know the rules.

3.

Wet in the windy counties of the dawn
The lone crow skirls his draggled passage home:
And God (whose sparrows fall aslant his gaze,
Like grace or confetti) blinks and he is gone,
And you are gone. Your scarecrow valor grows
And rusts like early lilac while the rose
Blooms in Dakota and the stock exchange
Flowers. Roses, rents, all things conspire
To crown your death with wreaths of living fire.
And the public mourners come: the politic tear
Is cast in the Forum. But, in another year,
We will mourn you, whose fossil courage fills
The limestone histories: brave: ignorant: amazed:
Dead in the rice paddies, dead on the nameless hills.

The Repeated Journey

for Marian

Again and again I make the intolerable journey:
First three days in the locked train, passing my home
On the stormy midnight when no light burns and all the
    houses

Are shut; then pinesmell, rain, confusion, a cold camp;
Again and again

I make the winter voyage: first the narrow
Sea-passage between the mountains where like frozen
Smoke the waterfalls hang and the scenery becomes por-
    tentous,
Dream-like and sullen, charged with a higher reality
Than our own; then, shadowy

As clouds in the roaring night-black ocean, islands
Plunge, fog-bound, nameless; finally, driving
Seaward, the headlands, and the crooked harbor: wreckage,
Spume like spiders crawling, gun-metal water;
Again and again

I climb the hill: past the cemetery, the dead
Fighter aircraft, past the shops where the great
Machines rust in their beds and know it is
Useless, useless, the night-journey inbound and cannot,
Can not turn back—

What am I hunting? I cannot remember. Rain
Slats like shot on the empty tents. The flaps
Are all closed tight on nothing. On ghosts. The night
Comes screaming down on the wind. Boredom. Loneliness.
Again and again

I return to the hunt for something long buried
In Time, like the dead in the cliff-face cemetery.
Loneliness, terror of death, splendor of living—
I rescued these wounded; but cannot reclaim my youth
Nor those lost violent years whose casual ignorant lovers
We were for a season.

The Odor of Blood

Odor of blood excites
The violent, powerless dead—

Compelled again and again
To the place of their suicide,

Or haunted by the house
Where forgotten murder was done,
They grow drunk on the smell of the past
As if on the fumes of wine.

So, summoned in sleep
From his civilian dream,
The buried soldier returns
To the scene of an old crime

Where innocence and blood
Were spilled in the ditch of war—
Compelled again and again
By fury of desire

Or memory, to return:
Ghosts weak, bloodthirsty, mad:
As ghost planes tirelessly orbit
The closed fields of the dead.

WILLIAM MEREDITH

A Boon

What I will ask, if one free wish comes down
Along with all these prodigalities
That we pick up like dollars in a dream,
And what I urge you ask, is not that we
Grow single in our passion without gap,
Losing with loneliness dear differences;
Nor lust, to burn a lifetime resinously,
Although that surely were a miracle
Worth asking, and a project for two saints,

Feeding themselves by bits into the smoke.
No, let us more ambitiously demand
What I'd go lonely and unpaid to hold,
The power I've heard the bravest lovers have,
Really to aid and injure one another.
Whereas there's no security, in dreams
Or waking, of the things we need the most,
The risk itself cries out to be possessed.

Perhaps the Best Time

O waly, waly,
But lovely is bonny
A little while when it is new,
But when it's old
It groweth cold
And fades away like morning dew.
—ANONYMOUS

This would be spring, if seasons could be found
In everything; or if times, this would be morning.
We dazzle at this first warm shy half-turning
As at a sunrise or at quickening of the ground.
There leafs along our boughs what would astound
Old botanists and set dead lovers yearning—
And yet October will see all this burning:
I know because I stay here year around.

We flourish now like Theban royalty
Before act one: right now Delphi seems far,
The oracle absurd. But in the wing
Is one who'll stammer later out of pity
—I know because I've seen these plays before—
To name his actions to the fatal king.

Starlight

Going abruptly into a starry night
It is ignorance we blink from, dark, unhoused.
We have a gaze of animal delight
Before the human vision; then, aroused
To nebulous danger, we may look for easy stars,
Orion or the Dipper. But they are not ours,

These learned fields. Dark and ignorant,
Unable to see here what our forebears saw,
We keep some fear of random firmament
Vestigial in us. And we think, Ah
If I had lived then, when these stories were made up, I
Could have found more likely pictures in haphazard sky.

But this is not so. Indeed, we have proved fools
When it comes to myths and images. A few
Old bestiaries, pantheons and tools
Translated to the heavens years ago—
Scales and hunter, goat and horologe—are all
That save us when, time and again, our constructions fall.

And what would we do, given a virgin sky
And this dearth of image? Our fears, our few beliefs
Do not have shapes. They are like that astral way
We have called milky, vague stars and star-reefs
That were shapeless even to the fecund eye of myth—
Surely these are no patterns to start a zodiac with.

To keep the sky free of luxurious shapes
Is an occupation for most of us, the mind
Free of luxurious thoughts. If we choose to escape,
What venial constellations will unwind
Around a point of light, and then can not be found
Another night or by another man or from other ground.

As for me, I would find faces there,
Or perhaps one face I have long taken for guide;

Far-fetched, maybe, like Cygnus, but as fair,
And a constellation anyone could read
Once it was pointed out; an enlightenment of night,
The way the pronoun *you* will turn dark verses bright.

A Korean Woman Seated by a Wall

Suffering has settled like a sly disguise
On her cheerful old face. If she dreams beyond
Rice and a roof, now toward the end of winter,
Is it of four sons gone, the cries she has heard,
A square farm in the south, soured by tents?
Some alien and untranslatable loss
Is a mask she smiles through at the weak sun
That is moving north to invade the city again.

A poet penetrates a dark disguise
After his own conception, little or large.
Crossing the scaleless asia of trouble
Where it seems no one could give himself away,
He gives himself away, he sets a scale.
Hunger and pain and death, the sorts of loss,
Dispute our comforts like peninsulas
Of no particular value, places to fight.
And what is it in suffering dismays us most:
The capriciousness with which it is dispensed
Or the unflinching way we see it borne?

She may be dreaming of her wedding gift;
A celadon bowl of a good dynasty
With cloud and heron cut in its green paste,
It sleeps in a hollow bed of pale blue silk.
The rice it bought was eaten the second winter.
And by what happier stove is it unwrapped
In the evening now and passed around like a meat,
Making a foliage in the firelight?

She shifts the crate she sits on as the March
Wind mounts from the sea. The sun moves down the sky

Perceptibly, like the hand of a public clock,
In increments of darkness though ablaze.
Ah, now she looks at me. We are unmasked
And exchange what roles we guess at for an instant.
The questions Who comes next and Why not me
Rage at and founder my philosophy.
Guilt beyond my error and a grace past her grief
Alter the coins I tender cowardly,
Shiver the porcelain fable to green shards.

The Rainy Season

As boring as the fact of a marvelous friend
Told at some length by strangers while you nod
From the booth of yourself and wait your turn,
Are these rains that detain these nights

               Until you think
What they say on each roof, awake in its own dismay:
Like the reproof of that singular good man,
Unknown to you, to whom you are not known,
Told at some length by strangers while you nod;
And not unlike the signs in rainy bars
That read themselves at the poor edge of sleep:
If you're so damn smart, why aren't you rich?

The Open Sea

We say the sea is lonely; better say
Ourselves are lonesome creatures whom the sea
Gives neither yes nor no for company.

Oh, there are people, all right, settled in the sea;
It is as populous as Maine today,
But no one who will give you the time of day.

A man who asks there of his family
Or a friend or teacher gets a cold reply
Or finds him dead against that vast majority.

Nor does it signify that people who stay
Very long, bereaved or not, at the edge of the sea
Hear the drowned folk call: that is mere fancy,

They are speechless. And the famous noise of sea
Which a poet has beautifully told us in our day
Is hardly a sound to speak comfort to the lonely.

Although not yet a man given to prayer, I pray
For each creature lost since the start at sea,
And give thanks it was not I, nor yet one close to me.

Picture of a Castle

Now I am tired of being Japanese,
The daimyo said, after a certain war.
Let there be a kempt jungle in a valley
And from it rise
So that you look through horizontal blossoms
A tall, unmoated fortress where the dolphins
On the gables, tails in the sky,
Swim from the separate quarters of the kingdom
Without thinking;
And with a balcony to every hour
Facing the hills, apart,
Where a sweet particular girl will say the truth
Over and over until I take it in.

The Chinese Banyan

There is no end to the
Deception of quiet things

And of quiet, every-day
People a lifetime brings.
Take a kind of Banyan tree
That grows in the temperate islands
Where a friend lived recently:
With what commendable violence
The shallow roots—as blunt
As earthworms in the dark,
As soft and as unremarked—
Make for what they want.
At night on their way to drink
They will rend like little dooms
(The last thing you would think)
Impediments of stone;
The last thing in the world
You would think of, seeing the crown
Of pale leaves just unfurled
That the breeze moves up and down.

And the friend himself who stayed
In the islands, his small roof
Taking a Banyan's shade—
That life was quiet enough:
Teacher, bachelor,
Hard forces both to measure.
With Sammy, a small white cur
Who would dance or yap for pleasure,
He lived in the four-room house
Under the small-leafed tree
Where counter to his wish
We said an obsequy.
The water had run in the sink
All night, for his heart had burst
While he drew the dog a drink;
And what he muttered first
Only Sammy the dog knew
Who stayed in the kitchen till dawn
As dogs have agreed to do.

A quiet, temperate man;
We have all known dearer loss.

But I speak of the unremarked
Forces that split the heart
And make the pavement toss,
Forces concealed in quiet
People and plants, until
At some silent blood riot
Or sap riot, they spill;
And this dark capacity
Of quiet looses a fear
That runs by analogy
On your page, in your house, for your dear.

JAMES MERRILL

The Bed

Where do we go, my love, who have been led
Afire and naked to our firelit bed?
For look! someone is sleeping there, his head

Pinned to the pillows by his own left arm,
Who sinks, who in swift currents of alarm
Sinks glistening (as though the night were warm)

Down through the rocking fathoms of the skin
To where the dreamers, brows on arms, begin
Bearing the dream each has been trammeled in.

Love at the sea's edge turns the turbulent waves
To sculpture, silken body that behaves
As if no paths were but the path love paves.

So with the stranger tangled in our sheet:
Seeing his mouth move, hearing his heart beat,
No lover hears the words his lips repeat.

And none dares question if the dream is good
That plunges him in nothing understood
Down down until, like bait beneath a flood

Suspended where the unseen mouthings feel
For food in darkness, it is him they steal;
And none knows—when to grasp the spinning reel

The mind wakes, winds it back in joy and fright—
If what has torn him in our own bed might
Not first have sought us there! Ah, for tonight

Let us seek out a bed that's less our own.
There is a kind of sleep which we have known
Both pleasurable and calm. Leave him alone,

Come, leave him to his dream. Too long we've kept
Watch by this bed familiar except
For one strange sleeper. It is time we slept.

Cloud Country

How like a marriage is the season of clouds.
The winds at night are festive and constellations
Like stars in a kaleidoscope dissolve
And meet in astounding images of order.
How like a wedding and how like travelers
Through alchemies of a healing atmosphere
We whirl with hounds on leashes and lean birds.

As though the air, being magician, pulled
Birds from a sleeve of cloud, birds drop
To warm grass dented by a smile asleep.
Long odysseys of sunlight at this hour
Salute the gaze that of all weariness
Remains unwearied, and the air turns young
Like reddening light in a corridor of pines.

The landscape where we lie is creased with light
As a painting one might have folded and put away
And never wished to study until now.
How like a marriage, how like voyagers
We come upon this season of right clouds,
Valors of altitude, white harbors, hills
Supple and green, these actions of the sun.

Variations: The Air Is Sweetest That a Thistle Guards

I

The air is sweetest that a thistle guards
And purple thistles in our blue air burn
And spiny leaves hold close the light we share.
The loose tides sprawl and turn and overturn
(Distant pearl-eaters gorging) on the shore,
While taut between those waters and these words,
Our air, our morning, the poignant thistles weave
Nets that bind back, garland the hungering wave.

II

Midsummer spreads the ticklish mullein-leaf,
Rambler and brambles, and his ankles bleed
Who wanders less than gingerly among them;
In winter, holly; later, the bittersweet rose;
Leaves harsh and somber, nettles in November.

Burr, cactus, yucca, the moral thorn that only
A snail can master; plants that bring to mind
Porcupines (bad for dogs), sea-urchins, scorpions:
Near by what silkiest blows a sharp thing grows
And this is good for lovers to remember.

III

Flowers are people
Enchanted by witches—

This we were able
To learn in the nursery,
But thought, being mercenary,
How witches brought candy,
Were easy to hide from
Or frighten with matches.

Listening to Nanny
We laughed till we died
At her warnings, her funny
Despairs, her enticements:
"Be good!"—while in basements
We broke eggs on grindstones,
Pulled apart flowers
And tracked snow inside.

Ah, people are flowers.
They fall helter-skelter
In their first witching weather
Or turn wry like thistles
Who, bristling together,
Brag of their shelters,
Insist that each latest
Is safest, is sweetest.

IV

When at midnight Jane took off her mask, the red-
Chequered-lavender and bordered with seed pearls,
She kissed her lover as though she had never had
Nor wanted another. Some girls
Snorted, for this was beautiful. One could
But wander alone then through the tropical dark
And ask what comforts lurk
In such disordered gleams from under the tide.

Now not the answer, for of course there were
No helpful answers, but the air of questioning
Is what one needs to remember, to let ring clear
As a sea-cave widening
The little noise of loss. What barrier

Holds up, what is not vulnerable? Down, down,
Sand on a sunken crown
Settles; but that shape is always there.

Just as beneath her mask there was always Jane:
She let it drop, we saw her jubilant smile,
Thought, "Beauty is not so temperate, nor is pain,
But that they burst the seal
We stamp upon them." Remembering love. but fearing
The memory of the beloved, I once cut
Three thistles which I put
In a glass of water, then sat beside them, staring,

Asking the flowers, silver under water,
To tell me about time and love and doom,
Those great blue grottos of feeling where the rank intruder
Is moved to think in rhyme;
But the thistles could indicate only that face which came
Abruptly to mock with its usual witty anger
My nakedness, my hunger,
And the thistles jabbed my wrist when I reached for them.

V

Three days I wept in the snow, feet bare,
Then to Canossa waved goodbye.
Absolution was a luxury
Only the innocent could snare.
I went where the pearl-eaters were.

The air was dazzling in my eye
Accustomed to the mountainous shade
So lately left behind: this showed
I was still far from purity
But it would come assuredly.

Pearl-eaters met me on the road,
Glimpsing me first as down foothills
I stumbled, rising from their meals,
And every courtesy bestowed
To make me at their tables glad.

In a chair of pearl I sat while gulls
Croaked Cheer! and ate the priceless food—
There was always more, my hostess said.
I knew those pearls were pure, or else
Purity was the pace that kills.

So with the pearl-eaters I stayed
Till memory drove me back inland
Where, to my wonderment, I found
Whatever I tasted wherever I strayed
Became at once of pure pearl made.

For a Second Marriage

Orchards, we linger here because
Women we love stand propped in your green prisons,
Obedient to such justly bending laws
    Each one longs to take root,
  Lives to confess whatever season's
Pride of blossom or endeavor's fruit
  May to her rustling boughs have risen.

But autumn reddens the whole mind.
No more, each swears, the dazzle of a year
Shall woo her from your bare cage of loud wind,
    Promise the ring and run
  To burn the altar, reappear
With apple blossoms for the credulous one.
  Orchards, we wonder that we linger here!

Orchards we planted, trees we shook
To learn what you were bearing, say we stayed
Because one winter twilight we mistook
    Frost on a bleakened bough
  For buds of green, and were afraid
To miss the old persuasion, should we go.
  And the spring came, and discourse made

Enough of weddings to us all
That, loving her for whom the whole world grows
Fragrant and white, we linger to recall
    As down aisles of cut trees
    How a tall trunk's cross-section shows
Concentric rings, those many marriages
    That life on each live thing bestows.

W. S. MERWIN

When I Came from Colchis

When I came from Colchis
Where the spring fields lay green,
A land famed for fine linen,
Bounded northerly
By the glistering Caucasus,
By the Euxine westerly,

Most I spoke of fine linen
But did, in truth, tell something
Of Jason who had come sailing
And poised upon that shore
His fabulous excursion.
All turned the incredulous ear.

From Troy, over the water
Returning, I recounted
The tale of wrecked walls, but said
That gray waves lap and surround
That shore as any other.
With a shrew smile they listened.

Now if, amazed, I come
From the deep bourn of your hand,
A stranger up from the sunned

Sea of your eyes, lady,
What fable should I tell them,
That they should believe me?

December: Of Aphrodite

Whatever the books may say, or the plausible
Chroniclers intimate: that I was mad,
That an unsettling wind that season
Fretted my sign and fetched up violence
From the vagaries of dream, or even that pride
Is a broad road with few turnings, do not
Believe them. In her name I acted.

(Vidal once, the extravagant of heart,
For the love of a woman went mad, mad as a dog,
And the wolves ate him; Hercules, crazed
By that jealous goddess, murdered his children;
Samson, from a woman's lap, woke blinded,
Turning a mill in Gaza; Adam, our father,
Eating from his wife's hand, fell from the garden.)

Not that from heaven she twisted my tenderness
Into a hand of rage, nor because she delighted
In burnt offering, I in my five senses
Cut throats of friends, burned the white harvest, waged
Seven months' havoc even among
Her temples; but because she waited always
There in the elegant shell, asking for sweetness.

And though it was in her name the land was ravaged,
Spilled and dishonored, let it not be said
That by her wiles it was done, nor that she gave
That carnage her blessing. All arrogant demons
Pretending changelessness, who came first when she called,
Have faded and are spent, till out of the strong,
Without death, she conjured the honeycomb.

She sits at evening under a gray arch
Where many marvels fell, where all has fallen:
The blue over her dolphins, the poplar leaves,
The cold rain, all but the grave myrtle
And the rings of her ringdoves. The doge of one calendar
Would give her a name of winter, but where I stand
In the hazed gold of her eyes, the world is green.

Colloquy at Peniel

Countenance like lightning, why do you stand
In ebony raiment after no invocation
Suddenly where I knew no face, as though
You had stood so forever?
          —Say that the light
That is today, after so long becomes me,
Or that love's pleading incense that rose once
For mercy pleads now no longer, whereupon
The air conceives new clarity, and there
Suddenly I am visible. But know
I was the urgency that framed that love
And made it cry for mercy, the question
And the voice of the woman whispering, "Be content,
Be content."
          I am that which you lost
Behind you which you seek before you, for I
Am certain: sullen under your gaiety
And still its root and entrepreneur; footloose,
Not musical, but moving in all your music,
Assumed in all apostrophes.
          Think of me
As of a dusk through which no herds go home,
Quiet, perhaps, yet inexcusably
Disquieting, with a voice of infinite patience,
Gentle until resisted, like sheep bells
In the next valley.
          And I am he
With whom on a desperate hill, because I was

The closest combatant, always last night
You wrestled, as with the angel of your dark,
And overcame, yet in defeat who found
Such re-creation, always I rose with dawn
Enlarged by falling, as though I were the angel,
Equally, of your day. Yet one day
—Heaven and hills having endured—your arm,
Hopeless long since of conquest, will strike upon
Fatal surprise and end me there; and through
The evening slanting always at hand among
Unstartled trees, under a world of birds
Settling like dust despite the clang of triumph,
It will be your body that will fall.

Ballad of John Cable and Three Gentlemen

He that had come that morning,
One after the other,
Over seven hills,
Each of a new color,

Came now by the last tree,
By the red-colored valley,
To a gray river
Wide as the sea.

There at the shingle
A listing wherry
Awash with dark water;
What should it carry?

There on the shelving,
Three dark gentlemen.
Might they direct him?
Three gentlemen.

"Cable, friend John, John Cable,"
When they saw him they said,

"Come and be company
As far as the far side."

"Come follow the feet," they said,
"Of your family,
Of your old father
That came already this way."

But Cable said, "First I must go
Once to my sister again;
What will she do come spring
And no man on her garden?

She will say 'Weeds are alive
From here to the Stream of Friday;
I grieve for my brother's plowing,'
Then break and cry."

"Lose no sleep," they said, "for that fallow:
She will say before summer,
'I can get me a daylong man,
Do better than a brother.' "

Cable said, "I think of my wife:
Dearly she needs consoling;
I must go back for a little
For fear she die of grieving."

"Cable," they said, "John Cable,
Ask no such wild favor;
Still, if you fear she die soon,
The boat might wait for her."

But Cable said, "I remember:
Out of charity let me
Go shore up my poorly mother,
Cries all afternoon."

They said, "She is old and far,
Far and rheumy with years,

And, if you like, we shall take
No note of her tears."

But Cable said, "I am neither
Your hired man nor maid,
Your dog nor shadow
Nor your ape to be led."

He said, "I must go back:
Once I heard someone say
That the hollow Stream of Friday
Is a rank place to lie;

And this word, now I remember,
Makes me sorry: have you
Thought of my own body
I was always good to?

The frame that was my devotion
And my blessing was,
The straight bole whose limbs
Were long as stories—

Now, poor thing, left in the dirt
By the Stream of Friday
Might not remember me
Half tenderly."

They let him nurse no worry;
They said, "We give you our word:
Poor thing is made of patience;
Will not say a word."

"Cable, friend John, John Cable,"
After this they said,
"Come with no company
To the far side.

To a populous place,
A dense city

That shall not be changed
Before much sorrow dry."

Over shaking water
Toward the feet of his father,
Leaving the hills' color
And his poorly mother

And his wife at grieving
And his sister's fallow
And his body lying
In the rank hollow.

Now Cable is carried
On the dark river;
Not even a shadow
Followed him over.

On the wide river
Gray as the sea
Flags of white water
Are his company.

Leviathan

This is the black sea-brute bulling through wave-wrack,
Ancient as ocean's shifting hills, who in sea-toils
Travelling, who furrowing the salt acres
Heavily, his wake hoary behind him,
Shoulders spouting, the fist of his forehead
Over wastes gray-green crashing, among horses unbroken
From bellowing fields, past bone-wreck of vessels,
Tide-ruin, wash of lost bodies bobbing
No longer sought for, and islands of ice gleaming,
Who ravening the rank flood, wave-marshalling,
Overmastering the dark sea-marches, finds home
And harvest. Frightening to foolhardiest
Mariners, his size were difficult to describe:

The hulk of him is like hills heaving,
Dark, yet as crags of drift-ice, crowns cracking in thunder,
Like land's self by night black-looming, surf churning and
    trailing
Along his shores' rushing, shoal-water boding
About the dark of his jaws; and who should moor at his edge
And fare on afoot would find gates of no gardens,
But the hill of dark underfoot diving,
Closing overhead, the cold deep, and drowning.
He is called Leviathan, and named for rolling,
First created he was of all creatures,
He has held Jonah three days and nights,
He is that curling serpent that in ocean is,
Sea-fright he is, and the shadow under the earth.
Days there are, nonetheless, when he lies
Like an angel, although a lost angel
On the waste's unease, no eye of man moving,
Bird hovering, fish flashing, creature whatever
Who after him came to herit earth's emptiness.
Froth at flanks seething soothes to stillness,
Waits; with one eye he watches
Dark of night sinking last, with one eye dayrise
As at first over foaming pastures. He makes no cry
Though that light is a breath. The sea curling,
Star-climbed, wind-combed, cumbered with itself still
As at first it was, is the hand not yet contented
Of the Creator. And he waits for the world to begin.

The Master

Not entirely enviable, however envied;
And early outgrew the enjoyment of their envy,
For other preoccupations, some quite as absurd.
Not always edifying in his action: touchy
And dull by turns, prejudiced, often not strictly
Truthful, with a weakness for petty meddling,
For black sheep, churlish rancours, and out-of-hand damning

The messes he got himself into were of his own devising.
He had all the faults he saw through in the rest of us;
As we have taken pains, and a certain delight, in proving,
Not denying his strength, but still not sure quite where it
    was;
But luck was with him too, whatever that is,
For his rightful deserts, far from destroying him,
Turned out to be just what he'd needed, and he used them.

Opportunist, shrewd waster, half calculation,
Half difficult child; a phoney, it would seem
Even to his despairs, were it not for the work, and that certain
Sporadic but frightening honesty allowed him
By those who loathed him most. Not nice in the home,
But a few loved him. And he loved. Who? What? Some still
Think they know, as some thought they knew then, which is
    just as well.

In his lifetime what most astonished those
Acquainted with him, was the amount of common
Detail he could muster, and with what intimate ease,
As though he knew it all from inside. For when
Had he seen it? They recalled him as one who most often
Seemed slow, even stupid, not above such things surely,
But absent, with that air maybe part fake, and part shifty.

Yet famously cursed in his disciples:
So many, emulous, but without his unique powers,
Could only ape and exaggerate his foibles.
And he bewildered them as he did no others,
Though they tried to conceal it: for, like mirrors
In a fun-house, they were static, could never keep up with
    him,
Let alone predict. But stranded on strange shores following
    him.

So the relief, then the wide despair, when he was gone;
For not only his imitators did he leave feeling
Naked, without voice or manner of their own:
For over a generation his ghost would come bullying

Every hand: all modes seemed exhausted, and he had left
    nothing
Of any importance for them do to,
While what had escaped him eluded them also.

For only with his eyes could they see, with his ears hear
The world. He had made it. And hard, now, to believe
In the invention: all seems so styleless, as though it had come
    there
By itself, since the errors and effort are in their grave.
But real: here we are walking in it. Oh what we can never
    forgive
Is the way every leaf calls up to our helpless remembrance
Our reality and its insupportable innocence.

White Goat, White Ram

The gaiety of three winds is a game of green
Shining, of grey-and-gold play in the holly-bush
Among the rocks on the hill-side, and if ever
The earth was shaken, say a moment ago
Or whenever it came to be, only the leaves and the spread
Sea still betray it, trembling; and their tale betides
The faintest of small voices, almost still.
A road winds among the grey rocks, over the hill,
Arrives from out of sight, from nowhere we know,
Of an uncertain colour; and she stands at the side
Nearer the sea, not far from the brink, legs straddled wide
Over the swinging udder, her back and belly
Slung like a camp of hammocks, her head raised,
The narrow jaw grinding sideways, ears flapping sideways,
Eyes wide apart like the two moons of Mars
At their opposing. So broadly is she blind
Who has no names to see with: over her shoulder
She sees not summer, not the idea of summer,
But green meanings, shadows, the gold light of now, familiar,
The sense of long day-warmth, of sparse grass in the open
Game of the winds; an air that is plenitude,

Describing itself in no name; all known before,
Perceived many times before, yet not
Remembered, or at most felt as usual. Even the kids,
Grown now and gone, are forgotten,
As though by habit. And he on the other side
Of the road, hooves braced among spurge and asphodel,
Tears the grey grass at its roots, his massive horns
Tossing delicately, as by long habit, as by
Habit learned, or without other knowledge
And without question inherited, or found
As first he found the air, the first daylight, first milk at the
      tetter,
The paths, the pen, the seasons. They are white, these two,
As we should say those are white who remember nothing,
And we for our uses call that innocence,
So that our gracelessness may have the back of a goat
To ride away upon; so that when our supreme gesture
Of propitiation has obediently been raised
It may be the thicket-snared ram that dies instead of the son;
So even that we may frame the sense that is now
Into a starred figure of last things, of our own
End, and there by these beasts know ourselves
One from another: some to stay in the safety
Of the rock, but many on the other hand
To be dashed over the perilous brink. There is no need
Even that they should be gentle, for us to use them
To signify gentleness, for us to lift them as a sign
Invoking gentleness, conjuring by their shapes
The shape of our desire, which without them would remain
Without a form and nameless. For our uses
Also are a dumbness, a mystery,
Which like a habit stretches ahead of us
And was here before us; so, again, we use these
To designate what was before us, since we cannot
See it in itself, for who can recognize
And call by true names, familiarly, the place
Where before this he was, though for nine months
Or the world's full age he housed there? Yet it seems
That by such a road, arriving from out of sight,
From nowhere we know, we may have come, and these
Figure as shapes we may have been. Only, to them

The road is less than a road, though it divides them,
A bit of flat space merely, perhaps not even
A thing that leads elsewhere, except when they
Are driven along it, for direction is to them
The paths their own preference and kinds have made
And follow: routes through no convenience
And world of ours, but through their own sense
And mystery. Mark this; for though they assume
Now the awkward postures of illustrations
For all our parables, yet the mystery they stand in
Is still as far from what they signify
As from the mystery we stand in. It is the sign
We make of them, not they, that speaks from their dumbness
That our dumbness may speak. There in the thin grass
A few feet away they browse beyond words; for a mystery
Is that for which we have not yet received
Or made the name, the terms, that may enclose
And call it. And by virtue of such we stand beyond
Earthquake and wind and burning, and all the uncovenanted
Terror of becoming, and beyond the small voice; and on
Another hand, as it were a little above us
There are the angels. We are dumb before them, and move
In a different mystery; but may there be
Another road we do not see as a road: straight, narrow,
Or broad or the sector of a circle, or perhaps
All these, where without knowing it we stand
On one side or another? I have known such a way
But at moments only, and when it seemed I was driven
Along it, and along no other that my preference
Or kind had made. And of these others above us
We know only the whisper of an elusive sense,
Infrequent meanings and shadows, analogies
With light and the beating of wings. Yet now, perhaps only
A few feet away in the shaking leaves they wait
Beyond our words, beyond earthquake, whirlwind, fire,
And all the uncovenanted terror of becoming,
And beyond the small voice. Oh we cannot know and we are
     not
What we signify, but in what sign
May we be innocent, for out of our dumbness
We would speak for them, give speech to the mute tongues

Of angels, Listen: more than the sea's thunder
Foregathers in the grey cliffs; the roots of our hair
Stir like the leaves of the holly bush where now
Not games the wind ponders, but impatient
Glories, fire: and we go stricken suddenly
Humble, and the covering of our feet
Offends, for the ground where we find we stand is holy.

ROBERT MEZEY

A Simpler Thing, a Chair

for C. B. M.

Although the bed, by hollow shadowing
And a slight sag, shows where she slept last night,
A simpler thing, a chair, or the very room,
Recalls her presence in her absent hours,
Deeper impressions than her body made.
Alone, I feel the soft wave of her spirit,
That touches every thing she sees or touches;
These bare things move, a trick of the late sunlight;
And I move also, her light hands on me.

But more than this, simplicity becomes
Itself her landscape and her room of sleep—
Terrain of massive forms, uncluttered space,
In which love spurs the motions of her mind.
Soft lights and deeper darknesses of sleep
Fall from its dim ascent and shape for her
The bare uplands and forests of her body—
While I, enamored of such simple things,
Learn with my hands the length of naked lines.

The Salesman

"Go, go, seek out some greener
thing.
It snows and freezeth here;
Let nightingales attend the spring.
Winter is all my year."

I think that if some faery spirit strewed
Acorns and blossoms of dogwood on the ground
Before my feet, I would observe the sound:
Falling like soft white tennis balls on gut,
And rolling on the hard earth where I stood.
Strange, that being roiled in a rut,
Long drenched to flooding, and dusty from a long road,
Where grinding pistons churned beside my own—
That carrying sample bags, I look behind.
It was a blazing road that beat me blind.

But still I did stop and I did observe,
And seeing things as simple as a flower,
I thought of a once time, when at this hour
A book lay open on a simple table,
And nothing was to sell and less to serve.
The world at evening was young voices able
To sing, that spoke to me; it was the curve
Of shaded light. There was a dozing fire.
But it was over in a little while,
And straying travellers smile a stupid smile.

So this is where my car has taken me:
Where no speedometer could ever quell
The flooding of the heart, the winds that fell
From dreams. But it was over in a while,
And near the highway here are dogwood trees
And acorns scattered from the squirrel's pile.
There are no swans, no lapis lazuli:
Brown acorns only cannot make me well,
Who need to labor under Queen Mab's spell.
I hear the faery spirits shriek in hell.

In Defense of Felons

Winter will not let go of earth. The lust
Of the listless sun finds April difficult,
Mildly astonished that frost fights so hard.
The black earth still is tough in my back yard,
The brittle stubble has not begun to melt,
And in the shed my frozen spade turns rust.

Possibly winter is ashamed of what
The softening soil may turn up to the sight.
Perhaps my spade would crack against a bone.
Perhaps a dying animal would groan,
Having survived with pain the season's might.
Possibly winter is afraid of that.

How many stiff-furred bodies has she buried,
How many coverts converted into graves
About my house? All that I want to know
Is underground or underneath of snow.
But white suspicious daggers hang from the eaves.
I know that winter is abroad, and worried.

Killers at large are caught when they relax;
Nature protects them with their undulant nerves;
And it is said that mild weather dulls
Their sense to signs of dragnets and pitfalls;
Therefore winter's unquiet power serves
To steel the grave to the inquisitive axe.

But how long can her universe be cold,
Can she in this arctic south lie safely curled?
Another month will do. I know that she
Is fearfully desirous that I be
Futile against the surface of her world—
For when she wanes, the clues may be too old.

But late or soon, the sun will have its day,
And send the winter fleeing to the north;

And with the murderess nowhere, there will come
Swallows venturing back to their summer home;
And into the soft moist air I shall step forth,
In the green wake of winter's getaway.

But what high law condemns her felony?
Perhaps she commits the necessary crime.
Her myriad deaths are life, and death is worth
The green and giant labor of the earth.
I call her conscience clear, her breath sublime,
Striving with heat for balance, harmony.

But winter knows what she is guilty of,
And stirred by her memories will return
To these same fields, again and again, until
This world's vast orbit burst at the sun's will
And fly up tangent to where that ball can burn
Winter and earth to ashes with its love.

In the Environs of the Funeral Home

In the environs of the funeral home
The smell of death was absent. All I knew
Were flowers rioting and odors blown
Tangible as a blossom into the face,
To be inhaled and hushed—and where they grew
Smothered the nostrils in the pungent grass.

Hyacinths of innocence, and yellow-hammers,
That beat the air at dawn, at dusk, to metal
Immortality, that flush where a bee clamors
For wine, are blooms of another color. See
How the flush fades as it descends the petal,
How deep the insect drinks, how quietly.

The point of this is a bitter paradox:
That violets flying a silver and blue elation,
And flapping ruffles of the white lilacs,

Shaking the air to tempt the golden bee,
Stiffen at the moment of consummation,
Swayed with guilt and weight of the bee's body.

These flowers, when cut and used, will remain ruddy,
As though made deathless in the very way
Their cutter kept the hue in the human body
That they were cut to celebrate and mourn.
The coffin has sprouted in dark mahogany
Out of them—edged, and shining like a thorn.

A Bedtime Story

Accidents will happen—still, in time,
The rigors of mortality may chill
The racing channels of the blood, and spin
Around the brain a cold and opaque skin.
Then, one might not remember pain so well;
One could sit back, and life, if not sublime,
Would be a sleep to dream pleasantly in,
Embellishing the heroics of one's prime.

But this is wishful thinking; generally,
The hardening of the arteries portends
A loosening of control, weakness of will,
And a wrecked body, frail, susceptible
To every shock. There is no second wind
Nor childhood but an alien infancy;
And life is a strangling thing, and pitiful,
And inches on, feeling that it must be.

But worse than the sphincter's failure or wry tricks
Of the steadfast heart, the worms of time embed
Their jaws most ravenously into the fork
Where the blood of either man or woman works
The power of human love to a pale thread,
And sever the fine filament, all that protects
Against the lonely, labyrinthine dark.
What does age trade the body for its sex?

A pity, but longevity is cruel.
When he was eighty, impotent Sophocles said,
"This well-loved instrument is finally out of tune.
Well, I am old, and have my work." And soon
Wrote *Oedipus Rex;* but when he went to bed,
He wept bitterly, being neither stoic nor fool;
His genitals were withered as a prune:
"It's better," he said, "to have never been born at all."

Alas, but the old fare badly at our hands,
And come to us already weather-beaten;
Grizzled and shrunken, with not long to live,
Blessed with the bitterest gift that the gifties give;
A meal for death, who leaves no meal uneaten;
Almost too fond to mourn the prostate gland.
Youth is food for thought, the years bring grief;
In good time, men, or bad, we are all unmanned.

Consider dying young. That madcap crew,
That made Chicago warm and had their fun
Distilling medicinal gin as fast as they could
And watching citizens slip in their own blood
Through the acrid smoke of a machine-gun,
Went where good killers go, all but a few,
Their flowers of bloody manhood nipped in the bud
By friendly bullets, or their own fiery brew.

They were the comic heroes of their day—
Or take devout Leonidas and his boys,
Who butchered at the pass and weren't unnerved
By whispering arrows or whatever served
A Spartan soldier in keeping a soldierly poise
And stiff prone posture. For us, the memory
Of youthful martial and sexual prowess lives
On the tiny slope where the silent battalion lay.

I think of Stanley Ketchel, whose cool love
And subsequent early death preserved his youth
And left his classic body middleweight slim;
Graceful and powerful we remember him,
His battering fists telling the brutal truth.

But there are countless tales. It is enough
To guess the fate of vigorous life and limb
And lose it young in grandiose rough-stuff.

The image of an old man's ugly phiz
Drifts in the gloom, wearing a dreadful smile.
Regard this absurd ghost, as he goes by;
Was he not thoughtless once as you and I
Of what must happen in a little while,
Who now despairs that he is come to this?
Let him go. For better ways to die—
Come, love, come close, and murder me with a kiss.

VASSAR MILLER

Adam's Footprint

Once as a child I loved to hop
On round plump bugs and make them stop
Before they crossed a certain crack.
My bantam brawn could turn them back,
My crooked step wrenched straight to kill
Live pods that then screwed tight and still.

Small sinner, stripping boughs of pears,
Shinnied past sweet and wholesome airs,
How could a tree be so unclean?
Nobody knows but Augustine.
He nuzzled pears for dam-sin's dugs—
And I scrunched roly-poly bugs.

No wolf's imprint or tiger's trace
Does Christ hunt down to catch with grace
In nets of love the devious preys
Whose feet go softly all their days:
The foot of Adam leaves the mark
Of some child scrabbling in the dark.

Apology

My mortal love's a rabbit skin
That will not reach around your bones
To charm the chill, to wrap you in
Against the wind whose undertones
Are death, or snow whose flakes are stones.
My word will never do for thread
To knit you garments snug and tight
Though I would fold you foot and head
Against the frost-fangs of the night
Killing whatever rose they bite.
My will is not enough to stretch
The tattered pelt around us two.
Pity, with each of us a wretch,
Comes dyed my hurt's deceitful hue
As rag for me, not robe for you.
The only cover from heart's weather,
The only comfort under which
Our naked souls may crouch together
Only immortal love, all-rich
In warmer wool than fleece, can stitch.

Autumnal Spring Song

When autumn wounds the bough
And bleeds me white and shaken,
Forbear to tell me how
The spring must reawaken
  And the trees bloom on forever,
  But with the same leaves never.

When autumn smears the sheen
Of leaf-lace, nature's lore
Affirms each season's green

To shimmer as before
  While the trees bloom on forever.
  But with the same leaves? Never.

When every branch is whole
The bitter sword of spring
Will scar the forest's soul
And mine remembering
  That the trees bloom on forever,
  But with the same leaves never.

Lord, You must comfort me
When woods are autumn's spoil,
Yet with another Tree
Unnourished by the soil
  Whence the trees bloom on forever,
  But with the same leaves never.

Bout with Burning

I have tossed hours upon the tides of fever,
Upon the billows of my blood have ridden,
Where fish of fancy team as neither river
Nor ocean spawns from India to Sweden.
Here while my boat of body burnt has drifted
Along her sides crawled tentacles of crabs
Smearing her timbers; on the waves upwafted
Crept water rats to gnaw her ropes and ribs.
Crashing, she has dived, her portholes choking
With weed and ooze, the swirls of black and green
Gulping her inch by inch, the seagulls' shrieking
Sieved depth through depth to silence. Till blast-blown,
I in my wreck beyond storm's charge and churning
Have waked marooned upon the coast of morning.

Ceremony

I can preserve your letters, not your love
As I might keep your likeness, not your life
For souvenir. Shades fluttered on and off
The wall proclaims at least that they derive
From substances, while these at most,
These scrawls, are only charms invoked upon
My grief and loneliness, but grace alone
Is the one means of grace—and grace is lost.
So, offering these follies up, these tokens
Of tokens in this fable of a fire
Upon an altar no man's structure likens,
I gesture beyond gesture to explore
For sign or symbol till the lack of any
Has clothed my nakedness in ceremony.

Epithalamium

Crept side by side beyond the thresh
And throb of noise, do not come near it,
But bind the bandage of the flesh
Upon the open wound of spirit.

Crouched in the corner of your lust,
Doctor your hurts till by the prod
Of some next moment you are thrust
Against the cauteries of God.

Before He burns and scars to kill
Infection, God, who is the cleaver
Of bone from bone to cure the ill,
Bids you alleviate the fever.

Love Song Out of Nothing

You, being less than either dew or frost
Which sun can melt, are deader than the dead
Who once at least had life. You never fled
Because you never came, were never lost
From me since never held; you cannot boast
Of having been a whole, so leave no shred,
No footprint on the ground you did not tread.
For where no flesh has been there is no ghost.

Mirage upon the desert of my mind
Are you to me who walked alone before
You formed from crooked heat waves of my thought.
For when I mourn the want of you, I find
I only mourn a part of me, no more,
Who, minus you, am nothing but a nought.

Paradox

Mild yoke of Christ, most harsh to me not bearing,
You bruise the neck that balks, the hands that break you;
Sweet bread and wine, bitter to me not sharing,
You scar and scorch the throat that will not take you;
Mount where He taught, you cripple feet not bloody
From your sharp flints of eight-fold benediction;
Bright cross, most shameful stripped of the stripped body,
You crucify me safe from crucifixion:
Yet I, who am my own dilemma, jolting
My mind with thought lest it unthink its stiffness,
Rise to revolt against my own revolting.
Blind me to blindness, deafen me to deafness.
So will Your gifts of sight and hearing plunder
My eyes with lightning and my ears with thunder.

Reciprocity

You who would sorrow even for a token
Of hurt in me no less than you would grieve
For seeing me with my whole body broken
And long no less to solace and relieve;
You who, as though you wished me mere Good Morning,
Would smash your heart upon the hardest stones
Of my distress as when you once, unscorning,
Would sleep upon the margin of my moans—
I yield my want, this house of gutted portals,
All to your want, this selfsame ravaged stack,
In testimony that between two mortals
No gift may be except a giving back.
What present could I make you from what skill
When your one need is me to need you still?

HOWARD MOSS

Elegy for My Father

Father, whom I murdered every night but one,
That one, when your death murdered me,
Your body waits within the wasting sod.
Clutching at the straw-face of your God,
Do you remember me, your morbid son,
Curled in a death, all motive unbegun,
Continuum of flesh, who never thought to be
The mourning mirror of your potency?

All you had battled for the nightmare took
Away, as dropping from your eyes, the sea-
Salt tears, with messages that none could read,
Impotent, pellucid, were the final seeds

You sowed. Above you, the white night nurse shook
His head, and moaning on the moods of luck,
We knew the double-dealing enemy:
From pain you suffered, pain had set you free.

Down from the ceiling, father, circles came:
Angels, perhaps, to bear your soul away.
But tasting the persisting salt of pain,
I think my tears created them, though in vain,
Like yours, they fell. All losses link: the same
Creature marred us both to stake his claim.
Shutting my eyelids, barring night and day,
I saw, and see, your body borne away.

Two months dead, I wrestle with your name
Whose separate letters make a paltry sum
That is not you. If still you harbor mine,
Think of the house we had in summertime,
When in the sea-light every early game
Was played with love, and if death's waters came,
You'd rescue me. How I would take you from,
Now, if I could, its whirling vacuum.

A Balcony with Birds

The mind drowned in the sun may dream of birds,
    All downed, too heavy to arise, but when
The trees release their shuttlecocks of wings,
    Which bank of birds is but imaginings?
The eye must follow form, but from this height,
    I see how softly summer parries weight
Till everything alive weighs less and less
    And, thinly felt, the weighted consciousness,

No thicker than green leaves, or the meridian,
    Grows thinner, even, to absorb the sun.
All heaviness goes up, and up the clouds—
    Those thin patricians thick as Roman crowds

Assumpted in white togas into blue—
   Yet painful in the light, the real, in view,
Drifts back to the roof and the ailanthus tree—
   Fern of impermanence, but heavenly.

The light that hangs in the ailanthus weaves
   The leaves' leavetaking overtaking leaves.
The actual is real and not imagined—still,
   The eye, so learned in disenchantment, sees
Two trees at once, this one of summer's will,
   And winter's one, when no bird will assail
The skyline's hyaline transparencies,
   Emptying its architecture by degrees.

Roundly in its fury, soon, the sun,
   Feverish with light, goes down, and on
Come ambitious stars—the stars that were
   But this morning dimmed. Somewhere a slow
Piano scales the summits of the air
   And disappears, and dark descends, and though
The birds turn off their songs now light is gone,
   The mind downed in the dark may dream them on.

Elizabethan Tragedy: A Footnote

That prudent Prince who ends Shakespearian plays
And wanders in to tell us how we wasted time
To hate or fall in love or be deranged
Would, three hours earlier, have ruined the play.
And so experience is, after all,
The heart of the matter. Even chatter
And babbling, or scenes in the worst of love affairs,
Like tears or throwing things or being pushed downstairs
Have value in the long run. Caution has its place.
Premeditation, though, I think, when face to face
With *Sturm und Drang* can never win the race.
Although the Prince is on the angels' side,
What got him there is wholesale homicide.

Winter's End

Once in a wood at winter's end,
The withered sun, becoming young,
Turned the white silence into sound:
Bird after bird rose up in song.
The skeletons of snow-blocked trees
Linked thinning shadows here and there,
And those made mummy by the freeze
Spangled their mirrors on cold air.
Whether they moved—perhaps they spun,
Caught in a new but known delight—
Was hard to tell, since shade and sun
Mingled to hear the birds recite.
No body of this sound I saw,
So glassed and shining was the world
That swung on a sun-and-ice seesaw
And fought to have its leaves unfurled.
Hanging its harvest in between
Two worlds, one lost, one yet to come,
The wood's remoteness, like a drum,
Beat the oncoming season in.
Then every snow bird on white wings
Became its tropic counterpart,
And, in a renaissance of rings,
I saw the heart of summer start.

Tragedy

Does a tear fall from the eye
When, falling from great heights,
The body usurps the sky
To die of its appetites?
Do the limbs seek the land
And the lungs a last song
When, burned by cruel wind,
They hurtle headlong?

When to that center hurled
Kings have far to fall—
So high, they see the world
Smooth as a round ball—
Perspective takes their wit,
And sceptre, crown, and ring
Must somersault to it,
The whole world darkening.

Those falls from pinnacles
Through miles of royal air
Turn widely in their wheels—
Beggar and priest are there.
All flights of steps may lead
To terror at the top,
The heart begin to bleed
Suddenly without stop,

As when old Caesar's whore
Tore Egypt from her skull,
Or Hamlet's Elsinore
Broke for a lack of will,
Or King Lear on his heath
Invoked the end of breath,
And fools fell out of myth
Into a real death.

All saviors of the city
Are lit by an unknown star;
Love, terror, pity
Walk where they are.
The kings of our great ills
Are dead, yet come to mind
When we fall from small hills
Into the common ground.

A Summer Gone

for Mildred Wood

I

The brilliant seaside glitters its farewell
To bathers who pack up their stripes and go
Home from all the cottages that water built;
Deserted on deserted dunes, those stilts
Of slipshod timber watch the sun run out
Among their crooked legs to meet the sea.
The windows, darker as the days go by,
Drink in the liquor of the autumn light.

II

The spiral shells, now empty of their hosts
That noiselessly would hunt the sands at night,
Are not more empty than a house I know
Whose windows, boarded up, are black with dark.
The inner and the outer night converge
On blind astronomers who used to search
The summer sky for stars. The stars that fall,
In quick succession, are not seen at all.

III

Say there was a tree that once you loved
That storms drilled downward. It was but a sign
Of how the seasons wither in a man.
Its leaves will spring into your winter mind,
Until your mind's a winter lacking spring,
Until your mind is nothing but a spring
That feeds the network of another tree
That storms will work at till the roots are free.

IV

Intrinsic as the crickets are to night,
The summer night is music made by them.
Uncritical, we listen to their themes.

The little orchestras that lure the stars
Down, down from fiery perimeters
Until we seem to touch them with our hands,
Have chirped into a silence. Where are they
Who plucked the hours of our sleep away?

V

Is it love that makes our summers shine?
Ideas of love, I mean. The naked limbs:
Bronze gears that cut the bluest sky to shreds
By running past reclining, sandy heads?
Sweet breasts that hold the very heart of love?
All shapely weights that we are mad to love?
Those beautiful outsides, those thin-skinned maps
Are part of love. Or all of it, perhaps.

VI

The insects scatter on their flimsy wings
And disappear. Sometimes one finds a trace
Of one, and sees a wingless carapace
Erosion has a mind to sculpture in.
Such tiny fans, fantastic skins are they,
One cannot hold them in the hand. The wind
Will bear, invisible upon the air,
Those cenotaphs to nothingness away.

VII

If you have listened to a summer rain,
You cannot think it will not come again:
Dead thunder that put tonnage in a drum,
Light rummaging to crack its fork on sky;
If, sleeping on a sun porch rinsed by rain
(A vine of morning-glories climbed the pane
Outside), you plumbed the very depths of sleep,
You know the silences through which sound seeps.

VIII

Sea purses lie on the September beach,
Miniature old-fashioned sleds of black,
The runners clawlike, paired parentheses.
These are egg cases of the skate or shark,

And if they ever held their dangerous young,
Indented by the hand, like dry seaweed,
The horny little shapes hold nothing now.
Each is an artifact that you can hold.

IX

There is a time when feeling knows two things:
The dead bird lying, and the whir of wings.
Those travellers who beat the upper air
Have clarities in mind—a south somewhere,
Where clouds are higher and the sea more blue.
Diviners of the tropics have to go
Where summer is still spoken. Autumn wings
Time the distances between two things.

X

Sad fall, a thousand dyings color you:
The sunburnt skin of leaves. Of love, the view
To take is but another wintry one,
To wait for the new nestings of the sun.
Happy for the leaves that make us sad,
We walk across your fields of richest plaid,
Grateful for the view. We'll have, someday,
That other weather that we salt away.

HOWARD NEMEROV

History of a Literary Movement

After Margrave died, nothing
Seemed worth while. I said as much
To Grumbach, who replied:
"The oscillations of fashion
Do not amuse me. There have been
Great men before, there will be
Other great men. Only man

Is important, man is ultimate."
I can still see him sitting there,
Sipping level by level his
Pousse-café. He was a fat man.
Fat men are seldom the best
Creative writers.

        The rest of us
Slowly dispersed, hardly
Ever saw each other again,
And did not correspond, for
There was little enough to say.
Only Impli and I
Hung on, feeling as we did
That the last word had not
Finally been said. Sometimes
I feel, I might say, cheated.
Life here at Bad Grandstein
Is dull, is dull, what with
The eternal rocks and the river;
And Impli, though one of my
Dearest friends, can never,
I have decided, become great.

The Salt Garden

for S. M. S.

I

A good house, and ground whereon
With an amateur's toil
Both lawn and garden have been won
From a difficult, shallow soil
That, now inland, was once the shore
And once, maybe, the ocean floor.
Much patience, and some sweat,
Have made the garden green,

An even green the lawn.
Turnip and bean and violet
In a decent order set,
Grow, flourish and are gone;
Even the ruins of stalk and shell,
The vine when it goes brown,
Look civil and die well.
Sometimes in the late afternoon
I sit out with my wife,
Watching the work that we have done
Bend in the salt wind,
And think that here our life
Might be a long and happy one;
Though restless over the sand
The ocean's wrinkled green
Maneuvers in its sleep,
And I despise what I had planned,
Every work of the hand,
For what can man keep?

II

Restless, rising at dawn,
I saw the great gull come from the mist
To stand upon the lawn.
And there he shook his savage wing
To quiet, and stood like a high priest
Bird-masked, mantled in grey.
Before his fierce austerity
My thought bowed down, imagining
The wild sea lanes he wandered by
And the wild waters where he slept
Still as a candle in the crypt.
Noble, and not courteous,
He stared upon my green concerns,
Then, like a merchant prince
Come to some poor province,
Who, looking all about, discerns
No spice, no treasure house,
Nothing that can be made
Delightful to his haughty trade,
And so spreads out his sail,

Leaving to savage men
Their miserable regimen;
So did he rise, making a gale
About him by his wings,
And fought his huge freight into air
And vanished seaward with a cry—
A strange tongue but the tone clear.
He faded from my troubled eye
There where the ghostly sun
Came from the mist.
                              When he was gone
I turned back to the house
And thought of wife, of child,
And of my garden and my lawn
Serene in the wet dawn;
And thought that image of the wild
Wave where it beats the air
Had come, brutal, mysterious,
To teach the tenant gardener,
Green fellow of this paradise,
Where his salt dream lies.

The Goose Fish

On the long shore, lit by the moon
To show them properly alone,
Two lovers suddenly embraced
So that their shadows were as one.
The ordinary night was graced
For them by the swift tide of blood
That silently they took at flood,
And for a little time they prized
    Themselves emparadised.

Then, as if shaken by stage-fright
Beneath the hard moon's bony light,
They stood together on the sand
Embarrassed in each other's sight
But still conspiring hand in hand,

Until they saw, there underfoot,
As though the world had found them out,
The goose fish turning up, though dead,
 His hugely grinning head.

There in the china light he lay,
Most ancient and corrupt and grey.
They hesitated at his smile,
Wondering what it seemed to say
To lovers who a little while
Before had thought to understand,
By violence upon the sand,
The only way that could be known
 To make a world their own.

It was a wide and moony grin
Together peaceful and obscene;
They knew not what he would express,
So finished a comedian
He might mean failure or success,
But took it for an emblem of
Their sudden, new and guilty love
To be observed by, when they kissed,
 That rigid optimist.

So he became their patriarch,
Dreadfully mild in the half-dark.
His throat that the sand seemed to choke,
His picket teeth, these left their mark
But never did explain the joke
That so amused him, lying there
While the moon went down to disappear
Along the still and tilted track
 That bears the zodiac.

The Vacuum

The house is so quiet now
The vacuum cleaner sulks in the corner closet,

Its bag limp as a stopped lung, its mouth
Grinning into the floor, maybe at my
Slovenly life, my dog-dead youth.

I've lived this way long enough,
But when my old woman died her soul
Went into that vacuum cleaner, and I can't bear
To see the bag swell like a belly, eating the dust
And the woolen mice, and begin to howl

Because there is old filth everywhere
She used to crawl, in the corner and under the stair.
I know now how life is cheap as dirt,
And still the hungry, angry heart
Hangs on and howls, biting at air.

The Sanctuary

Over a ground of slate and light gravel,
Clear water, so shallow that one can see
The numerous springs moving their mouths of sand,
And the dark trout are clearly to be seen,
Swimming this water which is color of air
So that the fish appear suspended nowhere and
In nothing. With a delicate bend and reflex
Of their tails the trout slowly glide
From the shadowy side into the light, so clear,
And back again into the shadows; slow
And so definite, like thoughts emerging
Into a clear place in the mind, then going back,
Exchanging shape for shade. Now and again
One fish slides into the center of the pool
And hangs between the surface and the slate
For several minutes without moving, like
A silence in a dream; and when I stand
At such a time, observing this, my life
Seems to have been suddenly moved a great
Distance away on every side, as though

The quietest thought of all stood in the pale
Watery light alone, and was no more
My own than the speckled trout I stare upon
All but unseeing. Even at such times
The mind goes on transposing and revising
The elements of its long allegory
In which the anagoge is always death;
And while this vision blurs with empty tears,
I visit, in the cold pool of the skull,
A sanctuary where the slender trout
Feed on my drowned eyes. . . . Until this trout
Pokes through the fabric of the surface to
Snap up a fly. As if a man's own eyes
Raised welts upon the mirror whence they stared,
I find this world again in focus, and
This fish, a shadow dammed in artifice,
Swims to the furthest shadows out of sight
Though not, in time's ruining stream, out of mind.

A Fable of the War

The full moon is partly hidden by cloud,
The snow that fell when we came off the boat
Has stopped by now, and it is turning colder.
I pace the platform under the blue lights,
Under a frame of glass and emptiness
In a station whose name I do not know.

Suddenly, passing the known and unknown
Bowed faces of my company, the sad
And potent outfit of the armed, I see
That we are dead. By stormless Acheron
We stand easy, and the occasional moon
Strikes terribly from steel and bone alike.

Our flesh, I see, was too corruptible
For the huge work of death. Only the blind
Crater of the eye can suffer well

The midnight cold of stations in no place,
And hold the tears of pity frozen that
They will implacably reflect on war.

But I have read that God let Solomon
Stand upright, although dead, until the temple
Should be raised up, that demons forced to the work
Might not revolt before the thing was done.
And the king stood, until a little worm
Had eaten through the stick he leaned upon.

So, gentlemen—by greatcoat, cartridge belt
And helmet held together for the time—
In honorably enduring here we seek
The second death. Until the worm shall bite
To betray us, lean each man on his gun
That the great work not falter but go on.

The Lives of Gulls and Children

Around the headland, at the end
Where they had not been before,
Paced by the white and the grey gull
With loud shrieking, and by the neat
Black-hooded tern, they found the place of death.
When they looked back along their way they saw
The footprints lonely and loud on the sand.

Few bones at first their feet kicked up,
Then more a flat thicket of bone
And tangled cartilage, dry white and clean,
Tasting of salt when the children licked them.
Further on were feathers, then flesh
Strung on the bone ragged and rotting,
With still red tendons curled. Twice they saw
The whole delicate skeletons with the hard
Hornlike feet peacefully displayed, and there
A loud few flies buzzed on the torn meat

And dishevelled feathers; a sick and wrong
Smell mingled with the heat of the salt wind.

Silence strangely was twisted there
By the voices of the children, by
The outcries of the living gulls aloft
Swinging over the wash and rush of the sea
Between the heat of the sand and the blind sun of noon.

They saw there a great gull dying,
Huddled in the sun and shuddering out
Now and again a heavy wing in cold
Effortful motion; he stared at them
Out of a steady and majestic eye
Like a sun part baffled in cloud,
So rheumed over with the morning of death.

They would have reached out hands to him
To comfort him in that human kind
They just were learning—how anything alive,
They thought, hated loneliness most; but he,
A grim great-uncle with a cane, struck out,
Sullen and weakly fierce, with hooked beak and a claw.
He would have flown, but had not strength to rise,
Could not even, ridiculous, waddle away.

The children watched him for a moment more,
But at a distance, and did not see him die;
For he, making his death, would out-endure
What interest they had, who, being humankind,
Had homes to go to, and a bed this side of death.

But they knew the Atlantic kind he was,
And for this moment saw him swaying
In the grey dark above the cold sea miles,
Wingtips ticking the spray of the slow waves,
Leaning on the unhavening air the dangerous
Sustaining of his own breastbone; they knew
The indifference of time dragging him down.
And when after silence they turned away,
"No one has ever been here before,"

They cried, "no one, no one, no one."
Their mournful word went out, no one,
Along the shore, now that they turned for home
Bearing the lonely pride of those who die,
And paced by the sweet shrieking of the quick.

ROBERT PACK

On the Seventh Anniversary
of the Death of My Father

Intuitive guilt and the sun's harsh light
Rode with the cars and their numbing ritual,
While I was hoping night would bring relief
To hide me from my insufficient grief.
For I repented the unfinished stories
We told among the woods and intimate trees
That now in my mind, like light on broken glass,
Reflected fragments of a fabled past.
Crowding the grave in black in the alien day,
Was it our ignorance that made us dumb
Or the way too many flowers were arranged,
Suggesting how death must have everything changed?
Although his suffering prepared him well,
And though it seemed to me that death was gentle
In removing mortal parts with surgeon fingers,
What is it of his early joy that lingers?
That little girl with her great childhood lost
Who knew of death a mother's shattered face?
She will remember his song and the long night free
From fear by the richness of her fantasy.
And standing there in that insubstantial air
With her wound that bled in the veins of my heart,
I needed despair that could never come
To pay for the freedom that I had won.

And the spoken words turned in my unholy ears
As the light leaped in when the casket dropped,
And I stopped at evening's border, alone,
At my back the reaching shadow of his stone;
And the undone deeds spun about my head—
A dead father unsung—too young to truly sing
Or to see revealed by the colors of shade
The two of us, at last, together laid.

A Bird in Search of a Cage

Said the bird in search of a cage,
This world is even large for wings;
The mindless seasons drive me down
Tormenting me with changing things.

A cage is not escape, but need,
And though once in, all travel's done,
I'll sing so every bird will know
My wanderings in moon and sun,

And all the crickets shall be stilled,
And stilled the summer air and grass,
And hushed the secrets of the wind
For when my final callings pass.

And if a friend should stop to talk,
Reminding me of what is past,
And ask the meaning of my song,
I'll say that only cages last.

The Faithful Lover

I hesitate to write about the spring;
There is a fear with all that loveliness.
A wilderness I feel in everything.

Though not alone, I think of loneliness,
Of God's late isolation in the sky,
Of wisdom turned despair, not happiness.

And while we are together, you and I,
Abandon promises of future bliss,
But love me with the truth now in your eye:

Regard the early falling leaf—a kiss,
Regard fidelity a passing thing.
(It gives me courage when I tell you this.)

O do not count on me for anything,
Although I love you as I do the spring.

The Way We Wonder

What has become of our astonishment
For simple things: colors, sounds, the hour of day?
We wonder, now our early gift is spent,

About imagined reasons to repent
For joy, and words we've heard our parents say.
What has become of our astonishment

For night and stars and things we can't invent?
(While crickets tick the perfect night away.)
We wonder, now our early gift is spent,

Whether some miraculous event
Will soon reveal (we're told old men are gay)
What has become of our astonishment.

The questioning of ultimate intent
Is still continued in the abstract way
We wonder, now our early gift is spent.

O who among us would have ever dreamt
The very best of our ideas betray?

What has become of our astonishment
We wonder, now our early gift is spent.

An Idyl in Idleness

"So many unlived lives," she said; and idle
As gulls in their sleepy drift, a hot and somber
Autumn day in umber, we talked of things
Beyond the fountains of the moon, and walked
Without a place to go, for we were free—
Within the shadow of a prophecy.

"Those marriages of flesh and dream that stand
Before no altar of reality
Have consummation only in a wish.
And what of you and me who drink from springs
Whose waters never cloy but drown all sense
Of urgency? We walk and watch the river
And the days, and lean an ear to find
A message in the mumbling of the wind."

Idle as morning and the putting-on of clothes,
Idle as noon with thoughts that never reach
The empty page, languid as shapeless night
In meditation flying up among
The stars and sinking, past forgetfulness,
In dreams—we saw the squirrels and the children
On the lawns for whom not games, but real
Tears alone, are strange; the water's cargo
Of monotony, we saw, a bench,
A tramp who rose and went, the chasing cop—
All flashed vivid as figures on a screen,
But who could know that there was life within?

"If consciousness is freedom," she remarked,
"What words can wed us to the scene and make
Us touch one common world, comfort our wandering
Senses with some certainty, that we

May know this world as home, and come to know
Fulfillment from desire, and learn to see
That love is no phantom of infirmity?"

No flowers gathered at this invocation
To a glory in the sun, no light
Leaped up in hallelujahs of belief,
And we must sing until our fevered longing
Fills those empty fields and hollow skies.
But idleness of heart returns when we
Recall that only possibility
Fills out the cadence of incompleted song,
And that our longing decorates the sky
With forms that live not, for they do not die.

"We bear what dying life we can," she said,
"And I still weep my childhood tears and dwell
Upon old fantasies through which you change
To be my many worshippers, coming
Down a holy clouded way to bless
Me through the ages of my loneliness."

The gulls came round again and lost a feather
To the wind which, drifting, drew a graph
Of choice, and entered in the simple meaning
Of the sea . . . I tremble at the terror
Of the law, of facing, for it is our fate,
Its full monstrosity of rage, and fear
To find all suffering in just a doubt;
Yet what is this to standing in the shadow
Of the grave? . . . I turned and would have touched her
Though it cost me all life long,
But she was that moment vanishing,
And something in our flesh was wrong.

The Departure

You had expected more. Now that I leave,
Fatigued with masterful pretense and doubt,

Again in me your empty life will thrive,
And once again you'll flourish as you grieve;
And all the while, that you may not find out,
I'll do the things that tied-down people talk about.

You had expected more, but found that giving
Was neither end nor was it consolation,
And learned the dead do not release the living,
Nor is there honesty in self-forgiving.
And when a mother fills and bears a son
She passes on the crime by which all loving's done.

Again, as to a dream, you turn to me,
And I will go where I have never been,
And see the things that you will never see
(Though nothing's new beyond its novelty.)
But in my letters all will sound serene,
And comfort you with meanings that I do not mean.

I lie, and do you lie when you believe?
I fear that first dependency returns.
I look to you to look to me, and give
Those things alone that I cannot receive.
My friends say you look tired, but who discerns
That we will lie together when the whole world burns?

Your hands have paled to a transparency,
There are the veins, the bones—how very thin,
How smooth they are, how cool, when they touch me
I feel the rocking of my infancy.
I lie, I lie, for both our deaths begin,
And you are old without, and I am old within.

Again you turn to me, as to a dream.
Dream, dream, for the time of dreaming is not gone.
Though we are guilty of the oldest crime,
It yet may be transformed within a dream:
Who wakes beyond this nightmare loves all men,
And wakening, you'll be expecting dreams again.

Poem for You

Always have these clear sounds been in your ear:
The goat's clatter climbing across the wall
To reach the olive branch where leaves flash darting
Like fishes, silver and green. Always you hear
The voice of morning, and afternoon's long call
Of open air, and the whip of evening smarting
The sky and herding in slow clouds like sheep
Over the horizon's hill—simple,
Simple as the taste of bread, simple as sleep,
And far away, farther than mountain people
In little white towns, dreaming chores of butter,
Milk and hay, without a cause to utter,
Without a dream within a dream reversing
Dreams away. And always in your eyes
Are shadows, blue and amber, interweaving,
And fabrics of bright grasses and rough skies,
While hunter and the frozen hare assemble,
While pinecones drop and all the forests shudder,
Though death is simple to the forest people;
And on the moss the orange salamander
Is like a wink of daylight, time's reminder
That nothing ends and nothing really matters
Except to you, except to you. Wind grew
With rain to shake the scarecrow into tatters—
And nothing really matters, except to you.
And always your hands learn, always your touch
Tells the season in the stone·or branch
With weather's words, with wet, with shivering,
And tells a tale of underwater people
Whose tides are like your own; like you they sing
All comings and all goings are so simple:
Nothing to take with us, nothing to bring.
You have not ever known that air can smother
Or that it is a foreign element,
That what you hear and see and touch together
Is never what you feel or what is meant,
That nothing ends and nothing really matters,

That what you love is always almost true
(Wind grew to shake the scarecrow into tatters)
And nothing really matters, except to you.

ALASTAIR REID

Who Can Say

Mother, I went to China this morning.
The trees were pagodas, the puddles were seas.
Dragons were hiding behind the begonias.
    I was a mandarin.
    Willows were bowing.
    Lies, lies, said she.
    And I hid from her frightening eyes.
       who can say, who can say?

Children, the gardens belong now to goblins.
The willows spread legends, the waterfall plays.
Fairytales wind like a web round the window.
    Goodnight to all birds now.
    The night's wings are folding.
    Lies, lies, said I.
    But I hid from her wonderful eyes.
       who can say, who can say?

To Lighten My House

Somehow come to the calm of this present, a Sunday in
    summer,
here, held and steady under the spread sky,
    I set this christened poem loose
       to lighten my house.

Rising, my eyes and the sea, for ever and this time more,
meet; and across the anonymous sea-shaped bay,
   the wind, my life, and the ground beneath
     all turn on this breath.

Far away, over several lives and this sea, Scotland is aging,
the shape of a humped sea-horse, mountain-headed,
   holding that kind and harboured home
     where I found my name,

on the inherited, mapped island I loved by its first name,
Arran, hunchbacked and hazy with family secrets,
   where, quartered in tidy seasons, I woke
     into shelters of talk.

My father's grave voice preaching, in a parish rich with
   fishermen,
the chanted parables for faith, while a dark god
   stormed in the unworded nights and wild eyes
     of the boy I was,

the hard-bitten heather on hills, the drowned bird nursed like
   a sister
wearing death in its sweet breast, all spelled my fear
   on the frightened nightfalling sea where I sailed,
     growing up and growing old—

years where my head, turned loose in burning chapels of
   doubt,
turned back on my blood, with all the words for journeys—
   war, and a war in my body to break
     that one way back.

I tell my stilled years to the sea, but the sea moves and is
   patient,
bearing all bottled wishes, faithful to all its fables,
   promising islands that will ask me back
     to take my luck.

Yet not in these seafared years, borne now in all my choices,
but in this firstborn day, in my opened house,

are my hands handed the chance to love
down one dear life.

And patiently into my bruised dark house, light breaks like a
birthday
as, shouldering the weather of this place, I wake in
the nowhere of the moment, single-willed
to love the world.

Pigeons

On the crooked arm of Columbus, on his cloak,
they mimic his blind and statuary stare,
and the chipped profiles of his handmaidens
they adorn with droppings. Over the loud square,
from all the arms and ledges of their rest,
only a bread crust or a bell unshelves them.
Adding to Atlas' globe, they dispose themselves
with a portly propriety, and pose as garlands
importantly about his burdened shoulders.
Occasionally a lift of wind uncarves them.

Stone becomes them; they, in their turn, become it.
Their opal eyes have a monumental cast,
and, in a maze of noise,
their quiet *croomb croomb* dignifies the spaces,
suggesting the sound of silence. On cobbled islands,
marooned in tantrums of traffic, they know their place—
the faithful anonymity of servants—
and never beg, but properly receive.

Arriving in rainbows of oil-and-water feathers,
they fountain down from buttresses and outcrops,
from Fontainebleau and London,
and, squat on the margin of roofs, with a gargoyle look,
they note from an edge of air, with hooded eyes,
the city slowly lessening the sky.

All praise to them who nightly in the parks
keep peace for us; who, cosmopolitan,
patrol and people all cathedraled places,
and easily, lazily haunt and inhabit
St Paul's, St Peter's, or the Madeleine,
the paved courts of the past, pompous as keepers—
a sober race of messengers and preservers,
neat in their international uniforms,
alighting with a word perhaps from Rome.
Permanence is their business, space and time
their special preservations, and wherever
the great stone men we save from death are stationed,
appropriately on the head of each is perched,
as though forever, his appointed pigeon.

Casa d'Amunt

However gracefully
the spare leaves of the fig tree
in fullness overhead
with native courtesy
include us in their shade,
among the rented flowers
we keep a tenant's station.
The garden is not ours.

Under the arching trellis,
the gardener moves below.
Observe him on his knees
with offering of water
for roots that are not his,
tendering to a power
whose name he does not know,
but whom he must appease.

So do we too accord
the windings of the vine
and whimsies of the olive

a distant mute oblation
and a respectful word,
aware of having put,
in spite of cultivation,
the worm within the fruit.

This garden tenancy
corrects our habitual eye.
Now, water and the moon
join what we do not own.
The rent is paid in breath,
and so we freely give
the apple tree beneath
our unpossessive love.

Dear one, our present Eden
lays down this one condition:
we should not ask to wait.
No angel will drive us out,
but time, without a word,
will show among the flowers,
sure as a flaming sword.
The garden is not ours.

A Game of Glass

I do not believe this room,
with its cat and its chandelier,
its chessboard-tiled floor,
and its shutters that open out
on an angel playing a fountain,
and the striped light spilling in
to a room that looks the same
in the mirror over my shoulder,
with a second glass-eyed cat.

My book does not look real.
The room and the mirror seem

to be playing a waiting game.
The cat has made its move,
the fountain has one to play,
and the thousand eyes of the angel
in the chandelier above
gleam beadily and say
the next move is up to me.

How can I trust my luck?
Whichever way I look
I cannot tell which is the door,
and I do not know who is who—
the thin man in the mirror,
or the watery one in the fountain.
The cat is eying my book.
What am I meant to do?
Which side is the mirror on?

ADRIENNE CECILE RICH

At a Bach Concert

Coming by evening through the wintry city
We said that art is out of love with life.
Here we approach a love that is not pity.

This antique discipline, tenderly severe,
Renews belief in love yet masters feeling,
Asking of us a grace in what we bear.

Form is the ultimate gift that love can offer—
The vital union of necessity
With all that we desire, all that we suffer.

A too-compassionate art is half an art.
Only such proud restraining purity
Restores the else-betrayed, too-human heart.

Orient Wheat

Our fathers in their books and speech
Have made the matter plain:
The green fields they walked in once
Will never grow again.
The corn lies under the locust's tooth
Or blistered in the sun;
The faces of the old proud stock
Are gone where their years are gone.

The park where stags lay down at noon
Under the great trees
Is shrill with Sunday strollers now,
Littered with their lees.
Poachers have trampled down the maze
And choked the fountains dry;
The last swan of a score and ten
Goes among reeds to die.

We were born to smells of plague,
Chalk-marks on every door;
We never have heard the hunting-horn
Or feet on the gallery floor—
The high-arched feet of dancers
Who knew how to step and stand.
We were born of a leaning house
In a changed, uneasy land.

Our fathers curse the crooked time
And go to their graves at last;
While some of us laugh at doting men,
And others sigh for the past.
And the dazzled lovers lie
Where summer burns blue and green,
In the green fields they'll be saying
Can never grow again.

Versailles

[Petit Trianon]

Merely the landscape of a vanished whim,
An artifice that lasts beyond the wish:
The grotto by the pond, the gulping fish
That round and round pretended islands swim,
The creamery abandoned to its doves,
The empty shrine the guidebooks say is love's.

What wind can bleaken this, what weather chasten
Those balustrades of stone, that sky stone-pale?
A fountain triton idly soaks his tail
In the last puddle of a drying basin;
A leisure that no human will can hasten
Drips from the hollow of his lifted shell.

When we were younger gardens were for games,
But now across the sungilt lawn of kings
We drift, consulting catalogues for names
Of postured gods: the cry of closing rings
For us and for the couples in the wood
And all good children who are all too good.

O children, next year, children, you will play
With only half your hearts; be wild today.
And lovers, take one long and fast embrace
Before the sun that tarnished queens goes down,
And evening finds you in a restless town
Where each has back his old restricted face.

The Celebration in the Plaza

The sentimentalist sends his mauve balloon
Meandering into air. The crowd applauds.
The mayor eats ices with a cardboard spoon.

See how that colour charms the sunset air;
A touch of lavender is what was needed.—
Then, pop! no floating lavender anywhere.

Hurrah, the pyrotechnic engineer
Comes with his sparkling tricks, consults the sky,
Waits for the perfect instant to appear.

Bouquets of gold splash into bloom and pour
Their hissing pollen downwind on the dusk.
Nothing like this was ever seen before.

The viceroy of fireworks goes his way,
Leaving us with a sky so dull and bare
The crowd thins out: what conjures them to stay?

The road is cold with dew, and by and by
We see the constellations overhead.
But is that all? some little children cry.

All we have left, their pedagogues reply.

Bears

Wonderful bears that walked my room all night,
Where are you gone, your sleek and fairy fur,
Your eyes' veiled imperious light?

Brown bears as rich as mocha or as musk,
White opalescent bears whose fur stood out
Electric in the deepening dusk,

And great black bears who seemed more blue than black,
More violet than blue against the dark—
Where are you now? upon what track

Mutter your muffled paws, that used to tread
So softly, surely, up the creakless stair
While I lay listening in bed?

When did I lose you? whose have you become?
Why do I wait and wait and never hear
Your thick nocturnal pacing in my room?
My bears, who keeps you now, in pride and fear?

Epilogue for a Masque of Purcell

Beast and bird must bow aside,
Grimbald limp into the wings.
All that's lovely and absurd,
All that dances, all that sings

Folded into trunks again—
The haunted grove, the starlit air—
All turns workaday and plain,
Even the happy, happy pair.

Harpsichord and trumpet go
Trundling down the dusty hall.
That airy joy, that postured woe
Like the black magician's spell

Fall in pieces round us now,
While the dancer goes to lie
With the king, and need not know
He will jilt her by and by.

We were young once and are old;
Have seen the dragon die before;
Knew the innocent and bold,
Saw them through the cardboard door

Kiss the guilty and afraid,
Turning human soon enough.
We have wept with the betrayed,
Never known them die for love.

Yet, since nothing's done by halves
While illusion's yet to do,

May we still forgive ourselves,
And dance again when trumpets blow.

Living in Sin

She had thought the studio would keep itself;
No dust upon the furniture of love.
Half heresy, to wish the taps less vocal,
The panes relieved of grime. A plate of pears,
A piano with a Persian shawl, a cat
Stalking the picturesque amusing mouse
Had been her vision when he pleaded "Come."
Not that at five each separate stair would write
Under the milkman's tramp; that morning light
So coldly would delineate the scraps
Of last night's cheese and blank sepulchral bottles;
That on the kitchen shelf among the saucers
A pair of beetle-eyes would fix her own—
Envoy from some black village in the mouldings . . .
Meanwhile her night's companion, with a yawn
Sounded a dozen notes upon the keyboard,
Declared it out of tune, inspected whistling
A twelve hours' beard, went out for cigarettes;
While she, contending with a woman's demons,
Pulled back the sheets and made the bed and found
A fallen towel to dust the table-top,
And wondered how it was a man could wake
From night to day and take the day for granted.
By evening she was back in love again,
Though not so wholly but throughout the night
She woke sometimes to feel the daylight coming
Like a relentless milkman up the stairs.

A Walk by the Charles

Finality broods upon the things that pass:
Persuaded by this air, the trump of doom

Might hang unsounded while the autumn gloom
Darkens the leaf and smokes the river's glass.
For nothing so susceptible to death
But on this forenoon seems to hold its breath:
The silent single oarsmen on the stream
Are always young, are rowers in a dream.
The lovers underneath the chestnut tree,
Though love is over, stand bemused to see
The season falling where no fall could be.

You oarsmen, when you row beyond the bend,
Will see the river winding to its end.
Lovers that hold the chestnut burr in hand
Will speak at last of death, will understand,
Foot-deep amid the ruinage of the year,
What smell it is that stings the gathering air.

From our evasions we are brought at last,
From all our hopes of constancy, to cast
One look of recognition at the sky,
The unimportant leaves that flutter by.
Why else upon this bank are we so still?
What lends us anchor but the mutable?

O lovers, let the bridge of your two hands
Be broken, like the mirrored bridge that bends
And shivers on the surface of the stream.
Young oarsmen, who in timeless gesture seem
Continuous, united with the tide,
Leave off your bending to the oar, and glide
Past innocence, beyond these aging bricks
To where the Charles flows in to join the Styx.

Love in the Museum

Now will you stand for me, in this cool light,
Infanta reared in ancient etiquette,
A point-lace queen of manners. At your feet

The doll-like royal dog demurely set
Upon a chequered floor of black and white.

Or be a Louis' mistress, by Boucher,
Lounging on cushions, silken feet asprawl
Upon a couch where casual cupids play
While on your arms and shoulders seems to fall
The tired extravagance of a sunset day.

Or let me think I pause beside a door
And see you in a bodice by Vermeer,
Where light falls quartered on the polished floor
And rims the line of water tilting clear
Out of an earthen pitcher as you pour.

But art requires a distance: let me be
Always the connoisseur of your perfection.
Stay where the spaces of the gallery
Flow calm between your pose and my inspection,
Lest one imperfect gesture make demands
As troubling as the touch of human hands.

JON SILKIN

Death of a Son

[who died in a mental hospital aged one]

Something has ceased to come along with me.
Something like a person: something very like one.
    And there was no nobility in it
        Or anything like that.

    Something was there like a one year
Old house, dumb as stone. While the near buildings
        Sang like birds and laughed
            Understanding the pact

They were to have with silence. But he
Neither sang nor laughed. He did not bless silence
    Like bread, with words.
        He did not forsake silence.

But rather, like a house in mourning
Kept the eye turned in to watch the silence while
    The other houses like birds
        Sang around him.

And the breathing silence neither
Moved nor was still.

    I have seen stones: I have seen brick
But this house was made up of neither bricks nor stone
    But a house of flesh and blood
        With flesh of stone

    And bricks for blood. A house
Of stones and blood in breathing silence with the other
    Birds singing crazy on its chimneys.
        But this was silence,

    This was something else, this was
Hearing and speaking though he was a house drawn
    Into silence, this was
        Something religious in his silence,

    Something shining in his quiet,
This was different this was altogether something else:
    Though he never spoke, this
        Was something to do with death.

    And then slowly the eye stopped looking
Inward. The silence rose and became still.
The look turned to the outer place and stopped,
    With the birds still shrilling around him.
        And as if he could speak

He turned over on his side with his one year
Red as a wound

He turned over as if he could be sorry for this
And out of his eyes two great tears rolled, like stones,
    and he died.

First It Was Singing

    From the first cry
I was given music with which to speak,
  Tramping the staring streets
      The amazed faces

    Turning, laughing with their
Windy voices at the mad singer in the common
  Street. From the first I was
      Given a voice

    To cry out with.
It was music, bread, blood, singing, love.
  Afterwards it was dying
      But it was singing

    First.
And from that it was I loved the hopping birds,
  The limping fly
      And the mad

    Bee, stung to anger
In worship of summer. It was their speech and my speech,
  The Jewish stone and the
      Animal rock

    Rolling together that made me sing
Of our common lash, the great white weal across
  Our black back, I and the hunted
      Fox, I and the huge

    Fly, his dangerous wings
Torn from his villainous body, I and the seal

Harming the human sea with his song,
  I and the bawling dog.

  It was our harm
Made me sing. Afterwards it was death,
  Afterwards it was our death,
    Death of the stone

    By stoning, the animal
By animals, but, first, singing,
  Jew and animal singing first.
    And afterwards death.

A Death to Us

A tiny fly fell down on my page
Shivered, lay down, and died on my page.

I threw his body onto the floor
That had laid its frail life next to mine.

His death then became an intrusion on
My action; he claimed himself as my victim

His speck of body accused me there
Without an action, of his small brown death.

And I think now as I barely perceive him
That his purpose became in dying, a demand

For a murderer of his casual body.
So I must give his life a meaning

So I must carry his death about me
Like a large fly, like a large frail purpose.

A Space in the Air

The first day he had gone
I barely missed him. I was glad almost he had left
    Without a bark or flick of his tail,
        I was content he had slipped

Out into the world. I felt,
Without remarking, it was nearly a relief
    From his dirty habits. Then, the second
        Day I noticed the space

He left behind him. A hole
Cut out of the air. And I missed him suddenly,
    Missed him almost without knowing
        Why it was so. And I grew

Afraid he was dead, expecting death
As something I had grown used to. I was afraid
    The clumsy children in the street
        Had cut his tail off as

A souvenir of the living and
I did not know what to do. I was fearing
    Somebody had hurt him. I called his name
        But the hole in the air remained.

I have grown accustomed to death
Lately. But his absence made me sad,
    I do not know how he should do it
        But his absence frightened me.

It was not only his death I feared,
Not only his but as if all of those
    I loved, as if all those near me
        Should suddenly go

Into the hole in the light
And disappear. As if all of them should go

Without barking, without speaking,
   Without noticing me there

But go; and going as if
The instrument of pain were a casual thing
   To suffer, as if they should suffer so,
      Casually and without greatness,

Without purpose even. But just go.
I should be afraid to lose all those friends like this.
   I should fear to lose those loves. But mostly
      I should fear to lose you.

If you should go
Without affliction, but even so, I should tear
   The rent you would make in the air
      And the bare howling

Streaming after your naked hair.
I should feel your going down more than my going down.
   My own death I bear everyday
      More or less

But your death would be something else,
Something else beyond me. It would not be
   Your death or my death, love,
      But our rose-linked dissolution.

So I feared his going,
His death, not our death, but a hint at our death. And I shall
      always fear
   The death of those we love as
      The hint of your death, love.

Death of a Bird

   A few days after.
After we had put him into the letterbox

And made a home for him
From this

Outrageous cage of wire
Long and shallow where the sunlight fell
    Through the air onto him;
      After

He had been fed for
Three days, suddenly in the late morning
    He was dead, without any
      Pretence.

He did not say goodbye
He did not say thank you. But he died
    Lying flat on the rigid
      Wires

Of his cage, his gold
Beak shut tight, which once in hunger
    Had opened enormously like
      A large

Trap, and closed again
Swallowing quickly what had been given him.
    How can I say I am sorry
      He died.

Seeing him lie there
Friendly with death I was angry he had gone
    Without pretext or warning,
      Without

A suggestion first he should
Go, since we had fed him and made him safe
    And bade him hop over our
      Hands. We

Asked him only that
He should desire life. He had become

Of us, a black friend with a
  Gold mouth

      Shrilly singing through
The heat. The labour of the black bird! I
    Cannot understand why
      He is dead.

I bury him familiarly.
His heritage is a small brown garden.
Something is added to the everlasting earth;
From my mind a space is taken away.

LOUIS SIMPSON

The Man Who Married Magdalene

The man who married Magdalene
Had not forgiven her.
God might pardon every sin . . .
Love is no pardoner.

Her hands were hollow, pale and blue,
Her mouth like watered wine.
He watched to see if she were true
And waited for a sign.

It was old harlotry, he guessed,
That drained her strength away,
So gladly for the dark she dressed,
So sadly for the day.

Their quarrels made her dull and weak
And soon a man might fit
A penny in the hollow cheek
And never notice it.

At last, as they exhausted slept,
Death granted the divorce,
And nakedly the woman leapt
Upon that narrow horse.

But when he woke and woke alone
He wept and would deny
The loose behavior of the bone
And the immodest thigh.

The Green Shepherd

Here sit a shepherd and a shepherdess,
He playing on his melancholy flute;
The sea wind ruffles up her simple dress
And shows the delicacy of her foot.

And there you see Constantinople's wall
With arrows and Greek fire, molten lead;
Down from a turret seven virgins fall,
Hands folded, each one praying on her head.

The shepherd yawns and puts his flute away.
It's time, she murmurs, we were going back.
He offers certain reasons she should stay . . .
But neither sees the dragon on their track.

A dragon like a car in a garage
Is in the wood, his long tail sticking out.
Here rides St. George, swinging his sword and targe,
And sticks the grinning dragon in the snout.

Puffing a smoke ring, like the cigarette
Over Times Square, Sir Dragon snorts his last.
St. George takes off his armor in a sweat.
The Middle Ages have been safely passed.

What is the sail that crosses the still bay,
Unnoticed by the shepherds? It could be
A caravel that's sailing to Cathay,
Westward from Palos on the unknown sea.

But the green shepherd travels in her eye
And whispers nothings in his lady's ear,
And sings a little song, that roses die,
Carpe diem, which she seems pleased to hear.

The vessel they ignored still sails away
So bravely on the water, Westward Ho!
And murdering, in a religious way,
Brings Jesus to the Gulf of Mexico.

Now Portugal is fading, and the state
Of Castile rising purple on Peru;
Now England, now America grows great—
With which these lovers have nothing to do.

What do they care if time, uncompassed, drift
To China, and the crew is a baboon?
But let him whisper always, and her lift
The oceans in her eyelids to the moon.

The dragon rises crackling in the air,
And who is god but Dagon? Wings careen,
Rejoicing, on the Russian hemisphere.
Meanwhile, the shepherd dotes upon her skin.

Old Aristotle, having seen this pass,
From where he studied in the giant's cave,
Went in and shut his book and locked the brass
And lay down with a shudder in his grave.

The groaning pole had gone more than a mile;
These shepherds did not feel it where they loved,
For time was sympathetic all the while
And on the magic mountain nothing moved.

John the Baptist

The Prophet, scourged by his own hand, progressed
Through wilderness inhabited by brutes
Whose hollow voices would not let him rest,
Feeding on honey-combs and cactus roots.

The leopard frolicked in her leafy marking;
A multitude of undetermined shapes
Walked parallel. He fled the wild dog's barking,
The buzzard's black umbrella and collapse.

And as he fled from white Jerusalem
"Make straight the crooked way!" would loudly cry,
And fled from people and discovered them
As shadows at the corner of the eye.

Against the gaudy red edge of the world
There came a caravan. The camels kneeled
Under the drivers' blows; the fires curled
And to and fro the white-robed Arabs wheeled.

Their melody the rocks replied again.
In veils and silver serpents at the fire
The women sinuated; the tall men
Danced arm in arm, apart from their desire.

A Negro, shaking like an epilept,
Beat with his bleeding knuckles on a gourd,
Two naked dancers in the circle leapt
Swinging a supple child across a sword.

Then, at a long-drawn bray from throats of bronze
A Roman legion rapidly debouched.
The drums, the piercing flutes, were stopped at once,
The dancers in a sullen silence crouched.

They carried on the column of their necks
The stone dome of the sky, their naked knees

Rolled out an iron street. Triumphant specks!
Their echoes had increased the silences.

A fearful discipline of little swords
And buckled mouths . . . The shields had shifted place
With the quick ruffle of an angry bird,
A slant of lances like one man's grimace.

They ruled the living and revered the dead . .
These were the last reflectors of the sun
And carried him in purple and in red,
Their braying shadows rampant at the throne.

The Prophet for his supper parched the locust
And of her little burden robbed the bee,
And laid his hairy cloak beneath a cactus
On the bright margin of eternity.

And all his dreams were of a marshy pool
Where the old Vices ran with backward glance:
Ingratitude, and Gluttony an owl
With human face, pot-bellied Ignorance.

An idiot with slack jaw and soiled rump
Was led upon a leash by sister crones—
Blind eye, flat dug, and amputated stump.
And there were mountain nymphs as smooth as stones

That kneel for centuries beside the waters
Under the leaves in the Italian wind,
Vases of clear song, the swan-necked daughters
Turned by divinity without a mind.

A centaur plashed in dappled dignity
Balancing a statue on his withers.
The forest flocked with gay stupidity,
The hoofs of goats and fluttering of feathers.

There, double-rooted, dark and ominous
The Tree of Knowledge screamed her triple text.

A pigmy, with a quiver of long arrows,
A monkey's head, both male and female sexed,

Fled from the shadow of pursuing Wisdom,
From the stained spear and the destroying shape,
And all the gods were guttural or dumb
To see Man separated from the Ape.

But was this Wisdom, with a woman's face?
She was not Wisdom, for she followed dancing.
Her mouth was smiling, an unholy grace
Flashed from her hands and from her eyes fell glancing.

And lightly lightly went the dancer's foot,
And as she danced she dazzled through a veil,
And softly softly played an Arab flute,
And on his throne a king sat stricken pale.

The Prophet woke. The stars were large with rain,
The moon upon a cloud lay soft and bright,
The pagan fires smouldered on the plain,
The tiger swung his lantern through the night.

And to the valley's winding ways he ran
Crying "Prepare the straight path for the Lord!"
And came to shallow Jordan, where began
The matter of the platter and the sword.

I Dreamed that in a City Dark as Paris

I dreamed that in a city dark as Paris
I stood alone in a deserted square.
The night was trembling with a violet
Expectancy. At the far edge it moved
And rumbled; on that flickering horizon
The guns were pumping color in the sky.

There was the Front. But I was lonely here,
Left behind, abandoned by the army.
The empty city and the empty square
Was my inhabitation, my unrest.
The helmet with its vestige of a crest,
The rifle in my hands, long out of date,
The belt I wore, the trailing overcoat
And hobnail boots, were those of a *poilu*.
I was the man, as awkward as a bear.

Over the rooftops where cathedrals loomed
In speaking majesty, two aeroplanes
Forlorn as birds, appeared. Then growing large,
The German *Taube* and the *Nieuport Scout*,
They chased each other tumbling through the sky,
Till one streamed down on fire to the earth.

These wars have been so great, they are forgotten
Like the Egyptian dynasts. My confrère
In whose thick boots I stood, were you amazed
To wander through my brain four decades later
As I have wandered in a dream through yours?

The violence of waking life disrupts
The order of our death. Strange dreams occur,
For dreams are licensed as they never were.

As Birds Are Fitted to the Boughs

As birds are fitted to the boughs
That blossom on the tree
And whisper when the south wind blows—
So was my love to me.

And still she blossoms in my mind
And whispers softly, though
The clouds are fitted to the wind,
The wind is to the snow.

WILLIAM JAY SMITH

American Primitive

Look at him there in his stovepipe hat,
His high-top shoes, and his handsome collar;
Only my Daddy could look like that,
And I love my Daddy like he loves his Dollar.

The screen door bangs, and it sounds so funny,
There he is in a shower of gold;
His pockets are stuffed with folding money,
His lips are blue, and his hands feel cold.

He hangs in the hall by his black cravat,
The ladies faint, and the children holler:
Only my Daddy could look like that,
And I love my Daddy like he loves his Dollar.

Elegy

For Bateman Edwards, d. 1 Sept. 1947

I stood between two mirrors when you died,
Two mirrors in a dimly lighted hall,
Identical in all respects.
Two mirrors face to face reflecting endlessly
Reflection's end.
The wind that had been blowing died away,
Or in the distance seemed about to die.
I stood between two mirrors in the hall.

Outside, the wheels had cut the gravel, and the sun-
Flower nodded to the sun; the air was still.

The deer that browsed upon a distant hillside
Lifted his antlers like a coral tree
Forgotten in midsummer undersea.
And from the delicate dark bridges which the spider
Spun from branch to branch,
In desolation hung
One leaf, announcing autumn to the world.

The world that evening was a world of mirrors
Where two great dragons from opposing caves,
Mirror their eyes and mirror all the scales
Of their long bodies and their giant tails,
Emerged. And all that had seemed human was confined
In terror in the limits of the mind,
And coiled, uncoiled within my memory.

In your sudden dying you became the night
Which I must add to darkness now
To make the morning bright,
To have day break, and daybreak
Melt the mirrors. But I know
You cannot hear me now although
I say, dear friend, good morning and good night.

Cupidon

'To love is to give,' said the crooked old man.
    'To love is to be poor.'
And he led me up his accordion stair,
    And closed his iron door.

'To love is to give.' His words like wire
    Dragged the ocean floor.
'Throw ten of your blankets on the fire,
    Then throw ten thousand more.'

His room was the prayer on the head of a pin.
    As clean as a diamond cut

Was the iron door which opened in
  And would not open out.

'To love is to give, to give, to give.
  Give more and more and more.'
And the wind crept up his accordion stair,
  And under his iron door.

Morning at Arnheim

I

From the cassowary's beak come streaks of light,
Morning, and possibility.
In the countries of the north
Ice breaks, and breaking, blossoms forth
With possibility; and day abounds
In light and colour, colour, sounds.

II

In Holland there are tulips on the table,
A wind from the north on the grey stones
That breaks the heart, and sits upon the shoulder,
And turns the mill, the pine cones.

Waking below the level of the sea,
You wake in peace; the gardens look
Like roofs of palaces beneath the water,
And into the sea the land hooks.

In Holland there are tulips on the table,
A wind from the north on the grey stones
That breaks the heart, and turns, with the mill at cockcrow,
Over the quiet dead, the pine cones.

III

From the cassowary's beak come streaks of light;
A wrought iron angel mounts a weathervane; you might

Be anywhere in Europe now that night
Is over, and you see that life begins like this
In tragedy: in light that is entangled in the leaves,
And morning shaken from an angel's sleeves;
And you can turn to face the mouth
Of the great black lion of heaven,
The terrible, beautiful south.

The Closing of the Rodeo

The lariat snaps; the cowboy rolls
    His pack, and mounts and rides away.
Back to the land the cowboy goes.

Plumes of smoke from the factory sway
    In the setting sun. The curtain falls,
A train in the darkness pulls away.

Goodbye, says the rain on the iron roofs.
    Goodbye, say the barber poles.
Dark drum the vanishing horses' hooves.

The Wooing Lady

Once upon the earth at the midnight hour,
When all the bells are ringing in the wood,
A lady lies alone in a palace tower,
And yet must woo, and yet must still be wooed.

She glides upon the stair, a bird on water,
In costly sable clad, in seven sins,
To lie beside her knight, a king's white daughter,
A scullery maid beneath the marten skins.

The stars are out, and all the torches lit.
Below the window is an orange tree,

Catching the light and then returning it,
A juggler in an antique tapestry.

Horses gallop away; the boughs are shaken
So gently it can hardly be believed.
And over all the world the birds awaken
As he awakens, beautifully deceived.

W. D. SNODGRASS

From *Heart's Needle*

—for Cynthia

II

Late April and you are three; today
    We dug your garden in the yard.
To curb the damage of your play,
Strange dogs at night and the moles tunnelling,
    Four slender sticks of lath stand guard
        Uplifting their thin string.

So you were the first to tramp it down.
    And after the earth was sifted close
You brought your watering can to drown
All earth *and* us. But these mixed seeds are pressed
    With light loam in their steadfast rows.
        Child, we've done our best.

Someone will have to weed and spread
    The young sprouts. Sprinkle them in the hour
When shadow falls across their bed.
You should try to look at them every day
    Because when they come to full flower
        I will be off away.

IV

No one can tell you why
the season will not wait;
the night I told you I
must leave, you wept a fearful rate
to stay up late.

Now that it's turning Fall,
we go to take our walk
among municipal
flowers, to steal one off its stalk,
to try and talk.

We huff like windy giants
scattering with our breath
grey headed dandelions;
Spring is the cold Wind's aftermath.
The poet saith.

But the asters, too, are grey,
ghost-grey. Last night's cold
is sending on their way
petunias and dwarf marigold,
hunched sick and old.

Like nerves caught in a graph,
the morning-glory vines
frost has erased by half
still crawl over their rigid twines.
Like broken lines

of verses I can't make.
In its unravelling loom
we find a flower to take,
with some late buds that might still bloom.
back to your room.

Night comes and the stiff dew.
I'm told a friend's child cried
because a cricket, who

had minstrelled every night outside
    her window, died.

VI

    Easter has come around
again; the river is rising
    over the thawed ground
and the banksides. When you come you bring
    an egg dyed lavender.
We shout along our bank to hear
our voices returning from the hills to meet us.
We need the landscape to repeat us.

    You lived on this bank first.
While nine months filled your term, we knew
    how your lungs, immersed
in the womb, miraculously grew
    their useless folds till
terrible air rushed in to fill
them like two shrubs bursting with leaves. You took your
    hour,
caught breath, and cried with your full lung power.

    Over the stagnant bight
we see the hungry bank swallow
    flaunting his free flight
still; we sink in mud to follow
    the killdeer from the grass
that hides her nest. That March there was
rain; the rivers rose; you could hear killdeers flying
    all night over the mudflats crying.

    You bring back how the red-
winged blackbird shrieked, slapping frail wings,
    diving at my head—
I saw where her tough nest, cradled, swings
    in tall reeds that must sway
with the winds blowing every way.
If you recall much, you recall this place. You still
    live nearby—on the opposite hill.

After the sharp windstorm
of July Fourth, all that summer
through the gentle, warm
afternoons, we heard great chain saws chirr
like iron locusts. Crews
of roughneck boys swarmed to cut loose
branches wrenched in the shattering wind, to hack free
all the torn limbs that could sap the tree.

In the debris lay
starlings, dead. Near the park's birdrun
we surprised one day
a proud, tan-spatted, buff-brown pigeon.
In my hands she flapped so
fearfully that I let her go.
Her keeper came. And we helped snarl her in a net.
You bring things I'd as soon forget.

You raise into my head
a Fall night that I came once more
to sit on your bed;
sweat beads stood out on your arms and forehead and you wheezed for breath,
for help, like some child caught beneath
its comfortable woolly blankets, drowning there.
your lungs caught and would not take the air.

Of all things, only we
have power to choose that we should die;
nothing else is free
in this world, to refuse it. Yet I,
who say this, could not raise
myself from bed how many days
to the thieving world. Child, I have another wife,
another child. We try to choose our life.

VII

Here in the scuffled dust
is our ground of play.
I lift you on your swing and must
shove you away,

see you return again,
    drive you off again, then

stand quiet till you come.
    You, though you climb
higher, farther from me, longer,
    will fall back to me stronger.
Bad penny, pendulum,
    you keep my constant time

to bob in blue July
    where fat goldfinches fly
over the glittering, fecund
    reach of our growing lands.
Once more now, this second,
    I hold you in my hands.

VIII

I thumped on you the best I could
    which was no use;
you would not tolerate your food
until the sweet, fresh milk was soured
    with lemon juice.

That puffed you up like a fine yeast.
    The first June in your yard
like some squat Nero at a feast
you sat and chewed on white, sweet clover.
    That is over.

When you were old enough to walk
    we went to feed
the rabbits in the park milkweed;
saw the paired monkeys, under lock,
    consume each other's salt.

Going home we watched the slow
stars follow us down Heaven's vault.
You said, let's catch one that comes low,
    pull off its skin
    and cook it for our dinner.

As absentee bread-winner,
I seldom got you such cuisine;
we ate in local restaurants
or bought what lunches we could pack
        in a brown sack

with stale, dry bread to toss for ducks
        on the sun-scummed lagoons,
crackers for porcupine and fox,
life-savers for the footpad coons
        to scour and rinse,

snatch after in their muddy pail
        and stare into their paws.
When I moved next door to the jail
        I learned to fry
Omelettes and griddlecakes so I

could set you supper at my table.
As I built back from helplessness,
        when I grew able,
the only possible answer was
        you had to come here less.

This Hallowe'en you come one week.
        You masquerade
        as a vermilion, sleek,
fat, crosseyed fox in the parade
or, where grim jackolanterns leer,

go with your bag from door to door
foraging for treats. How queer:
        when you take off your mask
my neighbors must forget and ask
        whose child you are.

Of course you lose your appetite,
        whine and won't touch your plate;
                as local law
I set your place on an orange crate
in your own room for days. At night

you lie asleep there on the bed
    and grate your jaw.
Assuredly your father's crimes
    are visited
on you. You visit me sometimes.

The time's up. Now our pumpkin sees
    me bringing your suitcase.
        He holds his grin;
the forehead shrivels, sinking in.
You break this year's first crust of snow

off the runningboard to eat.
    We manage, though for days
I crave sweets when you leave and know
They rot my teeth. Indeed our sweet
        foods leave us cavities.

X

The vicious winter finally yields
    the green winter wheat;
the farmer, tired in the tired fields
    he dare not leave, will eat.

Once more the runs come fresh; prevailing
    piglets, stout as jugs,
harry their old sow to the railing
    to ease her swollen dugs

and game colts trail the herded mares
    that circle the pasture courses;
our seasons bring us back once more
    like merry-go-round horses.

With crocus mouths, perennial hungers,
    into the park Spring comes;
we roast hot dogs on old coat hangers
    and feed the swan bread crumbs,

pay our respects to the peacocks, rabbits,
    and leathery Canada goose

who took, last Fall, our tame white habits
    and now will not turn loose.

In full regalia, the pheasant cocks
    march past their dubious hens;
the porcupine and the lean, red fox
    trot around bachelor pens

and the miniature painted train
    wails on its oval track:
you said, I'm going to Pennsylvania!
    and waved. And you've come back.

If I loved you, they said, I'd leave
    and find my own affairs.
Well, once again this April, we've
    come around to the bears;

punished and cared for, behind bars,
    the coons on bread and water
stretch thin black fingers after ours.
    And you are still my daughter.

April Inventory

The green catalpa tree has turned
All white; the cherry blooms once more.
In one whole year I haven't learned
A blessed thing they pay you for.
The blossoms snow down in my hair;
The trees and I will soon be bare.

The trees have more than I to spare.
The sleek, expensive girls I teach,
Younger and pinker every year,
Bloom gradually out of reach.
The pear tree lets its petals drop
Like dandruff on a tabletop.

The girls have grown so young by now
I have to nudge myself to stare.
This year they smile and mind me how
My teeth are falling with my hair.
In thirty years I may not get
Younger, shrewder, or out of debt.

The tenth time, just a year ago,
I made myself a little list
Of all the things I'd ought to know;
Then told my parents, analyst,
And everyone who's trusted me
I'd be substantial, presently.

I haven't read one book about
A book or memorized one plot.
Or found a mind I didn't doubt.
I learned one date. And then forgot.
And one by one the solid scholars
Get the degrees, the jobs, the dollars.

And smile above their starchy collars.
I taught my classes Whitehead's notions;
One lovely girl, a song of Mahler's.
Lacking a source-book or promotions,
I showed one child the colors of
A luna moth and how to love.

I taught myself to name my name,
To bark back, loosen love and crying;
To ease my woman so she came,
To ease an old man who was dying.
I have not learned how often I
Can win, can love, but choose to die.

I have not learned there is a lie
Love shall be blonder, slimmer, younger;
That my equivocating eye
Loves only by my body's hunger;
That I have poems, true to feel,
Or that the lovely world is real.

While scholars speak authority
And wear their ulcers on their sleeves,
My eyes in spectacles shall see
These trees procure and spend their leaves.
There is a value underneath
The gold and silver in my teeth.

Though trees turn bare and girls turn wives,
We shall afford our costly seasons;
There is a gentleness survives
That will outspeak and has its reasons.
There is a loveliness exists,
Preserves us. Not for specialists.

The Marsh

Swampstrife and spatterdock
    lull in the heavy waters;
some thirty little frogs
    spring with each step you walk;
a fish's belly glitters
    tangled by rotting logs.

Over near the grey rocks
    muskrats dip and circle.
Out of his rim of ooze
    a silt-black pond snail walks
inverted on the surface
    toward what food he may choose.

You look up; while you walk
    the sun bobs and is snarled
in the enclosing weir
    of trees, in their dead stalks.
Stick in the mud, old heart,
    what are you doing here?

MAY SWENSON

Frontispiece

In this book I see your face and in your face
your eyes holding the world and all else besides
as a cat's pupils rayed and wide
to what is before them and what more alive
ticks in the shadows flickers in the waves

Your hair in a slow stream curves
from your listening brow
to your ear shaped like a sea-thing found
in that water-haunted house where murmurs
your chaste-fierce name The vow

that corners your mouth
compelled you to that deep between words and acts
where they cross as sand with salt
There spills the layered light
your sockets lips and nostrils drank

before they sank
On stages of the sea the years tall
tableaus build The lighthouse you commanded
the room the oak and mutable Orlando
reoccur as the sea's pages to land's mind The wall

the steep and empty slate
your cane indented until you laid it as a mark
above where the tide would darken
is written in weed and shell how you were sane
when walking you wrapped your face

in the green scarf
the gray
and then the black

The waves carve your hearse and tomb
and toll your voyage out again again

Question

Body my house
my horse my hound
what will I do
when you are fallen

Where will I sleep
How will I ride
What will I hunt

Where can I go
without my mount
all eager and quick
How will I know
in thicket ahead
is danger or treasure
when Body my good
bright dog is dead

How will it be
to lie in the sky
without roof or door
and wind for an eye

Without cloud for shift
how will I hide?

The Key to Everything

Is there anything I can do
or has everything been done
or do

you prefer somebody else to do
it or don't
you trust me to do
it right or is it hopeless and no one can do
a thing or do
you suppose I don't
really want to do
it and am just saying that or don't
you hear me at all or what?

You're
waiting for
the right person the doctor or
the nurse the father or
the mother or
the person with the name you keep
mumbling in your sleep
that no one ever heard of there's no one
named that really
except yourself maybe

If I knew what the name was I'd
prove it's your own name
twisted in some way the one you
keep mumbling but you
won't tell me your
name or
don't you know it
yourself that's it
of course you've
forgotten or
never quite knew it or
weren't willing to believe it

Then there *is* something I
can do I
can find your name for you
that's the key to everything once you'd
repeat it clearly you'd
come awake you'd
get up and walk knowing where you're

going where you
came from

And you'd
love me
after that or would you
hate me?
no once you'd
get there you'd
remember and love me
of course I'd
be gone by then I'd
be far away

The Garden at St. John's

Behind the wall of St. John's in the city
  in the shade of the garden the Rector's wife
    walks with her baby a girl and the first
      its mouth at her neck seeking and sucking
        in one hand holding its buttocks its skull
          cupped by the other her arms like a basket
            of tenderest fruit and thinks as she fondles
              the nape of the infant its sweat is like dew
                like dew and its hair is as soft as soft
                  as down as the down in the wingpits of angels

The little white dog with the harlequin eye
  his tail like a thumb feet nimble as casters
    scoots in the paths of the garden's meander
      behind the wall of St. John's in the city
        a toy deposed from his place in her arms
          by this doll of the porcelain bone
            this pale living fruit without stone

She walks where the wrinkling tinkling fountain
  laps at the granite head of a monk
    where dip the slippery noses of goldfish
      and tadpoles flip from his cuspid mouth

A miracle surely the young wife thinks
from such a hard husband a tender child
and thinks of his black sleeves on the hymnbook
inside the wall of St. John's in the city
the Ah of his stiff mouth intoning Amen
while the organ prolongs its harmonious snore

Two trees like swans' necks twine in the garden
beside the wall of St. John's in the city
Brooding and cool in the shade of the garden
the scrolled beds of ivy glitter like vipers
A miracle surely this child and this garden
of succulent green in the broil of the city

she thinks as setting the bird-cries apart
she hears from beneath the dark spirals of ivy
under the wall of St. John's in the city
the rectal rush and belch of the subway
roiling the corrugate bowels of the city
and sees in the sky the surgical gleam
of an airplane stitching its way to the West
above the wall of St. John's in the city
ripping its way through the denim air

WESLEY TRIMPI

To Giotto

Giotto, I have not found
The passion nearer thought
Than on these chapel walls;
Nor one whose hand has bound,
Bright in the lucent dust,
Precision that recalls
More meaning than you knew
When Joachim prayed and Anna,

Mother of Mary, knelt
In so intense a blue
To wrap the newborn child
And close the golden belt
About her waist. Your brush
Drew Spirit, which, like mirrored
Sunlight, returned unspent:
The angels' soft bright rush
Through stillness to the cross,
Sweet emanations sent
To bear Him home. And must
The paint which holds your thought,
Dissolving flake by flake
To dust, now join your dust
In final dissolution?
You hoped too much to make
These figures always stay
Ageless and calm, for now
Even your blues and greens
Cause meaning to decay,
And none can comprehend
What dissolution means.

Lines for a Wedding Gift

for E. H. and C. B.

Accept each gift, though it be small,
And poorly wrapped when it arrives:
From us this music Haydn praised,
From Erica these butter knives.

Though blades and grooves will slowly wear
With the years' use, may they find you
The same, when they are worn, as now,
When knife cuts deep and groove sounds true.

May they say well how they were sent
With that intention to your hand

Which you toward one another hold:
That is, that each shall understand.

On a Bas-Relief

The winged horses descend to drink.
The bird breaks upward and the hare
Startles while shepherds watch them sink
In that unmoving air.

While the years' stain on the white stone
Shades it as dust the glare of sun,
The horses in the air have thrown
No shadows where they run.

Unreal, descending through the mind
Until the artist's hand could seal
The concept in the stone it lined,
They prove the concept real.

But nothing more. They bring no news
Of peace to you; their quietness
Was won by nothing you could lose,
By nothing they express.

Do not await them here. Below,
Waters which they shall never taste
Through marble pastures overflow
And do not run to waste.

Oedipus to the Oracle
[from Colonus]

Tête complète et parfait diadème,
Je suis en toi le secret changement.

I

Your will is done. Its promise, that I fled,
Drove me from friends and from the high homeland,
Where bear-grass stung like snakebite and my skin
Chilled, as with fever, when the thin air stirred.
I came from foothills, down through mesa draws,
Past stunted-yucca slopes to cottonwood
And willow wash. Quick movements cooled my eyes,
Till each thing grew as clear as if it stood,
And rested with more meaning when it ceased,
As, when a lake wind drops, reflected leaves
Tremble an instant longer than the water
As clear in motion as when they are still.
I stayed, an honored guest. Refusing there
All choice, I tried to break your prophecy.
Feasted to sleep, I lay without my fear.
Straight, with light flesh moving on waist and thigh,
Young women bending naked held my eyes,
Or, if they came in darkness, their bare feet
Fell sweeter than lutenotes. As contours shift
In the lithe haze, each object I once sought
Lost its identity in new sensations
And faded till desire for it had ceased.
My calm increased, but when my anger came
I could not hold it, and the stranger died.

II

I left and travelled back through ease to choice.
With partial knowledge, grown ambitious, sure,
I answered your enigma to the Sphinx.
Pretendant to the throne, I came to Thebes

So that I might have heirs, and heirs, a kingdom.
The queen became my bride; I gained the crown,
And Creon watched, mistrusting most what seemed
Most innocent. Again deceived, I found
Peace in the ceremonial love of wealth,
Its end the pestilence, and joy in marriage,
Its consummation incest—all this to breed,
And who is bred must learn again what error,
Perversion, and deceit conceive a child,
A riddle's answer on a dusty road.
Tiresias knew my crime; I sought his vision
But did not know that I should tear my eyes
For so much darkness and so little light.
Blind in the noon I stood and cursed you, seeing
Of all I had been once that there remained
Only a lingering brutality,
Worn to a thinness that is age. I felt
The desert drying after centuries
Of wind and drying; no time can cool this heat,
Nor teach me how to expiate your will.

III

Barefoot, with thin chiton, Antigone
Led me from Thebes. Her eyes moved in my mind,
And, as she spoke, I saw the buzzard's shadow
Wrinkle over rock and the lizards catch
On the edge of shade. Apollo sent us on:
"There is a grove that stands close by Colonus
Called Eumenides, consecrate to them
Who shall restore your power." Your thought is fact,
And, centered in your mind, my course swung true,
Enclosing what is real from what is not,
Till my experience seemed reality—
While memory, unabsolute with hope
And disappointment, changed with what I knew
Without my knowing. What I did not perceive
Ceased to exist; what I could not endure
I could deny: I had assumed your power.
When we came to the grove, I sought no more
From Theseus than this shade and learned that I
Controlled the fate of Thebes. Through the night wind

In a dream, part by part, I quieted
The leaves to hear your voice, and yet one part
I could not still: Creon stood in those trees—
Above, an old nest in a leafless web
Of branches still heaved like a dying wasp.

IV

He seized my daughters, swore to have me come
Or a whip make their naked, loosened flesh
Leap on the bone. Their cries would be your words
Which I could neither silence nor endure.
Distinct from what I could not change, no longer
The perfect agent of a perfect cause,
I struck in your pure crystal of events
The imperfection of fortuity—
My own identity beyond prediction.
For even now, while I fulfill your words,
We grow apart. You have not thought or felt
What I have felt; what you did once, or said,
Does not affect you now. I learn and age,
While you, pure knowledge, touching all, like time,
Have no remembrance or maturity.
One is what one has done; choice must relate
The past to circumstance: though you prevent
What I would do, you force me still to choose.
I called, and Theseus intercepted Creon,
Bound him, and freed my daughters, left me true
To their past love and each son's hate which shall
At last be true to him. Betraying either,
I should have, day by day, betrayed myself,
Though pride, with nothing to defend, should pass.

V

Then, from Poseidon's altar, my son came,
Begging through shadows for my body,
Lest it return to Thebes to save those walls
He tried to save once by my banishment.
He spoke as softly as Antigone.
Holding her hand, cautious of Creon's eyes,
The seventh of the seven against Thebes
Urged peace and for forgiveness promised me

The robe of justice to avenge my sight,
Slaves from each household, and his brother's house
And lands and wife—or, were the seige too long,
A ruined city for a private tomb.
He offered all I came there once to find—
A queen and power—and all I found and left—
A city ruined by my coming there.
He heard my curse, drawn, like an arrow, back
In memory. Feathered by ghostly hands,
It flew along the vision that remains:
Laius dying, Tiresias healing Thebes,
And there, so still her body did not turn,
Jocasta hanging in the silent court.
I banished him to Thebes. Let him seek you
To find the way there; I am free to go
From darkness into darkness to my peace.

JON MANCHIP WHITE

The Rout of San Romano

after the picture by Paolo Uccello

I watch the battle in the orange-grove
    And wonder who retreated, who advanced,
And why the staid and steady knighthood strove,
    And why the gaudy rocking-horses pranced.

Uccello, somewhat troubled by recession,
    Set the plumed warriors in this flowery place,
And I for one much welcome the digression
    That lends a combat atmosphere and grace.

The vulgar infantry, uncouthly armed,
    Wrestle and run behind with oaths and cries.
The nobles, who infrequently were harmed,
    Engage as cavaliers before my eyes;

A credit to the scroll of chivalry,
　　They chase each other in and out the bushes;
The rider with the ivory baton, he,
　　In his brocaded mob-cap leads the rushes.

Magnificent his head-dress and his manner,
　　Conductor of the antique symphony,
Young Dragon-Casque behind him bears his banner,
　　A stiff page holds his helmet on his knee.

And oranges felicitous motif,
　　In verdant clouds meticulously glow,
They bulge with a solicitous relief,
　　Refulgent, courtly, painterly they grow.

But there, behind, those low-bred rascals scurry,
　　Six rogues at butchery upon a hill,
Slower than nightmare must the pikeman hurry,
　　And though the screams are numb, they echo still.

Strange how I linger on this far-off highway
　　To catch Black Will and Shakebag at their deeds,
While splendid coursers skirmish in the byway,
　　A figured dream of which the scholar reads.

O I too sweated, fumbling with a gun:
　　I never swung a sword or feutred lance,
In common garb I stumbled on the run
　　And grappled coarsely in an awkward stance.

The old knights have my fancy for dominion,
　　Yet these half-dozen foot-men have my pity—
Worthless and breathless minion hacks at minion,
　　A dirty city sacks a dirty city.

The vagabonds lash out for no fine houses,
　　Bestride no chargers with a classic ease,
Rating no ransom, rewarded with carouses,
　　Their cadavers will dung the orange-trees.

I know the blackguards for my ancestors,
    Hemmed as we are by rail-and-wire mesh,
The wags anticipate these later wars
    Where crude steel battens cheaply on our flesh.

Well rest you, knights, that struck a blow for beauty,
    You errant, comely crop of hardihood!
God rest you, myrmidons, who did some duty,
    Brothers in blood, a beastly, bitter brood.

The Captain

*'Then cam Lungeus with a spere
And clift his hart in sonder.'*

Slowly he rode home at the end of day
    Over the plain toward the silken tent.
With shield and helmet hacked and surçoat rent
    Homeward the Captain rode. The air was grey,

The courser stumbled in the sword-strewn way,
    The broken-toothed and shattered battlement
Towered with vacant grinning as he went
    Home from the fight in triumph and dismay.

His wounded side still bled. The stars were pale.
    Beyond the blackened wall, against his orders,
Busy lieutenants hanged the caught marauders,
    Felon and mutineer and beaten foeman.
The aching Captain in his coat of mail
    Sought his pavilion sobbing like a woman.

Count Orlo in England

This rain like silver corn, this northern rain
    That rushes inward through the arrow-slit,

Is fine and soft and comforting to feel
   And looks as cold and beautiful as steel.
I brood beside the damp grey stone: I sit
   And watch the shooting fall of shining grain.

Today my narrow thoughts are full of sadness.
   I wish the dart and slant of rain would weave
The shift of fancies into tapestry,
   And catch the threads of thought, and knit for me
Tissues of memory and make-believe
   Reminding me of times of youthful gladness.

Among the patterns of the plunging trees
   Bound by the heavy downpour's misty ropes,
I see dim battles that my squadrons fought,
   Campaign and siege and holocaust I wrought,
The whole ambitious skein of early hopes,
   The acrid plains and scented classic seas.

Ah, those cerulean waves where once I sailed
   And knew the almond breath of eastern winds,
Where with Duke Robert, that old grim Guiscard
   Who shook the purple empires into shard,
I voyaged to the Isle of Tamarinds
   Through fish-shoals emerald-eyed and ruby-tailed!

And I remember how the vessel drove
   Through odorous gales, until one dusk it came
To the pale coastline of an unknown land
   With lemon-trees upon its pleasant strand,
And how the young stars burned with clear green flame
   As we dropped anchor in the placid cove.

The last grey bird swung down the empty sky
   With ghostly pulse of wings. Beside a brook
I found asleep upon a mossy bed
   A girl whose limbs were painted white and red.
She woke to me with rapture in her look,
   She held her arms out with a savage cry.

Around her brow she wore a chain of coins,
    Her hair was bronze and tawny were her eyes.
Was she, I wonder, peri or princess,
    Or merchant's errant wife, or shepherdess?
No man need ask the question, who is wise,
    I stooped and took the cestus from her loins.

I heard the stride and roar of leaves and waves,
    The lunge of captive winds in lemon-trees,
The lurch of dappled water over stone.
    I heard dark Nature swell and heave and groan
And lash the elements with winds and seas
    That fled her quivering to boughs and caves.

Upon the bed of moss till dawn we lay;
    First we made love, then afterwards we slept.
Time fluttered by me like a velvet moth
    In dreams of red kings on a painted cloth;
And I awoke, and from her side I crept
    Before the sharp and diamond light of day.

O in the hungry North my rich blood freezes!
    I sit in this great castle wet and cold
And watch the shimmering hawberk of the rain,
    And all my one desire to go again
Beneath the tingling branches where the bold
    And brown wench gave her flesh to pungent breezes.

The marrow in my bones runs weak and thin,
    The Saxon women smell of bacon-fat,
The numb encounters of provincial skirmish
    Have bruised my arms and made their strength diminish;
For ten years on my backside I have sat
    And listened to a lean priest talk of sin.

And every dream is shrunk, and Guiscard dead,
    And I grow old enduring crude assault
By sullen tribesmen sired in rain and swamp.
    These chilling rains have caught me in a cramp.
Where is the fire in the heavenly vault,
    The lemon-scented girl, the long green bed?

Orlo's Valediction

I am Count Orlo come to say farewell:
    A cold and crazed old man, a brutal pawn
Thrust forward by a cunning hand to tell
    A tale of pride and violence, power and scorn.

I roamed the ramps of ice, the battlefields,
    The castle lawns, the lists, the murderous heath,
Only that this young anti-self could wield
    A sword long since corroded in its sheath.

I saw the slack fruit on the gallows-tree,
    The crimson toadstools in the magic wood,
The harlot-merry cut-throats of the sea,
    Only that this young man might fret your blood.

I lay at rest upon the chequered grass
    For one brief moment, and was lost to love,
In order that my puppet's tears of glass
    Might this young whelp, this cub, arouse and move.

I heard the soft commotion of birds' wings
    And watched them stretch across the evening sky,
And like a harassed falcon jessed with strings
    Uttered my jealous, lingering, hooded cry.

I was the thing my young creator is:
    A misprized moment in the womb of time.
My pulses and my appetites were his,
    And his the shiftless promise of my prime.

I was the masked assassin in the scheme,
    The ancient ruffian skilled in subtle ways—
But free of his compulsive, living dream,
    The slavery and precipitancy of his days.

REED WHITTEMORE

A Treasure

Up in the attic, down in the cellar, and under
The sagging old porch in back lies the treasure,
Uncharted, in this box, that box, this trunk, that trunk,
Awaiting the tireless hunter, the scholar, the drudge
Now on his way on a generous grant to search
The depths of this dark cellar, attic and porch.

History rests quietly here in the dust
Of dry corners and crumbling timbers; the lost
Are still lost; the gone are still gone; the forgotten
Have not been remembered. There is no motion
Where no motion should be, no voices, no breath.
The past is present as past; the present is death.

But here is a scholar coming among the cobwebs
On a generous grant to finger the frail latches
And open all the boxes and trunks for the treasure—
Papers, clothing, letters, trinkets, and ledgers
Of someone who, though he knows it not, will be led
Out in due time from this timeless house of the dead,

While the scholar, the drudge, the tireless hunter sinks
Deeper and deeper into the boxes and trunks
Of this attic, cellar and porch on his generous grant
Until, in these depths, in this dust, in this present past,
He is who rests forgotten, another treasure
For later scholars on generous grants to discover.

A Week of Doodle

Monday

I will now address myself to the problem of writing
A few lines, a very few lines each day
During this winter of waiting and waiting and waiting
For something to say,

So that this special skill by which I live,
This talent of mine with an image, a rhyme and a pen,
Will suffer as little from cold and snow and neglect
As a well-oiled gun,

On the theory that one spring day I'll get up early,
Walk out with vigor and find on a tree a bill
Announcing that verse is once again in season—
Gridley, fire at will.

Tuesday

This kind of thing (these lines) might be likened to those
Hobbies with hammers and drills
Practiced in all the best basements by men who'd dispose
Of some of a long day's cache of bills and ills

In the evening. Manual therapy.
Even physicians practice it. It is approved.
The mind is soothed by the hand as the hand pounds a
    rickety
Chair or table together; violently soothed,

As, in this instance, this unregenerate mind
Seeks to dispose of some of its winter's reverses
By letting this ink in this pen in this clumsy hand
Make (for this mind) these verses.

Friday

You see how quickly the system has broken down.
Already two days have elapsed since I last entrusted

A line to this journal; already my modest design
Has proved too complex; I'm bested.

This brings me to my point for today. You recall
An essay by Mr. Eliot some time ago
On minor poetry. What is it? he asked, and with all
The solemnity of the pope said he didn't know.

I know even less (of course anyone knows even less
Than T.S.), but I think of this journal
As evidence of some weight of a kind of verse
Neither major nor minor but merely (an old kind) doodle.

Saturday

Doodle is waiting raised to a fine art,
Waiting in phone booths for answers, in classrooms for tests.
It is done with but part of the mind, but a pleasant part.
It brightens deserts of notebooks, scratch pads and desks.

It does, in my case, for my work, what others expect
Of courses in writing—how to express and impress;
And improves my condition no end in a different respect
Since, in a pinch, I can sell it for (minor) verse.

But of course it has limits. Even a week seems extravagant
Of just it. So my readers all over the world will
                    (I hope) come to thank
Me for my notable wisdom and judgment
On those days of the week—just two, not counting
                    Sunday—when I was blank.

A Projection

I wish they would hurry up their trip to Mars,
Those rocket gentlemen.
We have been waiting too long; the fictions of little men
And canals,
And of planting and raising flags and opening markets
For beads, cheap watches, perfume and plastic jewelry—

All these begin to be tedious; what we need now
Is the real thing, a thoroughly bang-up voyage
Of discovery.

Led by Admiral Byrd
In the *Nina, Pinta* and *Santa Maria*
With a crew of one hundred experts
In physics, geology, war and creative writing,
The expedition should sail with a five-year supply of
Pemmican, Jello, Moxie,
Warm woolen socks and jars of Gramma's preserves.

Think of them out there,
An ocean of space before them, using no compass,
Guiding themselves by speculative equations,
Looking,
Looking into the night and thinking now
There are no days, no seasons, time
Is only on watches,
                and landing on Venus
Through some slight error,
Bearing

Proclamations of friendship,
Declarations of interstellar faith,
Acknowledgments of American supremacy,
And advertising matter.

I wonder,
Out in the pitch of space, having worlds enough,
If the walled-up, balled-up self could from its alley
Sally.
I wish they would make provisions for this,
Those rocket gentlemen.

A Day with the Foreign Legion

On one of those days with the Legion
When everyone sticks to sofas

And itches and bitches—a day
For gin and bitters and the plague—
Down by Mount Tessala, under the plane trees,
Seated at iron tables, cursing the country,
Cursing the times and the natives, cursing the drinks,
Cursing the food and the bugs, cursing the Legion,
Were Kim and Bim and all those brave
Heroes of all those books and plays and movies
The remorseless desert serves.
And as they sat at the iron tables cursing the county,
Cursing the food and the bugs, cursing the Legion,
Some Sergeant or other rushed in from The Fort
Gallantly bearing the news
From which all those the remorseless desert serves
Take their cues:
"Sir!"
          "What is it, Sergeant?"
                              "Sir, the hordes
March e'en now across the desert swards."

Just like the movies.

Now in the movies
The Sergeant's arrival touches off bugles and bells,
Emptying bunks and showers, frightening horses,
Pushing up flags and standards, hardening lines
Of unsoldierly softness, and putting farewells
Hastily in the post so two weeks hence
A perfectly lovely lovely in far-off Canada
Will go pale and bite buttons and stare at the air in Canada.
And in the movies,
Almost before the audience spills its popcorn,
The company's formed and away, with Bim or Kim
Solemnly leading them out into a sandstorm,
Getting them into what is quite clearly a trap,
Posting a double guard,
Sending messengers frantic to Marrakech,
Inadvertently pouring the water away,
Losing the ammunition, horses and food,
And generally carrying on in the great tradition
By making speeches

Which bring back to mind the glorious name of the Legion,
And serve as the turning point,
After which the Arabs seem doped and perfectly helpless,
Water springs up from the ground, the horses come back,
Plenty of food is discovered in some old cave,
And reinforcements arrive led by the girl
From Canada.

But in this instance nothing from *Beau Geste*
Or the Paramount lot was attempted,
It being too hot, too terribly hot, for dramatics
Even from Kim and Bim
Aging under the plane trees,
Cursing the food and the bugs, cursing the Sergeant
Who gallantly bore the news because he was young,
Full of oats and ignorance, so damned young
In his pretty khaki; nothing at all,
So late in the day, with everyone crocked
And bitten to death and sweaty and all,
Was attempted despite the Sergeant,
Who whirled on his heel, his mission accomplished, and
        marched,
Hip hip,
Out of the bar, a true trooper, as if to the wars.

So the lights went on and the audience,
Pleasantly stupid, whistled and clapped at the rarity
Of a film breaking down in this late year of Our Lord.

But of course it was not the film; it was not the projector;
Nor was it the man in the booth, who hastened away
As soon as the feature was over, leaving the heroes
Cursing the food and the bugs, cursing the Legion
As heathendom marched and the Sergeant whirled, hip hip;
But some other, darker cause having to do
With the script perhaps, or the art.
Or not art—
None of these but still deeper, deeper and darker,
Rooted in Culture or . . . Culture, or . . .

Or none of these things. Or all.

What was it?

None of these things, or all. It was the time.
The time and the place, and how could one blame them,
Seated at iron tables cursing the country?
What could they do,
Seated under the plane trees watching the Sergeant
Whirl on his heel, hip hip, in his pretty khaki?
What could they say,
Drinking their gin and bitters by Mount Tessala,
What could they say?

For what after all *could* be said,
After all was said,
But that the feature had merely run out, and the lights
      had gone on
Because it was time for the lights to go on, and time
For them not to dash out in the desert,
But to rage
As befitted their age
At the drinks and the country, letting their audience
Clap, stamp, whistle and hoot as darkness
Settled on Mount Tessala, the lights went on,
The enemy roamed the desert, and everyone itched.

After Some Day of Decision

He doesn't know when it was that the last door closed,
But now it is closed for good. What he is doing
He will continue to do, and what he has not done
Will not be done. He can relax,
Letting a law of Newton's lay his tracks.

He is relieved. In the past the future was always
Troublesome, he being caught
In an onward and upward tradition. Not any more.
Now all the frontiers are closed where he could be other
Than what he has been, which is no bother.

It is called settling down. The time between waking
And sleeping shrinks, the days run together,
And all that was messily tentative, shaky and new
Is quietly stored away, that he may pursue
What, having been tried, is now his true.

And so forth. Stanza by stanza. If there is any
Slightest complaint he might possibly make
Against having made for his weary head such a bed,
It is merely that sometimes in it, as he was bred.
He dreams of being tried and pronounced—"Dead."

RICHARD WILBUR

Cigales

You know those windless summer evenings, swollen to stasis
by too-substantial melodies, rich as a
running-down record, ground round
to full quiet. Even the leaves
have thick tongues.

And if the first crickets quicken then,
other inhabitants, at window or door
or riding from table, feel in the lungs
a slim false-freshness, by this
trick of the ear.

Chanters of miracles took for a simple sign
the Latin cigale, because of his long waiting
and sweet change in daylight, and his singing
all his life, pinched on the ash leaf,
heedless of ants.

Others made morals; all were puzzled and joyed
by this gratuitous song. Such a plain thing

morals could not surround, nor listening:
not "chirr" nor "cri-cri." There is no straight
way of approaching it.

This thin uncomprehended song it is
springs healing questions into binding air.
Fabre, by firing all the municipal cannon
under a piping tree, found out
cigales cannot hear.

The Pardon

My dog lay dead five days without a grave
In the thick of summer, hid in a clump of pine
And a jungle of grass and honeysuckle-vine.
I who had loved him while he kept alive

Went only close enough to where he was
To sniff the heavy honeysuckle-smell
Twined with another odor heavier still
And hear the flies' intolerable buzz.

Well, I was ten and very much afraid.
In my kind world the dead were out of range
And I could not forgive the sad or strange
In beast or man. My father took the spade

And buried him. Last night I saw the grass
Slowly divide (it was the same scene
But now it glowed a fierce and mortal green)
And saw the dog emerging. I confess

I felt afraid again, but still he came
In the carnal sun, clothed in a hymn of flies,
And death was breeding in his lively eyes.
I started in to cry and call his name,

Asking forgiveness of his tongueless head.
. . . I dreamt the past was never past redeeming:
But whether this was false or honest dreaming
I beg death's pardon now. And mourn the dead.

Epistemology

I

Kick at the rock, Sam Johnson, break your bones:
But cloudy, cloudy is the stuff of stones.

II

We milk the cow of the world, and as we do
We whisper in her ear, "You are not true."

In the Elegy Season

Haze, char, and the weather of All Souls':
A giant absence mopes upon the trees:
Leaves cast in casual potpourri
Whisper their scents from pits and cellar-holes.

Or brewed in gulleys, steeped in wells, they spend
In chilly steam their last aromas, yield
From shallow hells a revenance of field
And orchard air. And now the envious mind

Which could not hold the summer in my head
While bounded by that blazing circumstance
Parades these barrens in a golden trance,
Remembering the wealthy season dead,

And by an autumn inspiration makes
A summer all its own. Green boughs arise

Through all the boundless backward of the eyes,
And the soul bathes in warm conceptual lakes.

Less proud than this, my body leans an ear
Past cold and colder weather after wings'
Soft commotion, the sudden race of springs,
The goddess' tread heard on the dayward stair,

Longs for the brush of the freighted air, for smells
Of grass and cordial lilac, for the sight
Of green leaves building into the light
And azure water hoisting out of wells.

Juggler

A ball will bounce, but less and less. It's not
A light-hearted thing, resents its own resilience.
Falling is what it loves, and the earth falls
So in our hearts from brilliance,
Settles and is forgot.
It takes a sky-blue juggler with five red balls

To shake our gravity up. Whee, in the air
The balls roll round, wheel on his wheeling hands,
Learning the ways of lightness, alter to spheres
Grazing his finger ends,
Cling to their courses there,
Swinging a small heaven about his ears.

But a heaven is easier made of nothing at all
Than the earth regained, and still and sole within
The spin of worlds, with a gesture sure and noble
He reels that heaven in,
Landing it ball by ball,
And trades it all for a broom, a plate, a table.

Oh, on his toe the table is turning, the broom's
Balancing up on his nose, and the plate whirls

On the tip of the broom! Damn, what a show, we cry:
The boys stamp, and the girls
Shriek, and the drum booms
And all comes down, and he bows and says good-bye.

If the juggler is tired now, if the broom stands
In the dust again, if the table starts to drop
Through the daily dark again, and though the plate
Lies flat on the table top,
For him we batter our hands
Who has won for once over the world's weight.

Years-End

Now winter downs the dying of the year,
And night is all a settlement of snow;
From the soft street the rooms of houses show
A gathered light, a shapen atmosphere,
Like frozen-over lakes whose ice is thin
And still allows some stirring down within.

I've known the wind by water banks to shake
The late leaves down, which frozen where they fell
And held in ice as dancers in a spell
Fluttered all winter long into a lake;
Graved on the dark in gestures of descent,
They seemed their own most perfect monument.

There was perfection in the death of ferns
Which laid their fragile cheeks against the stone
A million years. Great mammoths overthrown
Composedly have made their long sojourns,
Like palaces of patience, in the gray
And changeless lands of ice. And at Pompeii

The little dog lay curled and did not rise
But slept the deeper as the ashes rose
And found the people incomplete, and froze

The random hands, the loose unready eyes
Of men expecting yet another sun
To do the shapely thing they had not done.

These sudden ends of time must give us pause.
We fray into the future, rarely wrought
Save in the tapestries of afterthought.
More time, more time. Barrages of applause
Come muffled from a buried radio.
The New-year bells are wrangling with the snow.

Love Calls Us to the Things of This World

The eyes open to a cry of pulleys,
And spirited from sleep, the astounded soul
Hangs for a moment bodiless and simple
As false dawn.
                Outside the open window
The morning air is all awash with angels.

Some are in bed-sheets, some are in blouses,
Some are in smocks: but truly there they are.
Now they are rising together in calm swells
Of halcyon feeling, filling whatever they wear
With the deep joy of their impersonal breathing;

Now they are flying in place, conveying
The terrible speed of their omnipresence, moving
And staying like white water; and now of a sudden
They swoon down into so rapt a quiet
That nobody seems to be there.
                    The soul shrinks

From all that it is about to remember,
From the punctual rape of every blessed day,
And cries,
        "Oh, let there be nothing on earth but laundry,
Nothing but rosy hands in the rising steam
And clear dances done in the sight of heaven."

Yet, as the sun acknowledges
With a warm look the world's hunks and colors,
The soul descends once more in bitter love
To accept the waking body, saying now
In a changed voice as the man yawns and rises,

"Bring them down from their ruddy gallows;
Let there be clean linen for the backs of thieves;
Let lovers go fresh and sweet to be undone,
And the heaviest nuns walk in a pure floating
Of dark habits,
                    keeping their difficult balance."

A Voice from Under the Table

to Robert and Jane Brooks

How shall the wine be drunk, or the woman known?
I take this world for better or for worse,
But seeing rose carafes conceive the sun
My thirst conceives a fierier universe:
And then I toast the birds in the burning trees
That chant their holy lucid drunkenness;
I swallowed all the phosphorus of the seas
Before I fell into this low distress.

You upright people all remember how
Love drove you first to the woods, and there you heard
The loose-mouthed wind complaining *Thou* and *Thou;*
My gawky limbs were shuddered by the word.
Most of it since was nothing but charades
To spell that hankering out and make an end,
But the softest hands against my shoulder-blades
Only increased the crying of the wind.

For this the goddess rose from the midland sea
And stood above the famous wine-dark wave,
To ease our drouth with clearer mystery

And be a South to all our flights of love.
And down by the selfsame water I have seen
A blazing girl with skin like polished stone
Splashing until a far-out breast of green
Arose and with a rose contagion shone.

"A myrtle-shoot in hand, she danced; her hair
Cast on her back and shoulders a moving shade."
Was it some hovering light that showed her fair?
Was it of chafing dark that light was made?
Perhaps it was Archilochus' fantasy,
Or that his saying sublimed the thing he said.
All true enough; and true as well that she
Was beautiful, and danced, and is now dead.

Helen was no such high discarnate thought
As men in dry symposia pursue,
But was as bitterly fugitive, not to be caught
By what men's arms in love or fight could do.
Groan in your cell; rape Troy with sword and flame;
The end of thirst exceeds experience.
A devil told me it was all the same
Whether to fail by spirit or by sense.

God keep me a damned fool, nor charitably
Receive me into his shapely resignations.
I am a sort of martyr, as you see,
A horizontal monument to patience.
The calves of waitresses parade about
My helpless head upon this sodden floor.
Well, I am down again, but not yet out.
O sweet frustrations, I shall be back for more.

Mind

Mind in the purest play is like some bat
That beats about in caverns all alone,

Contriving by a kind of senseless wit
Not to conclude against a wall of stone.

It has no need to falter or explore;
Darkly it knows what obstacles are there,
And so may weave and flitter, dip and soar
In perfect courses through the blackest air.

And has this simile a like perfection?
The mind is like a bat. Precisely. Save
That in the very happiest intellection
A graceful error may correct the cave.

Lamarck Elaborated

"The environment creates the organ"

The Greeks were wrong who said our eyes have rays;
Not from these sockets or these sparkling poles
Comes the illumination of our days.
It was the sun that bored these two blue holes.

It was the song of doves begot the ear
And not the ear that first conceived of sound:
That organ bloomed in vibrant atmosphere,
As music conjured Ilium from the ground.

The yielding water, the repugnant stone,
The poisoned berry and the flaring rose
Attired in sense the tactless finger-bone
And set the taste-buds and inspired the nose.

Out of our vivid ambiance came unsought
All sense but that most formidably dim.
The shell of balance rolls in seas of thought.
It was the mind that taught the head to swim.

Newtonian numbers set to cosmic lyres
Whelmed us in whirling worlds we could not know,

And by the imagined floods of our desires
The voice of Sirens gave us vertigo.

Merlin Enthralled

In a while they rose and went out aimlessly riding,
Leaving their drained cups on the table round.
Merlin, Merlin, their hearts cried, where are you hiding?
In all the world was no unnatural sound.

Mystery watched them riding glade by glade;
They saw it darkle from under leafy brows;
But leaves were all its voice, and squirrels made
An alien fracas in the ancient boughs.

Once by a lake-edge something made them stop.
Yet what they found was the thumping of a frog,
Bugs skating on the shut water-top,
Some hairlike algae bleaching on a log.

Gawen thought for a moment that he heard
A whitethorn breathe *Niniane*. That Siren's daughter
Rose in a fort of dreams and spoke the word
Sleep, her voice like dark diving water;

And Merlin slept, who had imagined her
Of water-sounds and the deep unsoundable swell
A creature to bewitch a sorcerer,
And lay there now within her towering spell.

Slowly the shapes of searching men and horses
Escaped him as he dreamt on that high bed:
History died; he gathered in its forces;
The mists of time condensed in the still head

Until his mind, as clear as mountain water,
Went raveling toward the deep transparent dream

Who bade him sleep. And then the Siren's daughter
Received him as the sea receives a stream.

Fate would be fated; dreams desire to sleep.
This the forsaken will not understand.
Arthur upon the road began to weep
And said to Gawen *Remember when this hand*

Once haled a sword from stone; now no less strong
It cannot dream of such a thing to do.
Their mail grew quainter as they clopped along.
The sky became a still and woven blue.

A Baroque Wall-Fountain in the Villa Sciarra

for Dore and Adja

Under the bronze crown
Too big for the head of the stone cherub whose feet
    A serpent has begun to eat,
Sweet water brims a cockle and braids down

    Past spattered mosses, breaks
On the tipped edge of a second shell, and fills
    The massive third below. It spills
In threads then from the scalloped rim, and makes

    A scrim or summery tent
For a faun-ménage and their familiar goose.
    Happy in all that ragged, loose
Collapse of water, its effortless descent

    And flatteries of spray,
The stocky god upholds the shell with ease,
    Watching, about his shaggy knees,
The goatish innocence of his babes at play;

    His fauness all the while
Leans forward, slightly, into a clambering mesh

Of water-lights, her sparkling flesh
In a saecular ecstasy, her blinded smile

    Bent on the sand floor
Of the trefoil pool, where ripple-shadows come
    And go in swift reticulum,
More addling to the eye than wine, and more

    Interminable to thought
Than pleasure's calculus. Yet since this all
    Is pleasure, flash, and waterfall,
Must it not be too simple? Are we not

    More intricately expressed
In the plain fountains that Maderna set
    Before St. Peter's—the main jet
Struggling aloft until it seems at rest

    In the act of rising, until
The very wish of water is reversed,
    That heaviness borne up to burst
In a clear, high, cavorting head, to fill

    With blaze, and then in gauze
Delays, in a gnatlike shimmering, in a fine
    Illumined version of itself, decline,
And patter on the stones its own applause?

    If that is what men are
Or should be, if those water-saints display
    The pattern of our areté, *
What of these showered fauns in their bizarre,

    Spangled, and plunging house?
They are at rest in fulness of desire
    For what is given, they do not tire
Of the smart of the sun, the pleasant water-douse

    And riddled pool below,
Reproving our disgust and our ennui

* Note: *areté*, a Greek word meaning roughly "virtue."

With humble insatiety.
Francis, perhaps, who lay in sister snow

   Before the wealthy gate
Freezing and praising, might have seen in this
   No trifle, but a shade of bliss—
That land of tolerable flowers, that state

   As near and far as grass
Where eyes become the sunlight, and the hand
   Is worthy of water: the dreamt land
Toward which all hungers leap, all pleasures pass.

For the New Railway Station in Rome

   Those who said God is praised
By hurt pillars, who loved to see our brazen lust
   Lie down in rubble, and our vaunting arches
      Conduce to dust;

   Those who with short shadows
Poked through the stubbled forum pondering on decline,
   And would not take the sun standing at noon
      For a good sign;

   Those pilgrims of defeat
Who brought their injured wills as to a soldiers' home;
   Dig them all up now, tell them there's something new
      To see in Rome.

   See, from the travertine
Face of the office block, the roof of the booking-stall
   Sails out into the air beside the ruined
      Servian Wall,

   Echoing in its light
And cantilevered swoop of reinforced concrete
   The broken profile of these stones, defeating
      That defeat

And straying the strummed mind,
By such a sudden chord as raised the town of Troy,
To where the least shard of the world sings out
In stubborn joy,

"What city is eternal
But that which prints itself within the groping head
Out of the blue unbroken reveries
Of the building dead?

"What is our praise or pride
But to imagine excellence, and try to make it?
What does it say over the door of Heaven
But *homo fecit?*"

JAMES WRIGHT

To the Ghost of a Kite

Winter has wrecked the legend of your wings
And thrown you down beside the cold garage.
The silken gold that caught the air at large
Wrinkles and fades among some rusted springs.
There was a wind that sang below your breast,
Astonished air blown seaward on your breath.
That summer sound, lifted away and lost,
Mutters around the corners of the earth.

The season wrecks the legend of my child
And blows his image of the summer down.
He found the relic of your feathers blown
To common birds, depleted and defiled.
He was the child who ran below your flight,
The dark hair flopping leaf-like over eyes,
Who saw you leave your ballast for the light
And shouted your escape across the skies.

Back to the winter like a root he goes
To nurture some great blossom of your fire,
To bring the year back and the pure desire
For silken wings that never touch the grass.
Winter has wrecked the legend of all wings.
The sparrows scatter as I reach to hold
One remnant of those proud, uncommon things:
A warping stick turned yellow in the cold.

Ghost of a dragon, tell me how to charm
The spirit back to fill the body now.
You vanished to the wind one year ago
And left a broken string across my arm.
Tell me the rune, the ballad, or the song
To fling a rag upon a wand and build
Some high magnificence to last as long
As the clear vision of the summer child.

Paul

I used to see her in the door,
Lifting up her hand to wave
To citizens, or pass the hour
With neighboring wives who did not have
Anything more than time to say.

I used to see her in the door,
Simple and quiet woman, slim;
And hence, I think, Paul cared the more
The night they carried her from him,
The night they carried her away.

The doctor did not even ask
For any neighborly advice;
He knew he had a simple task,
And it was obvious from his eyes
There was not anything to say.

The doctor had a word for Paul;
He said that she was resting now,
And would not wake, and that was all.
And then he walked into the snow,
Into the snow he walked away.

And did Paul shriek and curse the air,
And did he pummel with his fist
Against the wall, or tear his hair
And rush outside to bite the mist
That did not have a thing to say?

He sat upon her ruffled bed,
And did not even look at me.
She was lovely, she was dead.
Some sparrows chirruped on a tree
Outside, and then they flew away.

The Assignation

After the winter thawed away, I rose,
Remembering what you said. Below the field
Where I was dead, the crinkled leaf and blade
Summoned my body, told me I must go.
Across the road I saw some other dead
Revive their little fires, and bow the head
To someone still alive and long ago.
Low in the haze a pall of smoke arose.

Inside the moon's hollow is a hale gray man
Who washed his hands, and waved me where to go:
Up the long hill, the mound of lunar snow,
Around three lapping pebbles, over the crossed
Arms of an owl nailed to the southern sky.
I spun three times about, I scattered high,
Over my shoulder, clouds of salt and dust.
The earth began to clear. I saw a man.

He said the sun was falling toward the trees,
The picnic nearly over. Small on the lake
The sails were luring lightning out of dark,
While quieter people guided slim canoes.
I hid in bushes, shy. Already cars
Shuttled away, the earliest evening stars
Blurred in a cloud. A lone child left his shoes
Half in the sand, and slept beneath the trees.

With fires demolished, everybody gone
To root in bushes, congregate by trees
Or haul the yellow windows down to haze,
I lost my way. Water in water fell,
The badgers nibbled rootlets up the shore
For dancing more than food, where long before
Women had gossiped. Chanting a soft farewell,
Canaries swung. Then everything was gone.

No hurry for me there, I let my dress
Fall to the lawn, the pleasure of the silk
Wind with the subtle grass, berries and milk
Of skin sweeten me. Snuggling, I lay prone,
Barren yet motherly for what might come
Out of the emptied branches, man or flame.
I shivered slightly. Everything was gone,
Everyone gone. I kicked aside my dress.

O then it was you I waited for, to hold
The soft leaves of my bones between your hands
And warm them back to life, to fashion wands
Out of my shining arms. O it was you
I loved before my dying and long after,
You, you I could not find. The air fell softer,
My snatch of breath gave out, but no one blew
My name in hollowed weeds. Lonely to hold

Some hand upon me, lest it float away
And be as dead as I, thrown in a sack
Of air to drown in air, I rose, lay back
In trees, and died again. The spiders care

For trellises they hold against the sky,
Except for walls of air the houses die
And fall; and only for my flesh of air
Your flesh of earth would lean and drift away;

But you cared nothing, living, false to me.
What could I do but take a daemon then
And slouch about in dust, eager for pain
Or anything, to keep your memory clear.
A thing came down from the dark air on wings
And rummaged at my limbs, to hold my wings
Down in the dirt; I could not see for fear.
The thing withdrew, full of the dark and me.

And I was riven. Even my poor ghost
Can never stand beside your window now;
I stir the wind, I chatter at a bough,
But make no sound. Your cowardice may keep
You from your assignation with my ghost,
The love you promised me when I was dust,
Not air. And yet I cannot even sleep,
I cannot die, but I will feel my ghost

Driven to find this orchard every year,
This picnic ground, and wait till everyone
Tires of the sundown, turns the headlights on,
To float them off like moths into the dark.
I will stand up to strip my hunger off,
And stare, and mumble, knowing all your love
Is cut beside my name on the white rock,
While you forget the promise and the year.

You sat beside the bed, you took my hands;
And when I lay beyond all speech, you said,
You swore to love me after I was dead,
To meet me in a grove and love me still,
Love the white air, the shadow where it lay.
Dear love, I called your name in air today,
I saw the picnic vanish down the hill,
And waved the moon awake, with empty hands.

On the Skeleton of a Hound

Nightfall, that saw the morning-glories float
Tendril and string against the crumbling wall,
Nurses him now, his skeleton for grief,
His locks for comfort curled among the leaf.
Shuttles of moonlight weave his shadow tall,
Milkweed and dew flow upward to his throat.
Now catbird feathers plume the apple mound,
And starlings drowse to winter up the ground.
Thickened away from speech by fear, I move
Around the body. Over his forepaws, steep
Declivities darken down the moonlight now
And the long throat that bayed a year ago
Declines from summer. Flies would love to leap
Between his eyes and hum away the space
Between the ears, the hollow where a hare
Could hide; another jealous dog would tumble
The bones apart, angry, the shining crumble
Of a great body gleaming in the air;
Quivering pigeons foul his broken face.
I can imagine men who search the earth
For handy resurrections, overturn
The body of a beetle in its grave;
Whispering men digging for gods might delve
A pocket for these bones, then slowly burn
Twigs in the leaves, pray for another birth.

But I will turn my face away from this
Ruin of summer, collapse of fur and bone.
For once a white hare huddled up the grass,
The sparrows flocked away to see the race.
I stood on darkness, clinging to a stone,
I saw the two leaping alive on ice,
On earth, on leaf, humus and withered vine:
The rabbit splendid in a shroud of shade,
The dog carved on the sunlight, on the air,
Fierce and magnificent his rippled hair,
The cockleburrs shaking around his head.

Then, suddenly, the hare leaped beyond pain
Out of the open meadow, and the hound
Followed the voiceless dancer to the moon,
To dark, to death, to other meadows where
Singing young women dance around a fire,
Where love reveres the living. I alone
Scatter this hulk about the dampened ground;
And while the moon rises beyond me, throw
The ribs and spine out of their perfect shape.
For a last charm to the dead, I lift the skull
And toss it over the maples like a ball.
Strewn to the woods, now may that spirit sleep
That flamed over the ground a year ago.
I know the mole will heave a shinbone over,
The earthworm snuggle for a nap on paws,
The honest bees build honey in the head;
The earth knows how to handle the great dead
Who lived the body out, and broke its laws,
Knocked down a fence, tore up a field of clover.

To a Defeated Saviour

Do you forget the shifting hole
Where the slow swimmer fell aground,
And floundered for your fishing pole
Above the snarl of string and sound?
You never seem to turn your face
Directly toward the river side,
Or up the bridge, or anyplace
Near where the skinny swimmer died.

You stand all day and look at girls,
Or climb a tree, or change a tire;
But I have seen the colored swirls
Of water flow to livid fire
Across your sleeping nose and jaws,
Transfiguring both the bone and skin
To muddy banks and sliding shoals
You and the drowned kid tumble in.

You see his face, upturning, float
And bob across your wavering bed;
His wailing fingers call your boat,
His voice throws up the ruddy silt,
The bleary vision prays for light
In sky behind your frozen hands;
But sinking in the dark all night
You charm the shore with bloomless wands.

The circling tow, the shadowy pool
Shift underneath us everywhere.
You would have raised him, flesh and soul,
Had you been strong enough to dare;
You would have lifted him to breathe,
Believing your good hands would keep
His body clear of your own death:
This dream, this drowning in your sleep.

PERMISSIONS AND ACKNOWLEDGMENTS

AMIS, KINGSLEY: "Masters," "Against Romanticism," "Departure," "A Bookshop Idyll," from *A Case of Samples*, copyright 1956 by Kingsley Amis. Reprinted by permission of Harcourt, Brace and Company, Inc., New York. BELL, WILLIAM: "To a Lady on Her Marriage," "A Young Man's Song," "On a Dying Boy," "Elegy X," "Sonnet," from *Mountains Beneath the Horizon*. Reprinted by permission of Faber and Faber Ltd., London. BLY, ROBERT E.: "The Man Whom the Sea Kept Awake," "Barnfire During Church," "Where We Must Look for Help," reprinted by permission of the author and *The Paris Review*. "The Puritan on His Honeymoon," and "A Missouri Traveller Writes Home: 1830," reprinted by permission of the author. BOOTH, PHILIP: "Heron," "The Wilding," "Barred Islands," "Vermont: Indian Summer," "Twelfth Night," "North" from *Letter from a Distant Land*, copyright 1953, 1954, 1955, 1956 by Philip Booth. Reprinted by permission of The Viking Press, Inc., New York. BOWERS, EDGAR: "From William Tyndale to John Frith," "Aix-la-Chappelle, 1945," "The Wise Men," "The Stoic: For Laura von Courten," "Grove and Building," "The Mountain Cemetery," "The Virgin Mary," from *The Form of Loss*, copyright 1956 by Edgar Bowers. Reprinted by permission of Alan Swallow, Denver, Colorado. CAUSLEY, CHARLES: "Recruiting Drive," "Ou Phrontis," "Cowboy Song," from *Survivor's Leave* and "A Ballad for Katherine of Aragon," from *Farewell, Aggie Weston*. Reprinted by permission of The Hand and Flower Press, Aldington, Kent, England. COULETTE, HENRI: "Antony and Cleopatra" reprinted by permission of the author and *The Paris Review*. "Intaglio" reprinted by permission of *The Hudson Review* and the author. DAVIE, DONALD: "The Garden Party," "Remembering the Thirties," "The Evangelist," from *Brides of Reason*. Reprinted by permission of Fantasy Press, Oxford, England. "Homage to William Cowper" and "At Knaresborough," from *The Fantasy Poets* (#13), reprinted by permission of the author. DAVIS, CATHERINE: "Nausea," "Insights," "After a Time," reprinted by permission of the author. DOUGLAS, KEITH:

345

"Oxford," "Cairo Jag," "Vergissmeinicht," "Aristocrats," "Landscape with Figures," "On a Return from Egypt," "Simplify Me When I'm Dead," "Song: Do I Venture Away Too Far," "Snakeskin and Stone," from *Collected Poems*. Reprinted by permission of Editions Poetry London, Ltd., Mandeville Publications. FINKEL, DONALD: "An Esthetic of Imitation," "The Clothing's New Emperor," "The Sirens," "Hunting Song," "Juan Belmonte, Torero," reprinted by permission of the author and *The Paris Review, Western Review, Quarterly Review of Literature*, and *Discovery #5*, in which they first appeared. GRAHAM, W. S.: "Letter II," "Baldy Bane," from *The Nightfishing*, and "The Hill of Intrusion" from *The White Threshold*. Reprinted by permission of Grove Press, Inc., New York. GULLANS, CHARLES: "Autumn: an Ode," "To a Friend," "Poema Morale," "Narcissus," reprinted by permission of *The Hudson Review, The Paris Review*, and the author. "First Love" reprinted by permission of the author. GUNN, THOM: "A Mirror for Poets," "The Wound," "Incident on a Journey," "Tamer and Hawk," reprinted by permission of Fantasy Press, Oxford, England. "Merlin in the Cave: He Speculates Without a Book," "The Corridor," "Before the Carnival," "The Nature of an Action," reprinted by permission of the author. HALL, DONALD: "The Sleeping Giant," "My Son, My Executioner," from *Exiles and Marriages*, copyright 1955 by Donald Hall. Reprinted by permission of The Viking Press, Inc., New York. Both poems were originally published in *The New Yorker*. "Sestina," which originally appeared in *The London Magazine* and *Audience*, "Munch's Scream," originally published in *Partisan Review*, and "Je Suis Une Table," "The Body Politic," "Marriage," "Abroad Thoughts from Home," reprinted by permission of the author. HAMBURGER, MICHAEL: "A Song About Great Men," "A Poet's Progress," "From the Note-Book of a European Tramp (XI)," "The Death of an Old Man," from *Flowering Cactus*, and "In October" from *Poems in Pamphlet 1952 (VI)*, reprinted by permission of The Hand and Flower Press, Aldington, Kent, England. HARROD, ELIZABETH B.: "Summer Afternoon," "Sonnet Against the Too-Facile Mystic," "August Night, 1953," "Calvinist Autumnal," reprinted by permission of *PS Magazine*, edited by Alan Swallow. Copyright 1956, 1957 by Elizabeth B. Harrod. HEATH-STUBBS, JOHN: "The Old King" from *The Charity of the Stars*, reprinted by permission of A. Watkins, Inc., copyright 1949. "Churchyard of St. Mary Magdalene, Old Milton," "A Charm Against the Toothache," "The Death of Digenes Akritas," "Epitaph," from *A Charm Against the Toothache*, reprinted by permission of Harold Ober Associates, Inc. HECHT, ANTHONY: "La Condition Botanique," "Samuel

DONALD HALL is poetry editor of *The Paris Review* and the author of *Exiles and Marriages* and *Dark Houses*. ROBERT PACK is the author of *The Irony of Joy, A Stranger's Privilege,* and *Wallace Stevens,* and co-editor and co-translator of *Mozart's Librettos.* LOUIS SIMPSON is the author of *Good News of Death and Other Poems* and *A Dream of Governors.*